America Through
a British Lens

America Through a British Lens
Cinematic Portrayals 1930–2010

JAMES D. STONE

McFarland & Company, Inc., Publishers
Jefferson, North Carolina

LIBRARY OF CONGRESS CATALOGUING-IN-PUBLICATION DATA

Names: Stone, James D., 1970– author.
Title: America through a British lens : cinematic portrayals, 1930–2010 / James D. Stone.
Description: Jefferson, North Carolina : McFarland & Company, Inc., Publishers, 2017. | Includes bibliographical references and index.
Identifiers: LCCN 2016031817 | ISBN 9780786498147 (softcover : acid free paper) ∞
Subjects: LCSH: United States—In motion pictures. | Motion pictures—Great Britain—History—20th century. | National characteristics, American, in motion pictures.
Classification: LCC PN1995.9.U64 S76 2017 | DDC 791.43/658—dc23
LC record available at https://lccn.loc.gov/2016031817

BRITISH LIBRARY CATALOGUING DATA ARE AVAILABLE

ISBN (print) 978-0-7864-9814-7
ISBN (ebook) 978-1-4766-2556-0

© 2017 James Stone. All rights reserved

No part of this book may be reproduced or transmitted in any form or by any means, electronic or mechanical, including photocopying or recording, or by any information storage and retrieval system, without permission in writing from the publisher.

Front cover: American star Robert Young turns on the charm with British starlet Jessie Matthews

Printed in the United States of America

McFarland & Company, Inc., Publishers
  Box 611, Jefferson, North Carolina 28640
    www.mcfarlandpub.com

For Rachel, Ashley,
Leo, and Madeleine

Acknowledgments

This book began life as a Ph.D. dissertation completed in the department of American Studies at the University of New Mexico. Beth Bailey, my committee chair in those days, deserves my wholehearted thanks for her incisive and inspiring comments and advice.

I'm hugely grateful to Susan Dever for her wise counsel and for encouraging in me a new appreciation for the comma. Gabriel Melendez and Gus Blaisdell should also be acknowledged for their unflagging enthusiasm regarding this project. Greg Strickland proved himself an exacting advisor on grammatical matters.

In searching for obscure and overlooked primary sources I was aided immeasurably by the staffs of the Library of Congress in Washington, D.C. (especially Rebecca Fitzsimons), the library of the British Film Institute in London, and the libraries of the University of East Anglia in Norfolk, England. David Herzl of the University of New Mexico's Zimmerman Library was ever a reliable ally.

Many thanks are due to my splendid wife, Rachel L. Stone, who was unwilling to countenance an unfinished book.

Table of Contents

Acknowledgments   vi
Preface   1
Introduction: Admitting America to British Life   4

1. "I used to like gangsters and newspaper films, but I'm not so sure now": The Hollywood Dreams of Jessie Matthews and the British Film Industry   27
2. "But he's so kind and friendly!" The Mysterious American in 1930s British Cinema   53
3. Johnny in the Clouds: Middle-Class Fantasies of the American G.I.   78
4. "Funny thing about controls, suddenly they go haywire": Debating the Necessity of Restraint in Postwar Britain   106
5. "A well-intentioned but inexperienced colossus": British Cinema, *Picture Post* and the Redefinition of National Identity in the Postwar Period   128
6. A World Worth Saving? Redefining National Identity in Margaret Thatcher's Britain   155
7. "You're his little English bitch and you don't even know it": Gendering Anglo-American Relations in Post–9/11 British Cinema   170

Chapter Notes   189
Bibliography   199
Index   207

Preface

In British movies, American characters are frequently depicted as the polar opposites of the Britons they encounter. The Chicago gangsters, Arizona cowboys, Hollywood starlets, and New York showgirls—plus a vast array of other imaginary U.S. citizens dreamt up by the United Kingdom's filmmakers over the last several decades—tend to be energetic, irreverent, and egalitarian. They often stand in stark contrast to markedly deferential, lackluster, and class-obsessed British characters with whom they interact. This book asks why British films have consistently portrayed Americans as a decidedly different breed, and chronicles the distinct phases of Britain's fascination with its transatlantic ally. Close readings of specific movies are combined with excerpts from the popular and quality press, from government documents on censorship and diplomacy, and from movie publicity materials that reveal much about the national mood.

For much of the twentieth century, Britain was enthralled by the United States' growing influence on the world stage. As they watched their empire crumble, the British saw America gaining international authority and, due to the persuasiveness of Hollywood imagery, an intoxicating glamour. The United States seemed a nation of go-getters unburdened by a rigid class system, its people apparently bereft of the emotional restraint that was so central to the self-image of many British citizens. This conception of America would prove very attractive to many working-class Britons, but horrifying to those members of the privileged classes that wished to preserve the status quo.

British Cinema used images of America to discuss social change occurring within the borders of the United Kingdom and to explore and reshape British national identity. In the 1930s, for instance, American stars appeared in British movies both as folk-devils—since they were regarded as harbingers of a supposedly deleterious mass culture—and as role models who embodied exciting new conceptions of class and gender. In *Gangway* (1935), while the British star Jessie Matthews realizes that an American gangster acquaintance is an unsophisticated bully, she can't help but be drawn to the prospect of social mobility and sexual equality portended by his thrilling tales of shootouts and screeching tires. After enjoying an American criminal lifestyle for a few scenes she—like all British stars of the era who embrace U.S. culture—rejects it as shallow. Just as British movies hinted that the citizenry should cut short any dalliance with America, so they implied that U.S. citizens would be unwise to meddle with the social order of the U.K. As a social-climbing American gangster says in *Murder in Soho* (1939), summing up the reasons for his defeat, "I tried to step out of my class, tried to reach too high."

In the late twentieth and early twenty-first centuries, British films continued their study of the United States. However, in these more recent works the meaning of America changes. Emerging from a nation that had, since World War II, steadily loosened the bonds of class, *Local Hero* (1983) and *Stormy Monday* (1988) do not regard America as a beacon of social mobility. Instead, they interrogate U.S. corporate power and the British response to it. In *Love Actually* (2003) and *28 Weeks Later* (2007) America's imperialist political stance, and its concomitant masculine posturing, become the focus.

In my research for this book, most of which took place at the British Film Institute, the Library of Congress, and the University of East Anglia, I found that, although British Cinema has regularly explored the subject of America, its depictions of U.S. citizens were fewest in number during the 1960s and 1970s. Certainly, some films that emerged from these decades are relevant to this study. *Gumshoe* (1971), for instance, finds Albert Finney playing a lowly, Liverpudlian bingo hall employee who dreams of being a hard-boiled private investigator. However, most of Britain's cinematic treatises on the United States were created before and after the sixties and seventies. Perhaps this is due to British cinema's inward-looking mood during much of this period, a time when a documentary spirit motivated the filmmakers of the British new wave, and a generation felt more eager to capture the social upheavals occurring in their home nation than cast an eye across the Atlantic. Whatever explanation might be offered, a dearth of relevant material from the sixties and seventies necessitates that, as soon as this book ends its study of the 1950s, it briskly moves on to explore the 1980s and the years after.

During the last several years, a number of books have considered the cinematic relationship between the U.S. and Britain. Sarah Street's *Transat-*

lantic Crossings: British Feature Films in the United States (Continuum, 2002) is a major study of the distribution and exhibition of British movies in America. *From Pinewood to Hollywood: British Filmmakers in American Cinema, 1910–1969* (Palgrave Macmillan, 2010) is Ian Scott's treatise on émigré cinematic artists. Mark Glancy's *When Hollywood Loved Britain: The Hollywood "British" Film, 1939–45* (Manchester University Press, 1999) examines American war-era films set in Britain. Glancy's *Hollywood and the Americanization of Britain: From the 1920s to the Present* (I.B Tauris, 2013) traces the British reception of Hollywood films. Each of these excellent books has shed new light on the Anglo-American cinematic dyad. My particular area of study—British cinema's portrayal of America—has not, until now, been the subject of a book-length examination.

Because the films discussed in this book are intimately related to developments within British society and culture, they are explorations, not just of a foreign land, but of home. Their creation may have been partly motivated by the question "who are they?" but they also, perhaps inevitably, answer the question "who are we?" The construction of America as everything Britain is not suggests that many of the films analyzed here are intent upon circumscribing British national identity, listing those attributes that denote insider and outsider status. Yet, though they suggest that national belonging rests on certain criteria, they also allow for the notion that national identity is, at least to some degree, malleable. In many of the films studied here, "Britishness" is largely preserved, but is also modified by the adoption of certain characteristics marked as American.

Introduction
Admitting America to British Life

Flabbergasted, the British patriarch surveys his household. The formerly tranquil space has devolved into chaos. Bobby Denver, the American singing star known as "the crying crooner," has finished an impromptu performance in the living room, charmed all women within earshot, and caused the maid to collapse in a fit of passion. The Briton, John Bentley, a man who aspires to the same quiet grace as the automobile that bears his name, can contain himself no longer and voices his exasperation: "Has everybody gone mad? This degenerate product of so-called modern civilization, this perishing weeper, barges into my house, wails his unadulterated mush into a microphone, and what happens? The maid faints all over the linoleum...."

In this early moment from the British comedy *As Long as They're Happy* (J. Lee Thompson, 1955) an American is identified as invasive, disruptive, irreverent, and excessive. He is also presented as the herald of a disquieting modernity that arrives on British shores in the form of pop music. Yet, although the scene is dominated by the father's condemnations, it also makes clear that other Britons, especially the working class maid, find the American an extremely attractive figure. It is this tension between the forces of acceptance and rejection that makes *As Long as They're Happy* typical of British films that focus on America and Americans.

Such movies have provided a forum within which Britain could allegorically present and explore its mixed feelings regarding the United States. As America became an ever more imposing force in British life, cinema analyzed the cultural traits trickling across the Atlantic and suggested which should be admitted to the nation and which should be kept out.

America Ascendant, Britain in Decline

It might seem that John Bentley has good reasons for rejecting America. As recently as 1930 his nation had been the world's preeminent power.[1] By the time Bobby Denver invaded the Englishman's castle, Britain was heavily in debt to the United States and watching its Empire crumble while American capital and culture wound their way around the globe. The power to steer the destiny of nations that had become known in the nineteenth century as the Pax Britannica had evolved into the Pax Americana.

To discover the origins of this transformation we must look to the late 1800s, a period when British and American fortunes began to be inextricably linked. The United States had been of interest to the British since the first colonists landed there, but it was in the late Victorian era that the ruling class began to feel increasingly affectionate toward America. Even though the U.S. was a former colony, the British maintained that shared heritage, language, and the ties of Anglo-Saxon blood could wash away any old animosities.[2] *The American Commonwealth*, a phenomenally successful 1888 book by British viscount James Bryce, was an instrumental text in creating feelings of kinship.[3] Other prominent Britons claimed that America was a natural ally of the imperialist project. Rudyard Kipling, for instance, used poetry to admonish America to "Take up the White Man's burden" and "Have done with childish days."[4] When, in the space of a few *fin de siècle* years, the United States exerted dominion over Hawaii, Puerto Rico, Guam, the Philippines, and Cuba, British dreams of colonial brotherhood appeared to be coming true.

The stage was set for an alliance and, indeed, Britain and America's similar international interests ensured that the two nations would be on relatively friendly diplomatic terms from the late nineteenth century onward. However, just as diplomatic links were being strengthened, British commentators began to voice their misgivings. Matthew Arnold, for instance, seasoned his kind words about the prospects for Anglo-American cultural exchange with notes of caution. In 1888 he wrote, "To us ... the future of the United States is of incalculable importance.... We have a good deal to learn from them; we shall find in them, also, many things to beware of, many points in which it is to be hoped our democracy may not be like theirs."[5] Like many Britons, he was most disturbed by America's apparent classlessness. British businessmen, fearing American incursion into their markets, offered graver warnings. In his 1902 book, *The American Invaders*, F.A. McKenzie, though he claims that "we are one kin, too closely knit together for trade disputes to sever,"[6] also points out that, "The purchase outright of British manufactories by Americans is a blow to our prestige."[7] A pattern had begun to emerge that would typify British dealings with the U.S. for many years to come. Since many Britons had an affinity and an admiration for America, they were keen to be an ally of a fellow Great Power. Yet, increased affiliation proved to be a double-edged sword. The United States had become so powerful that its influence on British society and culture was difficult to control. Britons who had opened the door to America soon realized that the portal could not be easily shut.

In the twentieth century, the Anglo-American relationship was characterized by uneasy alliance. American ascendancy occurred in tandem with, and was often largely responsible for, a gradual erosion of British power. The First World War was a major catalyst to this process. The U.S. emerged from the conflict a financial giant, usurping Britain's position as the world's most powerful economy and further expanding its foreign markets. Britain found itself saddled with war debt to the United States it could never pay and nervously eyeing the rapid growth of the American Navy. However, despite American advancement, at the close of the Great War Britain was still a hugely significant international force, largely due to its military might and its empire. Over the next few decades, the significance of both would be steadily stripped away.

In the twenties and thirties, British politicians and diplomats were repeatedly frustrated by American isolationism, the deadlock broken only after President Roosevelt convinced a skeptical American congress and public of the need to enter World War II. The war brought together the people and governments of the two nations in common cause but its outcome ensured the diplomatic supremacy of the United States. Britain's war debt to America was even greater than it had been after World War I and for many years after the conflict the nation was dependent on American loans. The United States propped up the ailing Britain because the latter's geographical position and continued, yet greatly diminished, bargaining power were essential to American interests in the cold war environment.

The postwar balance of power meant that the British had to become accustomed to playing second fiddle and, in the process, many were dismayed that America treated them somewhat tactlessly. Writing in a 1954 issue of *The Listener*, Harold Nicholson notes such behavior and suggests a reason for it:

> Although I think the Americans are the best mannered people that I know of—in the sense that they take off their hats in elevators and help weak women across the street—I do not think they possess much tact. Least of all do they possess the tact required by a great and powerful country in dealing with other countries, who were formerly as

great and powerful, but whose strength and wealth have been diminished in two very trying wars. The fact that they have been taught that all men are equal has rendered them clumsy in dealing with inferiors...[8]

It is perhaps more accurate to say that, instead of treating the British tactlessly, Americans refused to defer to them, a habit that was bound to upset Britons who had held great sway over the international arena.

If British pride were not sufficiently dented, the much-vaunted Royal Navy was now largely irrelevant due to U.S. atomic bombs and the British Empire was teetering on the brink of dissolution while America professed indifference. In the 1950s, as the colonized declared their desire for independence, the British clung to their imperialist legacy, a tendency that ensured a fraught relationship with the United States for most of the decade. Eisenhower advisers Herbert Hoover and George Humphrey viewed the British, according to historian Ritchie Ovendale, "as colonialists who wanted the Americans to pay for the safeguarding of British interests in the Middle East."[9] Diplomatic tensions culminated in the Suez crisis of 1956. After President Nasser of Egypt nationalized the Suez Canal, Britain sent troops to the region in order to reestablish control of the trade link. The United States failed to back the British effort, unimpressed by its air of outmoded imperialism and worried that an American endorsement would ensure Arab sympathy for the Soviets. The British were infuriated by American intransigence. The rift would be healed and the two nations would remain, throughout the 1950s, partners in an anti–Soviet alliance, but it was obvious that Suez constituted the last gasp of Britain's colonial endeavor. The episode also provided irrefutable evidence that the U.S. was now the dominant partner in the Anglo-American relationship.

The Rise of American Banality and Excess

As Long as They're Happy together with many other films discussed in the pages that follow, can be read as a response to Britain's declining diplomatic fortunes. The spectacle of John Bentley's anger may well have served a cathartic function for those who bridled at American dominance of the international scene. However, there is another component to Bentley's rage. His ire is specifically reserved for American culture. Since the 1930s many Britons, mostly from the privileged classes, had voiced concern not only about U.S. domination of the world stage, but also about the popularity of American-style products, styles, and behavior within Britain's borders.

English novelist and playwright J.B. Priestley was a prominent member of this group. In his 1933 state-of-the-nation book, *English Journey*, he identifies what he refers to as the "first England," a country rich in history; the "second England," brought about by the rampant industrialization of the nineteenth century; and a third incarnation:

> The third England, I concluded, was the new post-war England, belonging far more to the age itself than to this particular island. America, I supposed, was its real birth-place. This is the England of arterial by-pass roads, of filling stations and factories that look like exhibition buildings, of giant cinemas and dance-halls and cafes, bungalows with tiny garages, cocktail bars, Woolworths, motor-coaches, wireless, hiking, factory girls looking like actresses.[10]

Priestley is supportive of this Americanized England's egalitarian aspects ("It is, of course, essentially democratic. After a social revolution there would, with any luck, be more and not less of it"[11]) but he concludes despondently:

> Too much of it is simply a trumpery imitation of something not very good even in the original. There is about it a rather depressing monotony. Too much of this life is being stamped on from outside, probably by astute financial gentlemen, backed by the press and their publicity services. You feel that too many of the people in this new England are doing not what they like but what they have been told they would like. (Here is the American influence at work.)[12]

Priestley's ideas—that modern England was in many ways a version of America; that the process of Americanization was largely a "depressing" one; that the English and, by implication, the British as a whole, were under the control of Americana's onslaught—would be echoed by many British commentators over the next several decades.

The U.S. was resented because it had gained a reputation as the home of aesthetic banality. Members of the Britain's cultural elite claimed that Americans were unable to reach the artistic heights achieved by Europeans and, instead, settled for an uninspiring middle ground. Here was the realm of mass culture, where all the transcendent cultural products of old that had been available only to the few were now enjoyed by the majority, and consequently were regarded as a shadow of their former selves. British stage actor Hugh Walpole, writing in a 1937 edition of *World Film News*, notes that Hollywood reduces the craft of acting to a mechanical sham:

> When I first arrived in California I knew practically nothing about films. I soon began to realise how false was the whole procedure of picture making. I saw actors borrowed from the stage, placed on a chalk line and told to do their stuff. The finished product was an illusion of acting, but it was (and could be) nothing more than an illusion.[13]

This idea that, in American hands, art was robbed of its true potential would be a favorite of British journalism well in to the 1950s. An American obsession with money was blamed for the apparent soullessness of its cultural realm. Writing in *The Listener* in 1958, Alan Pryce-Jones suggests that America's preoccupation with the dollar has meant:

> Art comes to mean some splendid new repository like the Guggenheim museum now building on fifth avenue. Religion becomes a form of kindness to a God imprisoned in vast, warm buildings. Literature, similarly, as far as possible attempts to put together a cannon of sacred books containing unexceptional notions....[14]

While attacking the banality of American culture, British commentators, somewhat incongruously, voiced concerns about its excesses. According to a variety of moral guardians, the years between 1930 and 1960 saw Britain flooded with unaccustomed levels of sex and violence drawn from a distinctly American cesspool. In 1930 the Reverend Alfred Binks, Chairman of the London Public Morality Council, suggested that the tide of excessive Hollywood films should be stemmed, arguing:

> In America they have not quite the same idea of the sanctity of marriage to which we have been accustomed in this country, and there have been incidents of sex relation, shootings, murders, thefts and pictures of the underworld that have given us great concern.[15]

By the fifties it was the so-called horror comics, American illustrated magazines that specialized in lurid depictions of girls and gore, that caused alarm. *The Listener* drew upon the expertise of American correspondent Irving Sarnoff to explain the phenomenon. After noting that, "During the past year, horror comics, those unhappy bits of American export, have forced their way into the foreground of British public opinion," Sarnoff hypothesizes, "The essential problem lies within the fabric of ... [American] society with its fierce competition, its emphasis on the more and the material, and its lack of reward for those who would pursue other values."[16] Apparently, America produced such excessive pop cultural products because its society was ruled by desire, sexual according to the Reverend Binks, and material if we are to believe Mr. Sarnoff. In Britain, a nation in which self-restraint was especially prized, American excess seemed to challenge one of the cornerstones of the culture.[17]

Whether Britons offered explanations for American excess or not, they endlessly characterized the United States as a kind of freak show, a nation in which the extremes of human behavior found a natural home. From the late thirties to the late fifties, the popular British magazine *Picture Post* regularly published articles and photo-spreads that highlighted the more eccentric activities pursued by Americans. A 1938 piece covers a strange contest taking place in New York in which couples walk around an enclosed area, attempting to stay awake longer than their competitors.

The magazine revels in this lunacy ("New York's newest madness is the Walkathon") while maintaining a sanctimonious tone: "What draws people to watch such a contest? There is nothing to see but men and women in the final stages of exhaustion,"[18] notes the correspondent, apparently unaware of his hypocrisy.

As the preceding has hinted, it was widely believed that Hollywood was the main conduit through which mediocre, excessive, and eccentric American culture flowed to Britain. In the thirties, the British film press was peppered with articles that denounced the pernicious influence of the film capital. A 1937 article in *World Film News* suggests that the American film industry might encourage in British audiences a hero worship that, in the wake of Hitler and Mussolini's rise to power, could prove disastrous for the nation:

> Hollywood sold us sex, sold us crime, sold us horror, sold us history. Heaven forbid they sell us heroism, for it is a terribly dangerous thing, and if it is offered we will buy it and buy it and buy it, like strong drink: The Germans and the Italians seem to be quite drunk, but we must try to keep sober.[19]

Criticism of Hollywood was also rife in the postwar years, much of it revolving around the poor quality of product. Echoing the opinions of those who bemoaned American cultural banality, articles implied that the Hollywood movie was but a cheap imitation of the more artistic creations emerging from Europe. Writing in *Picture Post* in 1947, Simon Harcourt-Smith vents spleen at an American company that bought up the rights to the French film *Le Jour Se Leve* (Marcel Carné, 1939), destroyed all available prints and made their own version:

> The excuse of the vendors is the acquisition of dollars. But what would the civilized world say if some rich American spinster, after weeks of copying in the Uffizi Gallery, induced a dollar-starved Italian government to sell to her Botticelli's *Birth of Venus* so that she might destroy it, and that her daub might reign in place of the original?[20]

Britain's cultural sentinels saw Hollywood as the most harmful among a panoply of malignant American influences and regarded themselves as the last line of defense against pablum and propaganda.

In *As Long They're Happy*, John Bentley's exasperation is apparently a result of America's diplomatic and cultural hegemony. But what of his enraptured, swooning maid? While Bentley and his ilk loudly voiced their distaste for the U.S., a quieter constituency responded with adoration.

Even in the field of international relations, where there existed the greatest potential for resentment, America had its champions. Though the period from 1930 to 1960 was one of gradual, inexorable American ascendancy, it must be remembered that, through it all, Britain and the United

States remained allies. Indeed, the idea of Anglo-American kinship that had sparked the two nations' late-Victorian relationship would be cherished by members of the British ruling class well into the twentieth century. The notion was especially potent for two of Britain's most important twentieth-century prime ministers, Winston Churchill and Harold Macmillan, both the children of American mothers. Setting Britain and America apart from the rest of the world, Churchill noted that the two nations enjoyed a "special relationship." This relationship, as British author Christopher Hitchens comments, was based in a belief that "the two peoples were destined to be the lords of humankind."[21] Even after World War II had put paid to this dream, Macmillan remarked that his relationship with John F. Kennedy was like that of a father and son.[22]

But it was in the cultural realm, not the diplomatic, that a positive response to America would be most pronounced. The community that voiced its approval the loudest was Britain's working class. While their "betters" repeatedly stressed that banality and excess were colonizing the nation, ordinary Britons flocked to movie theaters to see the latest Hollywood fare or to their newsagent to buy Mickey Spillane and Coca-Cola. American products, though they doubtless gave rise to anti–Communist sentiment and tooth decay, were nonetheless empowering. To the workers, Hollywood was not a malignant force. Rather, it showcased a world of possibility in which citizens were not held back by the shackles of class. As British film critics E.W. and M.M. Robson pointed out in 1939, American films did not foreground the deference that was such an obvious component of British society and cinema:

> In England there is a division between the upper and lower strata of society. In America, too, there is a somewhat analogous division, but by comparison with the rigidity and frigidity that separates the upper layers of society from the lower in this country, the Americans are living in blissful brotherhood.
>
> You can see that clearly in any American film. There you will never find the abject deference which is accorded in this country to the doctor, the lawyer, the mayor, the councillor.[23]

America, through its cinema, provided a sense that social change was at least a possibility.

Press Books: Selling America to British Movie Audiences

Some evidence of what ordinary Britons wanted from America can be gleaned from publicity material associated with British films. For most

Constance Cummings in *Seven Sinners* (1936). The movie's press book makes sure to present the American as rebel.

of the twentieth century, movie studios routinely sent "press books" to movie theater managers. These were publications, tailored very specifically to the British market, that included plot synopses, movie stills, suggestions for advertising campaigns, and even "reviews" of films designed for inclusion in local newspapers. British studios knew that they catered to a predominantly working and lower middle class audience.[24] Therefore, if we make the reasonable assumption that studios, at least to some degree, knew what their public wanted, it can also be assumed that press books highlighted those aspects of a movie that would prove appealing to "ordinary folk." These publications, therefore, allow us a window into popular taste. They provide evidence that what most appealed to ordinary Britons about America was its sense of possibility. Press books stressed that the U.S. was a center of thrilling irreverence, chaos, and originality. Without mentioning the class system directly, they reveal a British thirst, predominantly slaked by Hollywood, for images of social change.

American stars appearing in British films were touted as rebels and, more specifically, rebels with an eye to shake up the system. For instance, the press book for *Seven Sinners* (Albert de Courville, 1936) a Hitchcockian romp about wise-cracking American investigators on the trail of gunrunners, presents its female lead as a crusader for social justice:

> Constance Cummings was once known as the "Anarchist"! It seems that "Connie" was more than a little bit independent in her chorus girl days and earned her nickname through repeated efforts to better conditions for herself and her fellow chorines.[25]

Her investigative partner is equally irreverent, the press book relating an episode in which he ignores accepted modes of behavior: "Edmund Lowe was so intrigued by the incredible immobility of the Horse Guards outside of Buckingham Palace, that he broke down and asked one of them a question. All he got in reply was a cool stare."[26] That Lowe should have a little fun at the expense of the Horse Guards, those icons of stability and tradition, marks him not just as impertinent but, more specifically, as disrespectful of the British status quo.

Plot summaries in press books stress that not only did Americans behave irreverently, but that this was what audiences came to see. For instance, the press book for *Orders Is Orders* (Walter Forde, 1933), a comedy about an American film crew attempting to make a movie in a British army barracks, clearly states that the film has been specifically tailored to audience tastes: "The situations arising out of this are riotously funny, being of the type that the British public love and which they are quick to appreciate."[27] The book goes on to reveal one of these beloved situations: "[The Americans] turn the barracks into a film centre and even rope in the Colonel as an actor. In the midst of scenes of very unregimental disorder the General makes a surprise descent upon the barracks, with what results may be readily imagined."[28] Of course the ridicule of an authority figure is a comedic staple, but the press book provides evidence that the film's main attraction is not the spectacle of authority brought low, but the sight of Americans as the primary cause of social disruption. Press books suggested that Britons did not have to enjoy America's disruptive ways from a distance. They hint that citizens might assimilate American behavior patterns and, in doing so, gain a sense of liberation. The press book for *Innocents of Chicago*, a 1933 British movie set in American gangland, contends that gunplay, that quintessentially American activity, can provide Britons, especially women, with a new self-confidence:

> [The British actress] Betty Norton, who until recently had only dared to touch a revolver with her fingertips to be on the point of swooning has amazed her friends by displaying a complete indifference to firearms. No longer does she tremble at the sight of a gun or put her fingers in her ears at its report. The reason for her contempt of

firearms, the sight of which hitherto almost sent her off into hysterics, is her frequent contact with revolvers, automatics, and machine guns in the gangster film *Innocents of Chicago*.[29]

The world of American violence, while it caused some raised eyebrows among the privileged classes, could be as empowering as it was thrilling.

The adoption of American speech patterns was another path to liberation touted by press books. The impact upon British society of "American English" should not be underestimated. Its infiltration infuriated British cultural guardians, especially when it was spoken by the working class and children. Commenting on a 1930s Hollywood film, G.A. Bryson, deputy chairman of Birmingham Justices, blustered: "We don't want our children to go about saying 'Oh yeah' and 'OK kid' and there is no doubt a tendency to Americanise the English language throughout the film that is, I think, deplorable."[30] American English was offensive because it challenged a tenet of British national identity—the mother tongue—that, because of the iconic status of writers such as Shakespeare and Dickens, was considered almost sacred. It was also anathema because English was an instrumental tool in sustaining Britain's class system. Historically, the way in which Britons used the English language determined their status in society. To use it "correctly" was a social asset, while ignorance of linguistic rules identified a person as a member of the lower orders. This was a system imposed from above. American English was filtering into the culture from below and therefore was largely outside the control of the elite. It was, therefore, not just a new form of expression. Because of the English language's role in sustaining the status quo, American English was an exciting and disruptive variation on the norm.

Press books presented it as such. Publicity material for *Innocents of Chicago* is typically exhaustive in its cataloging of American slang. After suggesting that theater owners entice audiences with the catch line "'It's Oke' sez you—'Oh, yeah' sez we—'well tell the cockeyed world,'" the booklet tells the story of the film's British hero: "Oblivious to his danger he jollies the tough he-men who have been detailed to 'take him for a ride,' and gently remonstrates with those who gather 'on the spot' when they are arguing as to who shall 'bump him off.'"[31] British studios knew that many ordinary Britons regarded American English as a symbol of irreverence and exploited the situation fully.

Britain's popular press joined the press books in portraying America as a beacon of change. In a 1938 article entitled "Dance Madness in the USA," *Picture Post* tempered its usual stress on American eccentricity with quotation from a U.S. source highlighting the hope for humanity that could be found in the Jitter-bug: "To viewers with alarm it might be as well to point out that the tap-tap, floy-floy of the Jitter-bugs' feet is sweet music compared with the martial tramp of countless booted feet in Europe as they goose-step along the path of glory to the well-known ending."[32] The quintessentially British publication was happy to offer America as "a land where fun isn't felony and where a killer-diller is a hot swing artist—not a poison gas expert."[33]

Picture Post bolstered the idea that America was a nation offering hope for the future by running articles that characterized the U.S. as dynamic and energetic. For instance, a 1941 piece on American "fitness camps" described campers as "good-lookers" and America as a "nation of natural athletes." American physicality is contrasted with British bookishness:

> Americans have a strong sense of fitness. They take their physical culture more seriously than any other race in the world. A crack instruction course for teachers, for instance, takes four years—or just the same slice out of life that a pre-war Oxford undergraduate spent in learning the whole of Greek and Latin literature, the whole of Greek and Roman history, and the whole of philosophy, ancient and modern.[34]

The images of America that can be gleaned from press books and popular press articles flew in the face of establishment notions that the Americanization of British culture was a disaster. Indeed, as cultural critic Duncan Webster pointed out in 1988—in response to late twentieth century debates on the Americanization of Britain—those on the lower rungs of society's ladder may be more burdened by certain British institutions than by any outside force:

> Where people do feel "colonized" in Britain is by the British State in Northern Ireland, Scotland or Wales, and where they feel humiliatingly dependent seems more likely to be in the Housing Benefit Offices, in DHSS queues, on hospital waiting lists, on Youth Training Schemes, in the cracks of a declining and undemocratic Welfare State rather than in the queue at McDonald's or Kentucky Fried Chicken.[35]

Press books and popular press articles, though they endlessly presented America as a blueprint for social change, rarely made explicit mention of the classlessness that many Britons perceived as integral to U.S. culture. It was left to more highbrow publications to occasionally champion American egalitarianism. For instance, in a 1955 edition of *The Listener*, Kenneth Lindsay holds forth somewhat idealistically on American society:

> The absence of caste and class structure has not only created a respect for man and for work, it has helped America to make use of talent which elsewhere would not be cultivated…. There are more Negro students in universities than the total number of students in British universities…. There is a healthy distrust of experts, bureaucrats, *elites*, and hierarchies. Secrets are considered discreditable; nobody is born to authority.[36]

Britain was certainly home to pro– and anti–American camps. Yet, despite this apparent bipolar division, it would be a mistake to suggest that the nation was simply divided into those who were positively disposed toward America and those who were not. A more likely scenario is that many people felt a multitude of emotions regarding the U.S. As K.W. Gransden points out in a 1958 letter to *The Listener*: "I love and revere the America of Robert Frost as well as being sometimes frightened by the America of Foster Dulles."[37] Most Britons could find as many reasons to embrace America as they could to keep it at arm's length.

At no time was this ambivalence more pronounced than during World War II. Though many believed that America was an excessive and morally corrupt nation, its participation in the war effort was admirable and essential. This disturbing confluence of ideas meant that Britons were faced with a conundrum—how could America be so bad and so good at the same time? The resulting puzzlement found expression in a 1942 *Picture Post* review of *No Orchids for Miss Blandish*, a play that takes place in, to quote the article's headline, a "brutal, sadistic, tawdry"[38] America. After spending the better part of two pages bemoaning the play's sensational violence and sexuality, the reviewer concludes by suggesting that, since America has sent troops to Britain to aid in the war effort, the U.S. must have hidden depths: "How strange! ... [The American sailors] come from the country inhabited, according to the author of *No Orchids for Miss Blandish*, by yeggs, hoodlums, and degenerate—homicidal—imbeciles. How very strange! And now they are here in England, to join in the fight for civilization."[39]

As Long As They're Happy: *The American as Invader and Exemplar*

British heads swam with conflicting ideas about America, and British films were packed with the same warring notions. *As Long as They're Happy* is one such film. It accommodates a wide range of British responses to the U.S., suggesting that America was both a hostile force exploiting a weakened Britain and a dynamic force for change.

The movie playfully presents an allegory of recent Anglo-American relations. The U.S., in the form of Bobby Denver (Jerry Wayne), challenges British power, embodied by the patriarch John Bentley (Jack Buchanan). Bentley will lose dominion over his house, his wife, his daughters and his staff. He is presented as a somewhat impotent figure, consistently unable to control his domestic environment. For instance, he plugs a speaker into

American singing cowboy Barnaby Brady (Hugh McDermott) serenades a highly Americanized English girl, Corinne Bentley (Susan Stephen), in *As Long As They're Happy* (1955).

a wall socket only to see it erupt in a plume of smoke and, in a barroom scene, repeatedly knocks his drink over a hapless barmaid. Such is his humiliation that he is soon driven to a crisis of confidence: "What's Bobby Denver got that I haven't got?" he asks. The answer to this question is self-evident. Denver has fame, fortune ("is it true you get $2000 a week?" he is asked), the affection of the British people, and poise that Bentley can only dream of. American competition is further highlighted by one of Denver's countrymen, Barnaby Brady (Hugh McDermott), a cowboy married to Bentley's daughter, Corinne (Susan Stephen). His disruptive behavior includes lassoing Bentley from horseback and practicing his rodeo act on the maid, snapping sticks out of her mouth with a whip.

The staples of British anti–Americanism are present throughout. American excess is stressed by Denver's habit of crying as he sings.[40] The supposed tactlessness of American diplomats finds expression in Denver and Barnaby's lack of respect for Bentley's authority and their insensitivity to his agitation. The crooner's popularity represents the triumph of American mass culture. His music is appreciated by those from all walks of life, cutting across the boundaries of social class, gender, and profession. The literal mass of humanity that, near the beginning of the film, chases him down the street includes private schoolgirls, garbage men, old and young women, even a policeman. In case we are under the impression that the coming of mass culture is a good thing, the movie ridicules Denver's lack of sophistication. When interviewed by journalists soon after his arrival in Britain, his words connote his ignorance of basic geography: "I want to see something of your wonderful country. You know, Stratford, Manchester, Scotland, towns like that." The repeated suggestions by British commentators that American mass culture was inherently empty are echoed by moments revealing Denver's inherent phoniness. A psychiatrist advises Bentley that his daughter's infatuation with Denver will wear off after she sees that he is "an ordinary, dull, uninteresting person like yourself." The psychiatrist's suggestion is born out by the revelation that the star has a wife—a blow to his sexual allure—and that his tears are produced by an onion rather than genuine emotion.

Apparently wishing to satisfy the broadest range of opinion, the movie combines this litany of reservations with more positive appraisal. Denver's visit offers many Britons the new realms of experience and excitement touted by press books and popular articles. In the light of the American's visit, Bentley's wife, Stella (Brenda de Banzie) offers a stunning reappraisal of her marriage: "For the last eighteen years, John, I've put up with your drab, dreary, dull, dismal, daily routine. In the short time that Mr. Denver's been in this house I've had more excitement and glamor than in all those eighteen years…. I'm sorry to say this John, but I would willingly leave you tomorrow for either Abbot or Costello."

The idea that the British might learn something productive from America is also well represented. From Denver, they learn to be more open with their emotions. The American star's dockside performance provokes an attendant policeman to burst into tears. Even Bentley, despite initial reservations, will eventually perform his own song and dance numbers in the Denver style. The lyrics of one such number confirm that the American's excessive approach is irresistible. "Let your hair down, go on and cry," croons Bentley. Toward the climax of the film, Bentley performs a dance, during which the telephone rings. He picks it up and further aligns himself with Denver and American mass culture by announcing brightly, "Gene Kelly speaking." By the time Denver returns to America, it seems even his harshest critics have taken to heart the cloying, saccharine statement he makes in his final song, "What the country needs is more moonlight, more people who sing I love you, I love you I do."

While the film is a broad enough vessel to accommodate a variety of views on America, its overall mood is conservative. Bobby Denver does change the British in some ways, but essentially the status quo is preserved. We might expect the American, bringer of chaos that he is, to impart some anti-establishment sentiment to Britain's youth. Instead, any whiff of rebelliousness about him is neutralized by the revelation that he is essentially a reactionary. He tells Pat (Jeannie Carson), another of Bentley's daughters, that her beatnik-style clothing is unbecoming: "No one as pretty as you should dress that way." His brand of apple pie wholesomeness proves so attractive that Pat gives up her life as an existentialist and singer in a rough Parisian café. She later reveals, "He has brought me to my senses. I'm never going back to the Boulevard Saint-Germain. I never want to hear the word existentialism again. I just want to live an ordinary, normal life with ordinary, normal people." Denver has been transformed from an agitator to a conservative's dream—a pop star who convinces the nation's youth that rebellion is just a phase and who wants nothing more from a teenage girl than a discreet dress sense.

Even though Denver does everything he can to prove himself innocuous, he is safely packed off to the U.S. at the end of the film. "I bet you're sure glad to get rid of me," he remarks to John Bentley. "Oh, I wouldn't say that," the Englishman replies. "You had me worried for a while though…. Now, don't forget, come and see us next time you're in England." After Denver leaves, the status quo is even more thoroughly restored. In place of the potentially dangerous American star, the movie offers a safe British alternative. Norman Wisdom, a British comedian who acted in many successful films of the 1950s and a man who could never be mistaken for a dangerous element, appears like a *deus ex machina* to restore predictability and order. Gwen, the daughter who had fallen for Denver, now directs her amorous attention at this boy-next-door. The film completes the process of homogenization by restoring the patriarch to power. "Dad was right," admits Pat, "He always is."

The structure of *As Long As They're Happy* is traceable in many a British movie between 1930 and 1960. An American is introduced as an exciting and fascinating force exerting great influence over the British populace. We are offered the chance to enjoy this spectacle or to decry it, until all debate over American merit is made irrelevant by a conclusion that undermines and/or rejects that which the American had stood for by sending him packing or in some way rendering him innocuous. It seems that however attractive the American may prove, his difference cannot be tolerated. Of the many movies discussed in this book that concern an American's visit to Britain, none ends with the outsider becoming an insider.

This policy of containment was the result of a draconian censorship tradition. For most of Britain's studio era—the period, lasting roughly from the 1920s to the early 1960s, in which films were created from pre- to post-production in factory-like film studios—movies were heavily invested in preserving the status quo. They did so by satisfying a system of censorship that served the interests of the powerful. From an early stage in British cinema history, the social elite made clear that they would not tolerate imagery that was in any way incendiary or seriously questioned the viability of the society they dominated. As film scholar Jeffrey Richards notes in a discussion of 1930s movies: "The cinema was *the* mass medium, regularly patronised by the working classes, and the potential of films for influencing, even inflaming, this huge audience was fully appreciated by the Establishment."[41] The British Board of Film Censors (BBFC) was, like America's Hays Office, concerned to police images of sex and violence, but they were also worried by imagery that hinted at impending chaos in British society. In the 1930s, Ivor Montagu, chief of the BBFC, listed among his reasons for censoring certain films: "References to H.R.H., The Prince of Wales; white men in a state of degradation amidst Far-Eastern and native surroundings; … officers in British uniform shown in a disgraceful light; … police firing on defenceless population."[42]

The film industry respected BBFC guidelines, taking great care to protect the reputation of official institutions. For instance, even though the 1933 film *Orders Is Orders* revolves around a British army unit dissolving into American-led chaos, its press book advises that in advertising the movie, "care should be taken that nothing is done in the nature of stunts, etc., that will bring disrepute to the British Army."[43] This repressive state of affairs remained in place with little modification until the late 1950s. A

1955 article on Arthur Watkins, then Secretary of the BBFC, reveals that British censors were still serving the interests of the powerful: "The censorship of Arthur Watkins is ... censorship by a cricket player for cricket players. Or perhaps we should say *intelligent* cricket players."[44] Watkins is seen as part of a rarified group—defined in terms of the middle and upper class sport of cricket—and is regarded as working on behalf of that group. The suggestion that he works for a privileged few is driven home by the italicized caveat that he only takes heed of "intelligent" cricket players.

With the status quo so carefully guarded, it is no surprise that images of America were stringently policed. Widely regarded as excessive, irreverent, energetic, and, most shocking of all, relatively classless, they provided perfect role models for a dissatisfied proletariat thirsting for change. The censors regularly made cuts in Hollywood films. Indeed, Watkins notes that he has just "banned six American films which we consider totally immoral."[45] When British filmmakers made movies about America or Americans they walked a tightrope between satisfying an audience that craved images of American dynamism and fulfilling their duty to the establishment/censor by rendering such images relatively innocuous. Therefore, no such movie is an all-out condemnation of the U.S., and none encourages a wholesale acceptance of American ways. The tension between attraction and repulsion is always there and, depending on each film's social/cultural context, one side of the divide is stressed over the other.

The Function of America in British Society and Culture

British society and culture are crucial to this study. The degree to which a film stresses the attractiveness or repulsiveness of America is greatly affected by Britain's socio-cultural climate at the time of its release. For instance, chapter one notes that the 1930s found Britain's mainly working class film audience drawn to Hollywood cinema and the glossy version of America it portrayed. At the same time, members of the British film industry were also being charmed by American images, but were much more ambivalent about them than their audience. Within the industry, Hollywood was admired for its technical brilliance, but also reviled for its crass commercialism. Such sentiment was certainly born of snobbery but also of jealousy, since it was patently obvious that American films were preferred by the British public, shown more often on British screens, and made more money than relatively small-scale British productions. Britain, a nation that was used to being in control, was forced—at least in terms of cinema—to admit to fragility. The industry's ambivalence gave rise to films that explored the allure of Hollywood, focusing on its charm and strength, but also its vapidity. Such movies admit to Britain's comparative weakness, but draw the conclusion that poor but honest is preferable to rich and phony.

Three such movies featured prominent British star Jessie Matthews. Each revolves around an impressionable young woman's attraction to and ultimate disillusionment with the machinations of the film capital. Matthews' mixed responses to Hollywood mirror those of the British film industry and, therefore, she can be seen as a representative of her national cinema. Through her, filmmakers explored their Janus-faced attitude to their transatlantic rival. Like the British industry, she feels torn between an attraction to Hollywood glamour and a growing awareness that it is shallow. Her eventual decision to reject the Hollywood lifestyle suggests that the American industry is essentially corrupt. This choice also confirms the viability of Britain's relatively small national cinema and its ability to compete with, and avoid absorption by, the American colossus. In deriding Hollywood, the films also engage in thinly disguised criticism of the United States, a nation that was often considered to share the shallowness of its cinema.

The thirties was also a period in which many well-to-do Britons feared that the nation's class system was under threat. Members of particular classes had begun to act in unexpected ways. As British historian Arthur Marwick puts it, "Men of moderate political opinions, or of none, began to talk the language of revolutionary violence; liberal intellectuals joined or flirted with the Communist Party."[46] Official pronouncements proffered the theory that it was becoming increasingly difficult to be sure in which class a person belonged. The authors of the government pamphlet "The Social Structure of England and Wales" asked: "Is it not a misreading of the social structure of this country to dwell on class divisions when, in respect of dress, speech, and use of leisure, all members of the community are obviously coming to resemble one another?"[47] An elite that cherished strict delineation between classes became alarmed at this development.

Since British films usually stressed the viability of the status quo, they did not directly confront this situation. However, as chapter two points out, they did so obliquely through the figure of the American. The new, classless mystery man appeared in the form of an enigmatic U.S citizen who refuses to "know his place." The conventional threat/containment structure ensures that the American's true self is eventually unmasked, but each film is at pains to point out that such individuals are becoming a disturbing reality.

Classlessness is foregrounded again in three wartime movies discussed in the third chapter. Like the 1930s, the 1940s saw a blurring of class lines in Britain. In 1948, a *Picture Post* article looked back on the previous ten years: "The war, with its common dangers and privations, and shared responsibilities, did develop in us a new sense of social solidarity. We realised our interdependence. Bombs and submarines do not recognise class distinctions. Some of this, I think, survived into this cloudy post-war Britain."[48] The forties, however, differed from the previous decade in that social changes, while they might have alarmed some members of the old guard, were officially sanctioned. As *Picture Post* put it, "Those human claims which in the 1930s were aspirations or slogans—the 'Right to Work,' 'Equality of Opportunity,' 'Fair Shares for All,' 'No Cake till All have Bread'—have become basic principles of national policy."[49] The advent of the welfare state was the most visible proof of this new approach to society by those in power.

The development of a less class-conscious Britain can be detected in many a wartime movie, including those that focus on American G.I.s. In these films, the American refusal to "fit in" is viewed positively. Though there is some initial friction between G.I.s and their British hosts, irreverent Americans eventually prove both charming and heroic. This outcome is certainly a result of the movies' basis in propaganda. One of the reasons such films were made was to encourage cooperation between Britons and the G.I.s who were currently living alongside them. But America's more casual approach to class is also presented as a blueprint for Britain's future.

The years linking the mid 1940s to the late 1950s saw a transition from a British society known for its restraint to one that would be made famous by moral guardians as a "permissive society." This transition was brought about by several factors, not least the increased explicitness of movies after the introduction of a new rating system; the publication of the Wolfenden Report on sexuality in 1957; the popularity of a series of scandalous plays and novels by the likes of Allen Sillitoe and John Osborne (soon to be dubbed the nation's "angry young men"); and the belated legalization of *Lady Chatterley's Lover* in 1960. Chapter four contends that Britain's incremental endorsement of American-style excess was also partly responsible for this change. The British have consistently described Americans as an excessive people, often doing so to champion their own comparatively restrained behavior. However, in the decade after World War II,

British films discussed American excess, not as an inadequacy, but as an antidote to postwar malaise.

Chapter five looks at Britain's changed diplomatic status in the 1950s. No longer the ruler of the waves, Britannia had to settle for the role of elder stateswoman. It was patently obvious that America now held the fate of the world in its hands, and this awareness gave rise to a group of British films that examine the changing of the guard.

British films of the 1950s tend to portray Americans as loud, overbearing, and overconfident of their skills. Such characterizations were almost certainly the result of a notion, widespread in British society, that the U.S., for all its military and diplomatic might, was essentially a child in the arena of international relations.[50] Though the films are intent upon casting aspersions on American belligerence, they are also concerned to explore how Britain might respond to such behavior. They offer the same answer as many contemporary British diplomats and politicians: Britain was to shepherd the inexperienced colossus and, whenever possible, put the upstart in its place.

The last two chapters of this book examine a British cinema freed from mid-twentieth century anxieties about class and culture. Americans in British films are no longer bringers of worrying egalitarianism or aesthetic banality. In the last few decades, cinematic definitions of the United States have become increasingly loose and varied. But one conviction remains: America is a force to be reckoned with. British movies continue to meet U.S. culture head-on in order to suggest which of its component parts should be accepted and which rejected.

Chapter six highlights four films of 1980s that show America coming to British shores in various forms: an oil company and its employees; gangsters and investors in urban renewal; the poet Joy Gresham; and the writer Helene Hanff. These are not the invasion narratives of old. The oil barons and criminals turn out to be less than rapacious. Indeed, the British characters they encounter easily outstrip them in terms of pugnacity. The American wordsmiths, Gresham and Hanff, are presented as every bit the intellectual equals of their British counterparts, thereby dispelling the many previous incarnations of America as barbarian at the gates. Indeed, these women seem more knowledgeable and appreciative of British culture than the Englishmen they fall in love with.

British filmmakers of the 1980s were ready to offer looser and more complex portrayals of American and British citizens, not only because the zeitgeist had radically altered, but because Margaret Thatcher, Prime Minister from 1979 to 1990, was attempting to solidify the meaning of Britishness. Harking back to the mid-twentieth century period that gave birth to the majority of films discussed in this book, Thatcher and her Conservative Party urged an increasingly divided nation to embrace a unified national identity drawn from Britain's imperial past. In apparent protest, British filmmakers seized upon the Anglo-American relationship to demonstrate that national belonging is not simply a matter of rallying round some well-worn imagery. Their movies make clear that, in a transnational world, national citizens are more indistinguishable than ever, and those aspects of Britishness that are often held up as the most valuable—for example, the emotional reserve enshrined in the phenomenon of "stiff-upper-lip"— may be highly counterproductive.

Chapter seven traces the influence of the United States on British national identity in the years following 9/11. This was a period of increased anti–Americanism in the United Kingdom. Historian John F. Lyons argues, "As the Bush administration responded militarily to the attacks ... broad sections of British society began to express an intense dislike of the American government, people and society."[51] Many reserved a special ire for George W. Bush and were particularly disdainful of the president's apparently cavalier and disrespectful attitude towards Prime Minister Tony Blair. The oft-repeated notion that Blair was "Bush's poodle" is explored in a series of movies presenting British and American men as rivals in matters sexual, political, and territorial.

It is often claimed that Americans appear in British movies simply to increase box-office revenue in Britain and especially in the United States. A website devoted to British movies argues, "Too often British producers have hired [American] actors because they thought their nationality would make it easier to sell the film in America."[52] Certainly, Americans are consistently cast in British films because they are popular with audiences, but their presence reveals far more than the astute business sense of British executives. As I have discussed, the way they are depicted tells us a great deal about British views on the U.S. and their own nation. The films in which they appear suggest that British cinema, and cinema in general, can function as a cultural watchdog. Each movie examines the pros and cons of admitting America to British life, then makes a judgment about which elements of U.S. culture should be let in and which kept out. Of course, this does not mean that audience members are unable to make their own judgments regarding the extent to which America should be embraced, but it does suggest that British industry personnel and censors have seen themselves as guardians of the nation's well being and a significant influence over public opinion.

British movies that focus on the U.S. reveal that the meaning of America changes as it travels and as time passes. While to a modern day resident of the Middle East, American culture might signify godless consumerism, in mid-twentieth century Britain it meant, amongst other things, classlessness and banality. Though American culture might leave U.S. shores in one particular form, the citizens of foreign nations use their own subjective experience to mold it into something new. With this in mind, because the films examined in this book portray a very British version of America, they can be regarded as an answer to those who see "Americanization" as an overwhelming force. They suggest that, rather than accepting a hypodermic injection of U.S. culture, it is possible for a nation to receive America on its own terms.

1

"I used to like gangsters and newspaper films, but I'm not so sure now"

The Hollywood Dreams of Jessie Matthews and the British Film Industry

Onscreen and off, transformation was a way of life for Jessie Matthews. In her autobiography she describes the screen persona that made her Britain's biggest star in the 1930s: "the waif with the great big eyes, who had become a sex symbol."[1] Matthews the chameleon was showcased in *Evergreen* (Victor Saville, 1934), in which she plays a character who rises to singing stardom by impersonating her famous mother, and in *First a Girl* (Victor Saville, 1935), in which she pretends to be a man in drag. Her fluid screen persona echoed her offscreen life. Born in the working class Soho district of London, she transformed herself from a street kid to an "it girl," complete with cut-glass English accent.

Transformation is again emphasized in three films she made for Gaumont-British, Britain's most prominent studio in the 1930s, about the attractions of Hollywood: *It's Love Again* (Victor Saville, 1936), *Head Over Heels* (Sonnie Hale, 1937), and *Gangway* (Sonnie Hale, 1937). *It's Love Again* finds her falling for an American show business reporter working in England. With his help, she becomes an instant star. In *Gangway*, a reporter herself, she becomes mixed up with American gangsters and alternately takes on the personae of Nedda Beaumont, American film star, and Sparkle, notorious jewel thief, who indulges in such characteristic Hollywood patois as, "I'm a dame who knows how to handle cops." The Matthews character in *Head Over Heels* is a poor showgirl offered the chance to travel to Hollywood and be "groomed for stardom." In each movie, after an initial fascination with the trappings of Hollywood, she rejects her aspirations as shallow. Hollywood and the form of stardom it could provide had become important enough topics to dictate the story line of three consecutive movies starring Britain's most prominent film actress. Why should this be so?

Certainly, stories about Hollywood provided ample opportunity for filmmakers to dazzle their audiences with glamour, and they offered a fresh way to present the conventional tale of an ordinary citizen aspiring to fame and fortune. While *It's Love Again*, *Gangway*, and *Head Over Heels* undoubtedly utilize Hollywood for these purposes, they are more than simple spectacles or wish fulfillment fantasies. They are arenas in which the British film industry's complex relationship with Hollywood is played out.

British Cinema and the Problem of Hollywood

In the 1930s the British industry was debating whether it should transform itself into a version of Hollywood by producing movies that were more American in appearance and tone. This debate took place in the mainstream and industry press, but also, I wish to claim, within the narrative of movies emerging from British studios during this period. In *It's Love Again*, *Gangway*, and *Head Over Heels* Jessie Matthews plays characters that embody the dilemma of the British industry, since they too must struggle with the decision to "go Hollywood." Because Matthews had become synonymous with transformation, she was the ideal medium through which the British industry could discuss its mixed feelings about aesthetic Americanization.

The desire to make British movies look and feel more like Hollywood product was born primarily of financial concerns. Those anxious to compete with Hollywood's global dominance of the cinematic market were painfully aware that Britain's mainly working class audiences preferred American films to the homegrown article. No less a figure than Alfred Hitchcock noted in 1937, "English audiences seem to take more interest in American life—I suppose because it has a novelty value. They are rather easily bored by everyday scenes in their own country."[2] Britons were drawn to American images not just because they were novel, but because they were thrilling and convincing, a fact born out by a 1938 Mass Observation questionnaire issued to cinema patrons in Bolton, England. A clear majority of the 559 respondents expressed their preference for Hollywood product because, in comparison to British, it was fast moving, slickly produced, and showcased natural, lifelike acting.[3] A typical respondent was eighteen year old William Turnock who, after noting his fondness for American films, writes: "As a complaint I don't like many British films owing to there not being sufficient action, and the actors are not acting their part properly."[4] British film industry personnel wisely surmised that cribbing from Hollywood would help domestic ticket sales. They also hoped that Americanizing their product would ensure more widespread distribution in the United States.

Accordingly, throughout the 1930s British studios produced a number of films centering upon iconographic Hollywood characters. Gangsters were a popular subject. *The Man from Chicago* (1930), *Innocents of Chicago* (1932), *This Is the Life* (1933), *The Avenging Hand* (1937), *Hey, Hey, USA* (1938), *Oh Boy!* (1938), and *Murder in Soho* (1939) all contain portrayals of American criminal life drawn from the Hollywood screen. The eccentric, wealthy Americans beloved of screwball comedy also proved appealing, appearing in *Lazy Bones* (1934), *Just Smith* (1934), and *Two's Company* (1936). The industry was responding to Hollywood's preeminence by aping it, and here the controversy began.

Hollywood presented an infuriating conundrum to British industry commentators who, while often disappointed by what they perceived as the shallowness and vulgarity of its films, were simultaneously dazzled by, and drawn to, its technical prowess. John Grierson, father of the British documentary movement of the 1930s, was typical of such voices. His film reviews often characterize Hollywood as a threat to civilization, churning out pablum and appealing to the lowest common denominator. For instance, he laments of *Frankenstein* (James Whale, 1932), "Hollywood has cheapened a great theme.... All Hollywood saw was a bogey man and a chance to whoop up the boys with straw in their ears."[5] Yet, as he often did, Grierson grudgingly admits that his Californian counterparts are, at least, skillful vulgarians. "I admit they have done it well," he writes, as if muttering the words under his breath. Paul Rotha, another luminary of the documentary movement, was similarly torn: "The American executives may be crude and possibly vulgar, but they have at least this merit—they possess the faculty for employing talent and are not afraid to do so."[6]

Such sentiments were not confined to the filmmaking community. John Betjeman, dubbed British poet laureate in 1972, but in the thirties a highly respected film critic, was also eager to point out that although Hollywood trafficked in empty glitz, it was expertly constructed empty glitz.

In 1937 he championed the low budget authenticity of the British stage over the extravagant artifice created by Hollywood choreographer Busby Berkeley. "Londoners ... know," he pointed out, "that the transformation scene in the Lyceum Pantomime is likely to be more moving and more beautiful than the most dazzling patterns of limbs, feathers and smiling dentals that ever wove itself into the theme song of a Warner Brothers' musical."[7] Yet, as did his critical peers, Betjemam concedes that Hollywood was doing something right. The Warner productions, he notes "open up exciting vistas of what might be made of a musical."[8] Perhaps the most succinct commentary summarizing Hollywood's recipe of shameless populism seasoned with technical brilliance was provided by *Cinema Quarterly* journalist Herman Weinberg. In a 1935 issue he argues: "one might say that the American movie is flawless. But one does not say that because the emotional content remains as sterile as ever."[9]

While British industry commentators found themselves able to bestow a modicum of praise upon Hollywood's technique, they found almost nothing positive to say about its star system. The American method of creating and publicizing cinematic celebrities was widely regarded within the British industry as a hindrance to quality filmmaking and the epitome of shallowness and vulgarity. Basil Dean, a head of Britain's Ealing Studios in the 1930s, argued that when British actors were lured away to Hollywood the star system impeded their craft:

> The almost inexhaustible supplies of dramatic talent which exist in this country are constantly called upon by Hollywood; despite the press ballyhoo, and despite the enormous material efficiency that goes to the polishing-up of the outward appearance of the women, euphemistically described as "grooming for stardom"—although why a phrase reminiscent of the stable and the horse-coper should be selected for this process may not be immediately apparent—the amount of genuine development of British-born talent by Hollywood is virtually nil. There is to be observed in the performances of the best of British artists, after they have spent some years in the film capital, a certain blunting of their characterisations, a drying-up of the rich juices of their personalities…. They have become just film actors or film stars.[10]

Though such concerns were widespread, it seemed to many that little could be done to rectify the situation. For example, British novelist Elizabeth Bowen, in a piece entitled "Why I Go To The Cinema," argues, "The star system may be all wrong—it has implications I hardly know of in the titanic world of Hollywood, also it is, clearly, a hold-up to proper art." Yet, she admits, "I cannot help to break it down."[11]

The sense that, reprehensible as it may be, the star system had become a fact of life, influenced the British industry's sporadic attempts to create its own stars. Indeed, in the 1930s, Jessie Matthews represented Britain's most successful challenge yet to the likes of Greta Garbo or Ruby Keeler. Ultimately though, Hollywood methods would never be fully embraced. As film scholar Sarah Street noted in 2000, the star system was often viewed as fundamentally incompatible with British values: "There has always been a tension between wanting British stars and resentment that, as a Hollywood invention, film stardom and its trappings of gossip, fandom, and scandal are somehow, unseemly, *unBritish*."[12]

British observers also frowned upon Hollywood because its films were thought to contain subversive messages. In 1930s Britain, Hollywood movies, and movies in general, were attended overwhelmingly by the working class. Those with direct influence over a movie's content were mainly from the privileged classes. Therefore, when commentators criticized Hollywood for its coarse tactics, a subtext to such criticism was that American movies were bad for the workers. They were bad because they were not "good art" and encouraged the worship of stars who did not deserve such a celestial title but, more worryingly, they might have an incendiary effect upon "the boys with straw in their ears." Such "boys" might be members of Britain's labor force or citizens of nations currently under British rule. As a prominent member of the London Public Morality Council put it: "a little group of men of southern European birth, with no Anglo-Saxon standard of morality and culture, have seized hold of the Motion Picture industry of the United States, and it is their type of thinking that is going out to the nations."[13]

Hollywood gangster movies were regularly singled out as catalysts to unrest because they centered upon men who escaped their working class roots through violent means. Such films were certainly popular amongst the British working class. It was noted in 1937 by Sidney L. Bernstein, chairman of a chain of theaters and one of the founders of the London Film Society, that, "[Hollywood] Films such as *Scarface*, *I am a Fugitive from a Chain Gang*, *Fury* and similar social documents have proved enormously popular in depressed, 'proletarian' districts, and less successful with the 'bourgeoisie.'"[14] Yet, gangster movies were not the only type of Hollywood product thought to provide potentially incendiary imagery. Virtually all films emerging from California specialized in presenting a world where social advancement and economic opportunity were within the grasp of all. In contrast, British films tended to promote social inertia. Scholarship by Peter Miles and Malcolm Smith contends that this fundamental difference ensured Hollywood films were required viewing for those jaundiced by British cinema's conservatism: "The vision of America that was so appealing to the interwar generation of British cinema-goers was of a violent but vibrant society, in which things went wrong but could be changed and were being changed, an apparently classless society which could be contrasted with the patronizing formal hierarchy of the British community."[15] The British industry, while under pressure to give the domestic audience the American-style images it craved, echoed with the voices of those who saw such images as a threat to the nation's deferential society.

British filmmakers attempted to defuse this powder keg by offering a compromise. They peopled their movies with generic Hollywood figures, such as the gangster and the screwball comic yet, simultaneously, contained the supposed threat these figures posed by presenting them as figures of fun. Most 1930s British films involving American gangsters, unlike those emerging from Hollywood, were comedies. Even a film like *Murder in Soho*, one of the few that are not straight comedy, includes comedic scenes making fun of the gangster's lack of taste and civilization. Moreover, in most such films the gangster meets his comeuppance at the hands of a British hero, an outcome reinforcing the notion that he is not a viable role model for the British working class. For instance, the child-like hero of the aforementioned *Oh Boy!* metes out some very traditional British justice by dispatching his gun-wielding American foes with medieval mace, lance, and sword.

To many in the British film industry Hollywood was a threat not only to box-office revenue, "good art," and the souls of ordinary people; Hollywood was a menace to Britain's international influence. Writing in 1937, Maurice Kann, the editor of the New York based *Motion Picture Daily*, noted that British government intervention to prop up their film industry against an onslaught of Hollywood product was motivated by an increasingly battered national pride. Discussing the Cinematographic Films Act of 1927 (an Act of Parliament that attempted to help the British film industry face down American competition by requiring British theater owners to show a certain quota of British films), he notes, "The quota law was designed to set up a fragile industry on more steady underpinnings, on the general theory that such a procedure eventually would earn for England a place in the international celluloid orbit commensurate with her prestige as a world power."[16] With its empire still relatively intact, Britain was not used to being discussed in terms of fragility, but commentators like Kann insisted on casting the nation as weak in the face of American dominance. Hollywood, he notes, is "the gargantuan rival England has set out to meet and to conquer if she can."[17] British self-esteem cannot have been bolstered by the alarmist rhetoric emerging from the serious film magazines of the era. A 1937 editorial in *World Film News* argues, "The American drive to obliterate every vestige of a native British film industry is succeeding admirably. Cynics are comparing the situation with the Italian conquest of Abyssinia.... So far as films go, we are now a colonial people."[18] Apparently, the conqueror was being conquered.

With such sedition in the air it is perhaps unsurprising that industry commentators on both sides of the Atlantic would begin to characterize Hollywood in terms of loud, rugged physicality and the British industry as considerably less virile. For instance, a 1934 article in America's *Photoplay* connotes that, while Hollywood studios are packed with sweaty, loud teamster-types, a British set is peopled with quiet, refined gentlemen:

> [Britain's] Pinewood studios ... is not a motion-picture lot in the ordinary sense of the word. It is the onetime ancestral estate of an illustrious line of English earls.... In this gracious atmosphere, Jessie Matthews makes her pictures. Even on the set everything seems strangely tranquil. The workmen don't rush around coatless, perspiring, as they do between scenes in Hollywood. No one shouts. No one gets excited.[19]

The picture painted here was not resisted by the British, who often characterized themselves as a rather listless bunch struggling to keep up with Hollywood. In a passage discussing British attempts to emulate Hollywood speech patterns, British producer Basil Dean describes American speech as "virile" and notes Britain's sense of inferiority in the face of hard-boiled language: "attempts to make the British actor speak as rapidly as his American rival have disastrous results, for this intensely virile, slangy speech is not our national medium, and if it were not for our inferiority complex in this matter of film production, attempts to reproduce the American method would have been sternly repressed long ago."[20] Any attempt on the part of British filmmakers to suggest their industry was every bit as robust as America's was faced with the derision of British critics who, by the 1930s, had acquired the habit of casting their nation's films as weak in comparison to Hollywood fare. British film historian Rachael Low argues:

> Once the idea of British inferiority became fashionable, few were brave enough to praise anything British without hedging. One could safely admire European films...; one could even be roguish about the enjoyable vulgarity and sentimentality from Hollywood; but to mention the good qualities of a British film maker without qualification might give the wrong impression.[21]

The harsh truths of the cinematic economy meant that Hollywood was repeatedly cast as a tough guy kicking sand in the face of the British weakling.

The Ambivalence of a Star and Her Studio

"Hollywood" had become an extremely charged word. While adopting its slick production values might ensure commercial success, those who did so ran the risk of being branded a philistine, an agitator, or a turncoat. These pressures affected the public pronouncements of prominent industry figures. When speaking of Hollywood, caution and tact were the order of the day. Britain's biggest star, Jessie Matthews, presented herself as torn between her desire to make films in Hollywood and her misgivings about life in America. "I've had several offers to star in American films since the success of *Evergreen* in the US, and I am considering them,"[22] she told reporters in 1935. "One of my great ambitions is to dance with Fred Astaire," she informed *Film Weekly* the same year. But in a 1937 edition of *Photoplay* she commented on a disastrous theatrical tour of the United States by noting "for the second time I felt that America was no place for me." Unlike other British actors such as Cary Grant and David Niven, who lit out for Hollywood in such great numbers during the 1930s that the formation of the Hollywood Cricket Club was a foregone conclusion, Matthews stayed behind. Her decision to stay in Britain, coupled with her yearning to dance with Fred Astaire, meant that she came to embody the British film industry's feelings of attraction and repulsion toward Hollywood.

Gaumont-British, the studio for which Matthews made *It's Love Again*, *Head Over Heels*, and *Gangway*, also became defined by its ambivalence regarding Hollywood. At first glance, it would seem that it was fully committed to Hollywood-style moviemaking. Michael Balcon, the head of the studio, argued in 1935, "It is necessary to bear in mind that in order to obtain a firm grip on the American market our pictures must bear comparison, not only with the average Hollywood product, but with the outstanding American films; this is our problem in a nutshell."[23] Gaumont-British attempted to solve this problem by employing Hollywood talent. *It's Love Again* was directed by Victor Saville, a British filmmaker who had spent some time working in Hollywood. *Head Over Heels* was principally written by the British screenwriter Marjorie Gaffney (who also wrote *Evergreen* and *First a Girl* for Matthews), but was helped in her task by American screenwriter Dwight Taylor. *It's Love Again* was written by the American Marion Dix and the British Austin Melford. The British actor, writer, and director Sonnie Hale was helped with the *Gangway* script by the American Lesser Samuels. Gaumont-British utilized this personnel to ensure that their creations looked as much like Hollywood films as possible.

They succeeded to a great extent, an achievement confirmed by British critics of the day. John Gammie wrote of *It's Love Again*, "In scope and magnificence the backgrounds rival those of Hollywood's most elaborate musicals."[24] G.A. Atkinson noted of *Gangway* that "the tempo is so snappy that the Atlantic dwindles to a ditch," and that the movie "flatters Hollywood technique more than anything produced in our studios this year."[25] C. A. Lejeune provided an insightful critique, sensing that *Gangway* was intended to conquer the United States. She called it "the sort of refined romp that England obviously supposes America thinks that English films should be."[26] Yet, despite the reliance on Hollywood personnel and aesthetic strategies, Gaumont-British professed a commitment to a specifically British cinema. They were quick to point out that their movies would retain an innate Britishness. Studio spokesman C.M. Woolf noted in 1934, "Although our pictures will be made for the world market, it is our intention to make them as strongly British in sentiment as they are today."[27]

The British film critic Andrew Higson argues that such statements are unconvincing, a bluff by a studio that had decided "the threat of denationalization ... [was] to be met not with a reaffirmation of English or British culture ... but with an attempt to exploit the colonized imagination even further."[28] Even in the thirties, some industry commentators suggested that noble words about preserving a specifically British cinema were so much hot air. Writing in *Cinema Quarterly*, American commentator Eric M. Knight chuckled "...although the British mogul shouts loud damnation of American films, excoriates their blatancy, their eternal sex appeal, their mob ideology, he doesn't really mean it. Scratch a British cinema mogul, and under his skin you will find a man with burning desire to learn how to create movies that are just as mob-appealing as the Hollywood product."[29] Higson and Knight are correct to some extent, but the idea that Gaumont-British and other British studios were fully committed to Hollywood methods is challenged by the narratives of *It's Love Again*, *Head Over Heels*, and *Gangway*. Certainly, the films are designed to look and feel American, yet they also suggest that the "reaffirmation of English or British culture" was of paramount concern. Rather than simple homages to American filmmaking, their narratives dramatize the British film industry's ongoing ambivalence regarding Hollywood.

Gangway, It's Love Again, *and* Head Over Heels: *Choosing Between Hollywood and Home*

Each movie revolves around the thrilling prospect that Jessie Matthews might become a Hollywood star, and raises an intimately related, and very topical, question: Will the actress known for her transformations abandon herself to Americanization? Attracted by Hollywood glamour, but repulsed by its shallow vulgarity, she finds herself in a quandary. Given the British industry's tortured relationship with its transatlantic rival, it is impossible not to see Matthews as embodying its mixed feelings, drawn to Hollywood's promises of excitement, wealth, and success, but wary of their price.

The British industry's attraction to American-style filmmaking is explored through Matthews's fascination with all things Hollywood, especially its men. In each film she is fascinated with a glamorous male character whose appearance and manners are copied verbatim from the American screen; in *Gangway* he is a Chicago gangster, in *Head Over Heels* a European "lover," and in *It's Love Again* a combination of screwball comic and newspaper man. The inference becomes clear: if Matthews, the embodiment of the British film industry's Janus-faced mentality, embraces this man, she will be embracing Hollywood.

In all three films, the Matthews character pines after the opportunity and adventure she perceives will be afforded by a Hollywood-style existence. For example, in *Gangway*, as journalist Pat Wayne, she yearns to be more like the newspaper women portrayed in American movies. In an early scene, she chats with Joe (Graham Moffatt), a young newspaper employee. Matthews hands him some movie tickets and the two embark on a rapid-fire homage to the newspaper genre.

> JOE: I've been wanting to see that flicker. It's one of those fast American newspaper films ain't it? The kind you like.
> PAT: That's the life Joe. You know you're alive then. Working for a newspaper means something real.
> JOE: Nothing ever happens in England. Those birds in America have all the fun. Gangsters!
> PAT: Riots!
> JOE: Fires!
> PAT: Earthquakes!
> JOE: Racketeers!
> PAT: Floods!
> JOE: Stickups!
> PAT: Murders!
> JOE: Gee, what a swell country to live in.
> PAT: Just think Joe. What fun it is to be a newspaper woman like the ones in the American movies. Wisecracking with the boss. Sitting around with the boys. Then the alarm, and off you go. If they'd only give me half a chance around here, I'd get some front-page news. If an American girl can do it, so can I!

While this speech makes clear that Matthews is drawn to America, it is a very specific incarnation of the United States that she pines after: that of Hollywood movies.

1. "I used to like gangsters and newspaper films…"

In *Gangway* (1937) "Smiles" Hogan (Nat Pendleton) enthusiastically informs Pat Wayne (Jessie Matthews) of the joys of the criminal life.

This world is rendered yet more attractive by the appearance in the narrative of American gangster "Smiles" Hogan (Nat Pendleton). A criminal whose appearance and attitude are copied from George Raft, Edward G. Robinson, and Humphrey Bogart, Hogan is an iconographic Hollywood figure. Although he is a criminal, he has many attractive qualities. As his nickname suggests and another character confirms, he is "one of the friendlier public enemies." Indeed, it is difficult not to be swept away by his enthusiastic evocation of the gangster life. Looking at the night sky, he holds forth on its inspiring qualities:

> Gives you pep to pull off a job. You jump in the car for a getaway, zigzagging in and out of traffic, turning corners on two wheels, all the while taking potshots at the cops trying to catch up with you. Then out into the open country. Ah, that's the part I like. The good fresh air, the sweet smelling flowers and all the time you're doing ninety in the old bus. Then you duck into the hideaway, split up the swag, a drink with the boys, then back into town for a movie.

This speech is so tonally similar to Matthews's speech about the excitement of being "a newspaper woman like the ones in the American movies" that the two, at least for a moment, seem kindred spirits. Matthews finds Hogan so attractive that she will take on some of his characteristics. For instance, she becomes enamored of the hard-boiled language he uses. Matthews is initially confused by this foreign tongue. When Hogan informs her that "There's a gat sticking right in your ribs," she replies ingenuously, "A gat?" Frustrated, Hogan spits his reply, "A gat. A rod. A gun." Despite this false start, Matthews soon shows a great facility for hard-boiled speech and, in the process, demonstrates her eagerness to model herself after her Hollywood hero.

It's Love Again also makes clear that Matthews's character aspires to a Hollywood lifestyle and a relationship with a Hollywood man who embodies such a world. As Elaine Bradford, she is a dancer who wishes to become a Hollywood star, an aspiration that becomes clear in a scene in which she auditions for a theatrical producer. After largely ignoring her, the producer gives his attention to a former protégé, the aging Hollywood starlet Francine Grenoble. As he and Grenoble discuss Hollywood, Matthews asks, "What's she got that I haven't got?" Her desire for Hollywood fame is fulfilled to some degree by a love affair with an American journalist working in England, Peter Carlton. He offers her access to Hollywood in three ways. Firstly, like "Smiles" Hogan, he is iconographic of Hollywood, alternately playing the roles of go-getting newspaper reporter and wise-cracking screwball comic. Secondly, he uses Hollywood's star making tactics to propel Matthews to fame. A society gossip columnist, he creates a non-existent celebrity, Mrs. Smythe-Smythe, whose daring and exotic exploits thrill the newspaper reading public. Matthews, hoping to give her career in show business a jumpstart, pretends to be Mrs. Smythe-Smythe and, therefore, embraces the world of shallow celebrity derided by the British press. Thirdly, he offers access to Hollywood because he is played by bonafide American movie star Robert Young. Matthews is not only courting an American journalist. Extradiegetically, she is courting an embodiment of Hollywood.

1. "I used to like gangsters and newspaper films..."

In *Head Over Heels*, Matthews plays Jeanne, a singer and dancer who dreams of becoming a star in America. An early scene finds her chatting to a friend about Hollywood, describing it as "marvelous." She goes on to say, "They tell me the climate in Hollywood's wonderful." Once again, a male character embodies the attractions of American cinema. Though Marcel (Louis Borell) is diegetically French, he is nonetheless a representative of Hollywood. Like the gangster and the screwball comic he is a type—the European "lover" who, from Rudolph Valentino to Maurice Chevalier, was a fixture in Hollywood throughout the 1920s and 1930s. Almost from the moment Marcel opens his mouth he is linked with Hollywood. One of his first lines is, "Of course I shall probably go to Hollywood quite soon." Indeed, the movie suggests that Marcel is attractive to Matthews precisely because he aspires to a Hollywood career. Though she has become involved with another man, Pierre (Robert Flemyng), when Marcel talks of Hollywood she is swept away. A dissolve that occurs during their conversation denotes that they discuss the subject for hours. A few scenes later, Marcel leaves for Hollywood to become a star after being spotted by talent scouts. For the rest of the movie Matthews's longing for him symbolizes her desire for a Hollywood career.

Each movie presents the Hollywood man as desirable, not only because he is iconographic, but because he exudes overt masculinity. His stereotypical manliness means that he stands in stark contrast to the movies' British men. Bereft of the conventional markers of masculinity, British males are variously presented as gay, effeminate, boyish, and nervous. The comparison of these types of men provides a concise metaphor for the cinematic imbalance of power, reminding us that commentators were discussing Hollywood in terms of strength and dominance, while they often constructed the British industry as its antithesis.

In *It's Love Again*, before we meet the American Peter Carlton, the film offers us a portrait of British manhood. The third shot of the movie depicts the dreamy, lackluster face of Archibald Raymond (Ernest Milton), a British theatrical producer. The camera pulls back to reveal that he is sitting in front of a female chorus line. Raymond then indulges in a fit of pique, lambasting the chorus girls for their poor performance. From this essentially feminine space we are transported to its antithesis, the bachelor apartment of Peter Carlton. Wearing smoking jacket, cocktail in hand, the American dances energetically to jazz music emanating from a blaring gramophone.

Across the hall from Carlton's apartment is the home of Archibald Raymond. Returning home from the theater, Raymond throws himself melodramatically about an ostentatiously decorated room, bemoaning the quality of the auditions he must endure and threatening to leave the profession: "I wash my hands of the theater. I hate the word. I hate the people." He threatens to run away to join a monastery. Cut to the hallway that stands between the two apartments. A man appears and rings the bell next to Raymond's door. A decidedly snooty butler appears.

> MAN: Mr. Peter Carlton?
> BUTLER: No, this is Mr. Archibald Raymond. Mr. Peter Carlton is over there.

This simple mistake, added to what we have already witnessed of the two men, seems designed to stress that Carlton is very definitely not Raymond. Moreover, the camera's position at this moment, equidistant from the two apartments, connotes the gulf that separates the two spaces and their occupants rather than stressing their proximity.

Back inside the Englishman's baroque apartment we are offered a Freudian slip. Raymond says, "I was about to enter a convent (he quickly recovers), ah, a monastery."

He utters this line with a shirt pulled over his head so that he resembles a wimpled nun. Raymond is not only painted as Carlton's feminized antithesis, he is in later scenes portrayed as gay. Carlton describes Raymond as "queer duck Archie." As if to back up this observation, it will soon be revealed that the impresario lives with a young man named Woolf.

This early comparison between Raymond and Carlton establishes a pattern in *It's Love Again* whereby British men appear gay and/or nervous in contrast to the American's hyper-masculinuty.[30] The man who rang Raymond's doorbell introduces himself to Carlton. He has come to take a job as the American's manservant. His role in the film is that of comic relief but it is a very specific type of comedy. Like Raymond, he exists to make the American appear even more masculine. His name, which he insists on spelling out loud, is Boys. Not only does the name suggest that he is a mere boy in comparison to Carlton, it may also suggest his sexual preference. Older, shorter, and no match for Peter's brilliantined good looks, Boys is a figure of impotence. To Carlton's question, "Were you ever in love, Boys?" he replies "Once, sir, but nothing came of it. I wasn't firm enough." Carlton's journalistic colleague is Freddie Rathbone (Sonnie Hale), another British foil. The first time we see him he is drunk and fearful of authority. Responding to Carlton's unwillingness to fulfill a journalistic assignment, he says, "You've got to write that column. The boss'll be furious." The nature of their partnership is spelt out by Freddie's comment about the creation of the fictional celebrity Mrs. Smythe-Smythe: "Aren't we the [he points to the American] father and the [points to self] … oh."

In *Gangway*, "Smiles" Hogan's overt masculinity is symbolized by his skill in gunplay and violence.[31] Like Peter Carlton, he appears even more masculine when compared to certain British men. Bob Deering (Barry Mackay) is a British policeman who falls in love with Matthews in *Gangway*. Rather than paint Bob as an exemplary tough cop, the movie stresses his gentle side. When we first meet Bob he is walking down a Scotland Yard corridor telling a colleague what we assume to be the story of an arrest. Excitedly, he proceeds: "Yes, I got him in the end, but what a time he gave me. I was on his trail for days and then finally we came to grips. I don't mind telling you it was a battle, but I got him." The apparent arrest story turns out to be a fishing tale. Bob brings a large, mounted fish into shot with the words: "Isn't he a beauty?" Bob's tough-guy credentials are further undermined by his politeness. Meeting Matthews for the first time he says, "I beg your pardon, I hope you don't think I'm following you." Compared to Hogan's opening gambit, sticking a gun into Matthews's ribs, Bob seems all the more lily-livered. Indeed, even though Bob is prone to make self-aggrandizing statements such as, "Just you point out a public enemy if you want to see Bob Deering do his stuff," he cannot prevent Matthews' abduction and does almost nothing to ensure her safety. One role that can be safely attributed to Bob is that of fairy godmother. As he and Matthews joke together about the latter's life of drudgery, Bob suggests that she put on some glamorous clothes and hit the town:

> PAT [JESSIE MATTHEWS]: Slaving away, sitting up 'til all hours of the night, while the world goes gaily by. Don't you think I want pretty dresses, wine, music, dancing?
> BOB: By gad you'll have them!
> PAT: You're crazy.
> BOB: That is not the way for Cinderella to talk. You know you ought to be thanking your fairy godmother.

One further reason that Bob seems less of a man than Hogan is that, although he is a lord, his estate is penniless and his mansion, Garminster Hall, derelict. In the class-bound Britain of the 1930s, there was perhaps no more potent symbol of masculine strength than a title. Bob's association with a useless title and a bankrupt estate ensures that he appears somewhat emasculated.

One of *Gangway*'s minor characters also suggests that British manhood may not be as potent as it once was. Taggett (Alistair Sim) is a nervous, bug-eyed insurance company investigator. The hapless Taggett tries to make conversation with Hogan the gangster by asking, "Going back to America for the shooting sir?" Revealing his gun, Hogan replies, "Oh, a wise guy, eh? Now beat it Limey." Taggett duly shuffles off. Bob Deering is forced to join forces with Taggett since he believes him to have information that will lead to the kidnapped Matthews. Taggett believes the club where she is being held is named after a nursery rhyme. So, while Matthews is dodging bullets and associating with gangsters, Bob and Taggett sit in a toy shop flicking through a book of nursery rhymes attempting to jog the latter's memory.

Hollywood masculinity is again compared to British in *Head Over Heels*. Marcel, the man with whom Matthews is infatuated, proves irresistible to women. This is made clear in a scene in which Norma Langtry (Whitney Bourne), a Hollywood star, watches Marcel and Matthews perform a double act. She chats with her manager (Fred Dupree) about his appeal:

> MANAGER: The girl's the act. What was so good about him?
> LANGTRY: Oh, I don't know. I like the way he carries himself.... He's got something.
> MANAGER: Just what?
> LANGTRY: Ask me when you're twenty-one.

Marcel's rival for Matthews's love is Pierre. Though the movie takes place in France and Pierre is ostensibly French, unlike Marcel, he speaks with a British accent. His accent ensures that we regard him as the British rival to Marcel, the Hollywood man. Pierre, unskilled in the ways of love and equipped only with boy-next-door looks, wonders how he can possibly compete. Having lost Matthews to Marcel, the Hollywood villain, he moans, "He can offer her the kind of life she wants. What have I got to offer her?" Pierre's romantic ineptitude is confirmed when he prepares to court Matthews by reading a book entitled *How to Make Love*. Acting on a friend's advice to be more aggressive in his pursuit, all he can do is grab her arms and shake her vigorously, while blurting out "I love you." Faced with Pierre's pathetic advances, Matthews returns to Marcel even after he has proven himself a cad.

In demonstrating the strength and glamour of the Hollywood man, the films suggest that Jessie Matthews's attraction to Hollywood and, by implication, the British industry's fascination with American film, are quite understandable. In portraying British men as his opposite, they hint that commentators who presented the British industry as inferior to that of the U.S. were justified in doing so. Are the films, then, exercises in masochism, admitting that Britain and its film industry are no match for the American tough guy?

To some extent, it seems the answer is yes. Historically, when Britain has felt confident of its place in the world, it has yielded images of a robust male populace. For example, in the late Victorian era the British male's prowess at sports and games was popularly regarded as one of the reasons for Britain's dominance of the international scene. Historian James Walvin argues, "British athleticism—original, manly, and pioneering—was but another illustration of the superiority of the British. Sports and games seemed to confirm the abundant evidence which was available on all hands—economic ascendancy, imperial prime, diplomatic assertiveness— that Britain was the world's pre-eminent power."[32] The Matthews films provide a very different image of British masculinity that seems directly related to feelings of decline and inferiority brought about by America's cinematic and geopolitical advance.

The comparison of Hollywood and Britain's men can also be interpreted, not only as an admission of inferiority, but as a suggestion that the British industry might begin to present male stars cut from American cloth. At the time the Matthews films were made, two very different ideas about manhood were competing for the hearts and minds of British cinemagoers. The men of Hollywood film, such as James Cagney, Clark Gable and Douglas Fairbanks, were young, handsome, knockabout guys who looked like they could change the world and often did. The British film industry did not traffic in such matinee idols. Popular comedians George Formby (a jug-eared boy-next-door) and Will Hay (a seedy, scruffy, idle, mean-spirited know-it-all) specialized in playing nobodies who succeeded more by luck than judgment. The leading men of more serious 1930s British cinema— Gordon Harker, a middle-aged curmudgeon in a bowler hat and raincoat; Leslie Howard, famously foppish in *The Scarlet Pimpernel* (1934); Ralph Richardson, more of a heavy than a hero in the *Return of Bulldog Drummond* (1934) and *Bulldog Jack* (1935); Tod Slaughter, scenery chewing villain of gaslight melodrama; and Charles Laughton, known primarily as a grotesque—endeared themselves to millions, but were largely bereft of the Hollywood man's go-getting glamour.

In 1933, Eric M. Knight, film critic of the Philadelphia Public Ledger, summarized the way many Americans, and probably the majority of the pro–Hollywood British audience, thought of Britain's male stars. He argues, "They ... appear to us like a lot of top-hatted silly asses of exactly the type that Americans delight to scorn."[33] Only Ivor Novello, the suave anti-hero of *The Lodger* (1927), and Robert Donat, who played the lead role in *The 39 Steps* (1935), had something in common with the Hollywood male. However, Novello and Donat made few British films in the 1930s compared to those actors just mentioned and so did not stamp their presence so thoroughly on the national medium. There existed a very definite gap in British films that the virile American could potentially fill. In foregrounding Hollywood men, the Matthews movies explored and enjoyed a form of masculinity that was largely absent from British cinema but, because of American dominance of British screens, was proving increasingly fascinating. In portraying the Hollywood male repeatedly triumphing over his British rival, it seems that the three films were, at least to some extent, championing Hollywood's brand of masculinity.

However, though "the British inferiority complex" (as Basil Dean put it) threads its way inexorably through the narrative of each film, so does a desire to see the American colossus humbled. The three movies combine Britain's stark realization that it was at the mercy of the Hollywood giant, with dreams of victory over its undeserving master. In the last act of each movie, Britain finally wins out, and the Hollywood man that Matthews had found so attractive is, in various ways, defeated. The three films that have spent much of their running time juxtaposing Hollywood's strength with Britain's weakness have apparently done so, not just as an exercise in self-laceration, but in order to establish a David and Goliath scenario.

Ultimately, Matthews rejects Hollywood and its men, thereby hinting that the British industry has no need of America's glamour or its stock characters. In *Gangway* and *Head Over Heels* Hogan and Marcel are rejected in favor of the British boy-next-door and, in *It's Love Again*, Peter Carlton ends his American tabloid tactics. Apparently throwaway lines, peppered throughout each film, hint that Hollywood may not be as wonderful as it first appears. In *Gangway*, on discovering that Nedda Beamont's film studio contract stipulates she may marry no more than seven times, Matthews scoffs, "Some things are sacred in Hollywood." In *It's Love Again*, as Archibald Raymond entertains the Hollywood star Francine Grenoble, he asks her, "How's Hollywood?" She replies only with a disdainful groan. Raymond answers, "So everyone says." Later in the same film we hear that a restaurant is "about as exclusive as a Hollywood party." In *Head Over Heels* the first we hear of Hollywood is that it has a "wonderful" climate, but we are then told "it always gets cold at night." These hints that the enticing warmth of Hollywood may turn out to be deceptive are portentous, since each movie proceeds to demonstrate that such a world is no place for a nice British girl like Jessie Matthews.

Hollywood, it turns out, is all gloss and no substance. In *Gangway*, after Matthews's initial enthusiasm about the excitement and opportunity on show in Hollywood movies, she has several disillusioning experiences. Trying to get ahead as a reporter, she attempts to steal the diary of Nedda

1. "I used to like gangsters and newspaper films..."

In *It's Love Again* (1936) Jessie Matthews is courted by Hollywood, here personified by Robert Young.

Beaumont (Olive Blakeney), a famous, but fading, Hollywood star staying in a London hotel. Disguising herself as a maid, Matthews soon learns that behind the star's glamorous image hides a pompous and mean-spirited woman. Beaumont, playing the American ugly sister to Matthews' British Cinderella, asks her, "Who cares about your best? It's my best that counts."

The British heroine later realizes that Hollywood-style excitement is less fun than she had hoped. Matthews follows Beaumont onto an ocean liner bound for the United States intent upon getting a story for her newspaper. While aboard, she is mistaken for an international jewel thief by Bob Deering, the Scotland Yard man, and by Smiles Hogan, the American gangster. After she is forced into working for Hogan's boss and experiences American tough guys and shoot-outs first hand, she admits, "I used to like gangsters and newspaper films, but I'm not so sure now." By the end of the movie, Matthews has plumped for the homespun safety of marriage to Bob Deering, the antithesis of "Smiles" Hogan.

Matthews realizes that Hollywood is essentially phony and ends the film disillusioned. However, as will be the case in all three movies, she is unwilling to totally reject its promises of a better life. *Gangway* allows her to keep something of her brief dalliance with American cinema. In the movie's climactic wedding scene, in which she marries her British beau, Bob, she asks the Justice of the Peace to proceed with the gangster slang, "OK brother, shoot." Moreover, the wedding scene suggests that Hogan and Matthews can be friends if not lovers. As the ceremony takes place, we realize that Hogan has strong-armed the official from his bed in order to perform it. Tenuous as they may be, Matthews retains some links to Hollywood and, in doing so, hints that the British industry too, though it should know better, still carries a torch for American cinema.

In *It's Love Again* Matthews experiences another sobering epiphany regarding the Hollywood star system. In the first two acts of the film, she is intent upon outstripping the fame of aging Hollywood star, Francine Grenoble. Initially, she is frustrated in this quest. Though she is young, pretty, and talented, she is not from Hollywood and therefore cannot command the attention enjoyed by the star. Despondently returning to her flat, Matthews tells a friend about the experience: "I've found out one thing. All you need is a big name. You don't have to have anything else." However, after Matthews has attained a big name and is therefore able to compete with Hollywood stars like Grenoble, she decides to reject her stardom, much to the consternation of her American boyfriend, Peter Carlton. She explains her decision by saying, "You can't spend your whole life at a fancy dress party." Peter's exasperated reply is, "Well, there's a girl for you. She wants to be. She is. And then she doesn't want to be." In rejecting her big name, she has rejected the superficiality of Hollywood fame.

Like *Gangway*, *It's Love Again* allows Matthews to retain some aspects of the Hollywood world she has briefly inhabited. Though she has cast aside her big name, she takes another Hollywood name, that of Peter Carlton AKA Robert Young, the American film star. In the last scene, in which Peter suggests they marry, he spells each letter of his name aloud, stressing that his name, not a big name, is all Matthews needs. Significantly, in the movie's last shot Matthews stands with Young on a British theatrical stage, not an American sound stage. The shot connotes that she can have the best of Hollywood, represented by Peter's strength and vitality, without its downside, the phoniness embodied by Grenoble. Moreover, by choosing Britain and its theatrical tradition she can enjoy a type of fame that results from genuine talent rather than journalistic hype.[34]

Head Over Heels demonstrates once again that Hollywood's glamorous surface conceals a fundamental emptiness. Matthews is aware from the outset that Hollywood, represented by Marcel, the European "lover," is phony. As he attempts to seduce her, she makes fun of his clichéd cinematic approach. After telling him that his next line will be, "Did anyone ever tell you that you're the most beautiful girl in the world, because you are," she notes that the scenario should proceed in the following manner: "and then I giggle and say 'don't be silly' and look away shyly. And then you seize me in your arms and kiss me fiercely and follow it up with two more." So knowledgeable is Matthews in the art of pat Hollywood screenwriting that she is able, not only to predict Marcel's next line, but to finish his sentences for him.

> MARCEL: I've been waiting for this moment...
> JEANNE [JESSIE MATTHEWS]: ...ever since I met you.
> MARCEL: You don't understand, for...
> JEANNE: ...the first time in my life.
> MARCEL: Are you being quite fair? I swear to you I've...
> JEANNE: ...never met anyone quite like you before.

Matthews, in full possession of the knowledge that Marcel is little more than a good haircut and a bundle of bad lines, kisses him anyway. Throughout the movie, Matthews must struggle to overcome her attraction to what she knows is shallow, vacillating between the glamorous but phony Marcel, and the honest, unglamorous "Briton" Pierre.

As British commentators often did, the film presents the decision to "go Hollywood" as a Faustian bargain. Indeed, at one point Marcel offers Matthews a contract: "I came here to offer you a contract. Hollywood. My leading lady.... All you have to do is sign." Matthews takes the whole movie to muster the strength to turn down such advances. The narrative revolves around a series of moments in which she succumbs to the charms of Hollywood and Marcel, then regains her senses, then falls once more under the apparently irresistible spell of her tormentors. In one such scene Marcel reveals his true colors when, after becoming a Hollywood star, he steals a song he once performed with Matthews, trying to pass it off as his own. Appearing on Matthews's radio show with his American girlfriend, Norma Langtry, Marcel introduces it as, "a song which we first introduced in America and has become the hit of the season over there." An argument ensues, hinting that Matthews has finally come to her senses about Marcel. She refuses to allow the couple to sing the number: "I'm sorry, but not that song," she insists. Langtry belittles Matthews's objections by demanding maniacally, "Who's going to stop me?" The defiant Matthews replies, "I am!" But these fine words prove to be empty. She is soon tempted once again by Marcel's offer of a Hollywood contract. A few scenes later she rallies, mustering the strength to turn it down. He whines in protest, "but it's what you've always wanted." She adamantly replies that "it's what I used to want."

Only in the final moments of the movie does she finally make up her mind to be with her "British" suitor. Yet, even then, it seems that Matthews is in thrall to Marcel and that Pierre must encourage her to do the right thing. As Marcel and Matthews conduct a dockside press conference discussing their imminent departure for Hollywood, Pierre races to save the day. Just after Marcel has uttered the line, "She will make tests and be groomed for stardom," Pierre enters the frame and punches him to the ground. Commandeering the microphone, Pierre addresses the assembled pressmen with the words, "Mademoiselle Courbet [Matthews] is not going to Hollywood! She's going to marry me, Pierre Brisar!" The fact that Pierre must help Matthews to finally reject Marcel suggests that, as in the other two films, she will retain some affection for Hollywood even after the credits roll.

Hollywood is largely rejected because it is inherently phony. Though the three movies seem ready to admit that the American industry is strong and they appear to revel in its version of masculinity, they are keen to point out that Hollywood's surface glamour conceals a sobering reality. Another reason that Hollywood is not allowed to triumph is that it represents social mobility and irreverence. In *Head Over Heels* Marcel, a starving artist living in a garret flat, is plucked from obscurity to achieve fame and wealth in America. A similar thrill lies at the heart of *Gangway*. Its gangsters wear their proletarian origins on their sleeve and still manage to retain positions of wealth and influence. Peter Carlton of *It's Love Again* is a similarly anomalous figure in British film since he has little respect for class. His role as a "society reporter" means that he makes his living delving into the private life of the aristocracy. He has no interest in perpetuating a traditional gentleman/servant relationship with his manservant, informing him that he does not need a butler to dress him or bathe him. Rather, a backgammon partner is what he seeks. In the Hollywood realm, the movies suggest, a person can choose his identity rather than have it thrust upon him. In the realm of 1930s British cinema, it was unthinkable that such a world-view should be victorious.

Debunking the American Utopia

There is yet another reason that Jessie Matthews is denied a lasting relationship with Hollywood. During the 1930s, the British journalistic and cinematic communities were engaged in an effort to discredit the nation from which Hollywood sprang. Since Hollywood was the United States's most prominent export, it was a natural target for what amounted to a campaign of anti–American propaganda. The Matthews films are part of cycle of movies and articles that aim to debunk utopian conceptions of America drawn from the Hollywood screen.

In 1937 the popular British film magazine, *World Film News*, ran a series of articles by Thomas Baird about the harsh realities of life in the United States. These were presented alongside, and presented a stark contrast with, more conventional pieces on the glamorous lives of Hollywood stars. In effect, the articles function as reminders that the Hollywood version of America proffered by most of the magazine's articles was little more than fantasy. Baird writes about African-American life in Washington, D.C., in an article entitled "An Innocent in Harlem." This muck-raking piece, the title of which encapsulates Baird's desire to take Britons who were innocent of American "truths" into environments closed off to them by the movies, appears, ironically enough, adjacent to an interview with Darryl Zanuck, Hollywood studio head and chief purveyor of American fantasy. Its opening lines reveal that the United States is a nation where apparent perfection conceals a sobering reality: "The White House, sitting like a forgotten wedding cake, dazzles in the sunlight. The capitol is like an architect's model. Everything is clean, neat and underlined like a schoolboy's prize copy-book. It is a Babbit's dream of organization and historicity."[35] Baird then argues that such images encourage us to forget the harsh truths of American race relations, so much so that, "It is quite astonishing to find pictures of the story of the Red Indian in the galleries and living negroes walking the streets."[36]

The previous month had seen a similar article by Baird, this time exposing the difference between fanciful depictions of the old west and the contemporary state of Native America. He begins by arguing, "No one who in his more tender years read with avidity the tales of Buffalo Bill and General Custer ... could maintain a steady heart-beat on waking up one morning in the home of it all," but is later forced to unhappily admit that "the ancient ceremonies of the Red Man are now the tea-time entertainment of the tourist."[37] When Baird's odyssey brings him to Hollywood, the town most responsible for creating an ersatz America, he notes that it is a place where image and reality have become hopelessly blurred: "They make films in Hollywood when the sun shines but it is difficult to know which are the 'sets' and which the hotels and restaurants. You get better food in the studios than you do in the restaurants and the studios look more like hotels than the restaurants look like restaurants. Everything looks like a set except a set. It is really very difficult."[38] Such articles suggest that the Matthews films not only expressed British dissatisfaction with Hollywood, but were part of movement to expose American phoniness.

The Matthews films function as anti–American propaganda because most Britons tended to view Hollywood and the United States as indistinguishable from one another. The conflation of nation with film industry meant that any indictment of Hollywood automatically became an indictment of America. The British tendency to think of America in terms of Hollywood and vice versa was a fact not lost on the writers of *Gangway*. The movie contains a scene in which Bob Deering suggests to Matthews that "Smiles" Hogan might be a gangster. She replies, "Oh, don't be so British and think every American's a gangster. He's probably just a cowboy." As thirties commentators often observed, most of Britain's ideas about America were gleaned from the movies. American critic Eric M. Knight asks incredulously after watching a popular Hollywood movie, "Do the girls in West Ham think we are like that? Do the lads in Lancashire imagine they are seeing us? ... It is almost with shock that I realize that, of course, they must accept us as we show ourselves by now."[39] Moreover, the behavior of Americans was often seen as closely tied to that of their screen counterparts. For instance, the business tactics of American studio personnel were discussed in the British trade press as if they were learned from the tough guys of the Hollywood screen. As an editorial in *World Film News* claims, "The American capacity for squeezing out has the long tradition of the gangster films behind it."[40] Britain's refusal to separate real Americans from their onscreen version meant that when a British film condemned the actions of a gangster or screwball comic, it also asked its audience to condemn the United States.

Such a request was made more blatantly in several British movies of the 1930s that portrayed a dark truth behind American glamour. *The Tunnel* (Maurice Elvey, 1935), a Gaumont-British picture that, at first glance, seems very different in spirit from the studio's Jessie Matthews vehicles, nonetheless warns that although American vigor is attractive, it may do more harm than good. Mac (Richard Dix), an American engineer, masterminds the construction of an undersea tunnel between Britain and the United States. At first, he seems the perfect man for the job. His manly, go-getting personality is established by his comment, "I'm better at doing things than I am talking about them." His grandiose plans ensure that he is attractive to women: "There's a certain charm about a dreamer, even if he dreams of iron and steel," comments an admirer. Robbie (Leslie Banks), a less overtly masculine Briton, is second in command on the project and is left to nurture Mac's family. His comparative dullness is confirmed by a female acquaintance who tells him, "Even marriage couldn't change your infinite monotony." Robbie does not possess the American's drive and enthusiasm. When he informs Mac that he is quitting the tunnel project, the American angrily rounds upon him, saying "you're not quitting. You're going through with it. Whatever happens, you're going through with it." Despite its suggestions that Americans are energetic and productive, the movie is keen to point out the price of Mac's go-getting ardor. He neglects his family, missing his son's birthday because he works so hard on the tunnel. A gas-leak in the tunnel causes his wife to go blind and a cave-in kills his son. While the Matthews movies discuss American shortcomings by focusing on Hollywood, *The Tunnel*, and other films like it, criticize the United States and its citizens more openly.

It is not only Gaumont-British films that suggest the United States is a nation whose glamorous image conceals a disturbing reality. The myth of American opportunity is a fundamental theme in *The Frozen Limits* (Marcel Varnel, 1938) a film released by Gainsborough studios. This movie, starring The Crazy Gang (a band of music-hall entertainers who also made madcap, surreal film comedies in the thirties and forties), concerns a group of friends who decide to travel to America in order to take part in a gold rush. Expecting to get rich quick, the gang encounters a ghost town whose only inhabitant is a fellow Briton who has seemingly been driven mad by his life as a gold prospector. Visiting a neighboring town, the gang enters a saloon that apparently offers free food and drink. "Blimey, this is the place to live in. Free lunch. Free beer," exclaims one of them. Yet, they soon discover that food is free only if they buy a drink.

Hey, Hey, USA (Marcel Varnel, 1938), a General Films release starring Will Hay, continues this revelatory trend by making fun of American claims to be a free and democratic country. Arriving in the United States, Hay is told by an ocean-liner steward that Ellis Island is "a sort of prison, sir, under the Statue of Liberty." Later, after Hay and Edgar Kennedy (playing a gangster) are arrested for laughing, Kennedy exclaims, "And they say America's a free country." Hay agrees "Yeah, it's a bit different from what I expected." The movie also includes an indictment of the shallowness of the American advertising industry. Asked to deliver a radio address, Hay attempts to do so, but is continually interrupted by a spokesman for the *Sweetie Wheaties* breakfast cereal company. The spokesman has no interest in the address, and periodically puts a hand over Hay's mouth in order to expound upon the benefits of eating his product. Such moments, and similar ones in the films just mentioned, suggest that the Matthews films were not only eager to explore the pros and cons of Hollywood because it was a fascinating cinematic rival. They also focused on Hollywood because it was a product of America, a nation that, as the British press and film industry repeatedly pointed out, was riven through with contradiction and failed to live up to its own hype.

It is often remarked that a film expresses the world-view of a particular director, writer, or other individual integral to its creation. Here I have attempted to show that a movie can incorporate a multitude of voices, not only those that directly shape the production, but also those that can be heard echoing through the industry from which it springs. While the Matthews movies were undoubtedly created to take a bite out of the American market and to increase ticket sales in Britain, their creators could not help but pay heed to the deafening cacophony of industry voices that urged caution in dealing with Hollywood. The sheer force of their presence in the cinematic zeitgeist meant that, though each film trades in Hollywood glitz, each one steps back from the brink of total Americanization. Matthews must reject the Hollywood lifestyle almost completely because, as British commentators pointed out, it was fundamentally false and potentially incendiary. Moreover, as British articles and movies of the time suggested, Hollywood was no place for Matthews because it was the product of America, a nation where the promise of utopia had yet to be delivered. The films' revelations about Hollywood and the United States have wider implications. They connote that Hollywood did not deserve its place as the preeminent cinematic power and, by casting Hollywood as an emperor with no clothes, the films suggest that America, its objective correlative, was also unfit to wield the international power it increasingly enjoyed.

2

"But he's so kind and friendly!"
The Mysterious American in 1930s British Cinema

American characters in British films of the 1930s are often figures of mystery. *Secret Agent* (Alfred Hitchcock, 1936), *Thunder in the City* (Marion Gering, 1937), *The Return of the Frog* (Maurice Elvey, 1938), and *Murder in Soho* (Norman Lee, 1938) all foreground enigmatic American men. In *Secret Agent*, Robert Marvin (Robert Young) is a spy who appears to be an American and then a German. At one moment he can seem a child-like playboy and, at another, a cold-blooded killer. *Thunder in the City* introduces Dan Armstrong (Edward G. Robinson), an American advertising executive who is equal parts businessman, huckster, and fraud. *The Return of the Frog* repeatedly raises doubts that Dale Sandford (Hartley Power) is the American policeman he claims to be, and suggests that he may instead be the criminal mastermind behind a notorious gang. *Murder in Soho* charts the progress of Steve Marco (Jack LaRue), an American nightclub owner who dresses like an English gentleman but acts like a Chicago gangster or, alternately, the epitome of petite-bourgeois aspiration. The elusive identities of these men ensure that they prove very confusing to the British characters with whom they come into contact. Indeed, their refusal to "fit in" is a crucial aspect of the films in which they appear. Why should British cinema be repeatedly drawn to American mystery men?

Enigmatic Americans became a common sight because they provided a means to confront Britain's rapidly changing social structure. In the 1930s, British society was built upon the idea that individuals were easily identifiable via the rubric of class and that they "knew their place" in the social hierarchy. However, to an unprecedented degree, Britain's working and middle classes were refusing to fit into their allotted roles. Political demonstrations by the workers made obvious their desire to live in a more equal and just society. The growth of a middle class whose members insisted on emulating their "betters" suggested that rigid social demarcation might soon be a thing of the past. British cinema was unable to confront these changes directly. Any film containing material that censors believed might challenge the status quo was heavily edited or banned and, therefore, it was nearly impossible to portray British citizens as square pegs refusing to fit neatly into society's round holes. Americans, however, as outsiders, could be portrayed this way.

An Unknowable Citizenry

In the inter-war period, many in the British establishment considered a heavily stratified class system an essential part of a civilized society. In an influential polemic of 1928, Clive Bell argues:

> Civilization requires the existence of a leisured class ... and a leisured class requires the existence of slaves—of people, I mean, who give some part of their surplus time and energy to the support of others.... This civilizing elite ... will merely live their lives; and living will be seen to have pleasures and desires, standards and values, an attitude to life, a point of view, different from those of the busy multitude.... You will keep the number as low as you can without jeopardizing the essential, that there should be a class of men and women of whom nothing is required—not even to justify their existence.[1]

With the advent of the Depression, this world of demarcation and inequality would be challenged. Working people engaged in a surge of political activism, epitomized by the Jarrow Hunger March of 1933 in which unemployed shipyard workers from the northern English town of Jarrow walked to London to raise awareness of their plight. Widely played newsreel footage of the event made it the most iconic image of Britain's economic slump. The cap-doffing mentality that the elite demanded of their "slaves" was apparently on the way out.

White-collar workers also began to behave differently. Advances in motor transport and the rapid growth of suburbs during the twenties and thirties made "the clerk," as the new breed of lower-middle-class office worker was popularly termed, as visible as the volatile unemployed.[2] Clerks posed a threat to a rigidly stratified class system because their appearance and tastes were becoming ever closer to those of the upper class. Their reproduction paintings, mass-produced china tea sets, and studied accents meant that they might be mistaken for those higher up on the social ladder. Clerks were yet more alarming because they appeared to be taking over the countryside, their rows of identical houses voraciously gobbling up the rural areas that the establishment regarded as its preserve.

The upper class had enjoyed a Britain in which the lower orders had apparently known their place, the workers suffering stoically, the middling sort serving the boss and not threatening his job. They now faced workers with Bolshevist tendencies and a bourgeoisie with delusions of grandeur. As historian David Cannadine notes, "'fear' and 'contempt' for organized labor ... [were] widespread among those of superior position."[3] He also argues that the British establishment regarded the burgeoning bourgeoisie as a heinous influence on society: "the middle classes were described ... as incompetent, vulgar, and unpleasant." He continues: "appeasement [of Hitler's Germany] was denounced as the sort of spineless foreign policy that had to be expected once the middle classes had taken over."[4]

According to many in the upper class, the social order was not only threatened by the changing behavior patterns of the general populace. It was also endangered by a process of "leveling-down."[5] This term described the perceived transformation of Britain into an increasingly classless society of average citizens with the same mediocre values, tastes, and morals. Instead of a nation divided into upper class and lower class, high culture and low culture, exceptional and unexceptional, it was argued that Britain was becoming defined by formless liminality. Commentators bemoaned the "dictatorship of the uncultured,"[6] but rather than a descent into barbarism, they predicted the far more sinister scenario of a drift into a middle ground where worlds that had been strictly demarcated were blended together.

Elite British novelists openly confronted leveled-down Britain. John Carey points out that Graham Greene's 1938 novel *Brighton Rock* is "a contemptuous indictment of England in the 1930s" that demonstrates the author's loathing for "clerks, hairdressers and fat, spotty girls."[7] As Carey notes, Greene presents vacationers who combine the worlds of lower and upper class, old world and new. His bathing beauties, all members of the middle and lower classes, take on the mannerisms and accent of the elite: "All down the front the girls sat in the two penny deck-chairs, waiting to be picked ... clerks, shopgirls, hairdressers.... Hale offered them cigarettes and they stared at him like duchesses with large cold eyes and said, 'I don't smoke, thank you.'"[8] Throughout the novel, it is quite obvious that a patrician Britain has been swept away by a coarse parody.

In the stratified social structure cherished by the powerful, an individual could be easily identified as a member of a particular social group.

This process of identification was a means to control and monitor access to power. If a person looked and acted in a particular way then he or she was given, or denied, admittance to a world of privilege. However, because the masses were refusing to play their allotted social roles, it was more difficult to know where a person stood in the social hierarchy and, therefore, patrician Britons began to fear that the corridors of power lay open to invasion.

A stratified social structure was one way to monitor the citizenry. A system of identity checks was another. World War I, and the inter-war years that followed, brought with them a crackdown on immigration, unprecedented surveillance of travelers, and a preoccupation with frontiers. The British government's attitude to immigration was radically altered.[9] Traveling became more difficult since passports were now routinely required and examined, while frontiers proliferated and were redrawn because the war had instilled an "irrational nationalism" in European leaders.[10] Travelers, then, were hugely threatening figures in the eyes of the authorities because they might be the agents of a hostile foreign power. It also seems likely that they were so closely monitored—especially in Britain where an amorphous citizenry had begun to alarm the elite—because travel afforded individuals an opportunity to reinvent their identity. Like the middle and working classes, travelers proved difficult to know.[11] With no peer group to regulate their behavior, they were free to defy the strictures of class and accepted behavior patterns. The traveler's identity could be defined less by their social position and more by individual ability, less by loyalty to a nation and more by loyalty to self.

Film Censorship and Social Control

British cinema was unable to confront these social changes directly because it was heavily invested in maintaining the status quo. To a great extent, British films were the voice of the elite. Many producers and directors came from upper class and/or moneyed backgrounds. Prolific and critically lauded director Anthony Asquith was the son of an ex-prime minister, and studio boss J. Arthur Rank was a millionaire flour magnate. Film critic Jeffrey Richards notes that the thirties film community included "a motley crew of maverick British aristocrats [and] eccentric millionaires."[12] The presence of such individuals in prominent studio posts was one reason that British cinema spoke for the elite. Most studio employees, however, were from the middle classes. Yet, any anti-establishment sentiment they may have harbored was stifled by a rigid code of censorship.

The primary task of the British censor was to protect the interests of the powerful. Since it was widely understood that the British film audience was largely working class, the elite was concerned that movies should not propagate revolutionary sentiment.[13] A number of draconian regulations were adopted. For instance, authority figures were not to be held up to ridicule. A 1929 leaflet issued by the British Board of Film Censors (BBFC) proposed a ban on:

> Stories and scenes which are calculated and possibly intended to ferment social unrest and discontent. Incidents which bring into contempt public characters acting in their capacity as such i.e. officers and men wearing His Majesty's uniform, ministers of religion, ministers of the crown, ambassadors and representatives of foreign nations, administrators of the law, medical men.[14]

More than their American counterparts in the Hays Office, who were primarily concerned with issues of morality, British censors were engaged in social control. For instance, the Soviet films *The Battleship Potemkin* (Sergei Eisenstein, 1925) and *Mother* (Vsevolod Pudovkin, 1926) were banned in Britain, while in the United States they encountered no censorship. This is not to suggest that British censors did not frown upon overtly sexual and violent imagery, but their objection to these was rooted more in a concern for social stability than moral uplift. As Jeffrey Richards has commented, "It is hard ... to see the moral censorship exercised by the BBFC as anything other than a coherently organized form of social control."[15] Thanks to censorship strictures, whether or not a filmmaker came from an elite background, his or her films were bound by law to protect the establishment.

Perhaps the most potent evidence that the elite considered the film industry to be a valuable tool is the frequency with which it decorated prominent producers for services to their nation. Alexander Korda, creator of lavish imperialist spectacles such as *The Four Feathers* (Zoltan Korda, 1939), and Michael Balcon, Head of Gaumont-British, MGM-British and, most famously, Ealing Studios, were knighted, while Basil Dean, Balcon's predecessor at Ealing, received the OBE.

Because they enjoyed a stranglehold on the industry's output, the elite used cinema to express its ideas. Paramount amongst these was the notion that the populace was divided into easily identifiable social classes. Onscreen, upper class and working class acted in very specific, predictable ways, thereby suggesting that in Britain a person's place in the social hierarchy was self-evident. Michael Powell's early film *Lazy Bones* (1935) is typical, portraying workers as shabby, dull-witted, and only interested in their pints, while the upper class drift about a mansion house, exchanging witticisms and loudly proclaiming their entitlement to a life of leisure ("You can't risk gossip by being actually seen at work," argues one of them). Significantly, the middle class was virtually ignored by British films of the thirties. As Alfred Hitchcock remarked in 1937:

> British Film Producers know only two strata of English existence, the poor and the rich.... Totally ignored by British film-makers is that vital central stratum of British humanity, the middle class. Forgotten are the men who leap on 'buses, the girls who pack in the Tube, the commercial travellers, the newspaper men, the girls who manicure your nails, the composers who write the dance numbers, the city-clerk.... In them lies the spirit of England that, for some unknown reason, is almost entirely ignored on the screen....[16]

By downplaying the existence of the middle class—the social stratum in which appearance and behavior were less likely to betray a person's background—thirties cinema avoided ambiguity and perpetuated the notion of an easily knowable citizenry.

Unsurprisingly, British films of the 1930s also transmitted the idea that the status quo should be sustained. The few moments when British movies admitted that citizens were discontented with their society were undercut by admonishments to be stoical in the face of hardship and, though films sometimes acknowledged the reality of the Depression, they attempted to defuse discontent by suggesting that, although Britain was made up of different social classes, the nation was one big happy family in which everyone knew their place.[17]

The American as Embodiment of Classlessness and Ambition

The establishment film industry, then, did not directly confront changes in Britain's social structure because one of its primary functions was to demonstrate the viability of that structure. It was possible, however, to address the threat to the status quo by attributing it to a foreign influence, an entity from outside the system exerting upon it a malignant influence. The American would fill this role. Though he is coded as "not British," he is an obvious stand-in for a newly enigmatic British citizen that the establishment feared, but was unable to look full in the face. An embodiment of "leveled-down" Britain, he blurs the borders of the class system, blending together working and upper-class behavior patterns, low and high culture, even encouraging others to follow his example. Like the working and middle classes, he wants more out of life, each movie presenting him as an ambitious individual who lets nothing stand between him and his desires. This man who refuses to "know his place" is portrayed as a disturbing enigma.

By presenting the American in this way, the industry avoided the incendiary image of a Briton refusing to know his place and, at the same time, demonstrated to the British audience that such behavior would lead to disaster. In each film, the American is a thorn in the side of the British authorities, but he is allowed onscreen so that the threat he poses can be identified and then obliterated. *Secret Agent*, *Thunder in the City*, *The Return of the Frog*, and *Murder in Soho* use Americans to introduce the threat of the enigmatic citizen, only to demonstrate how this individual's true self can indeed be unmasked, his ambition quashed, and his social mobility halted.

There was nothing coincidental about the use of Americans to portray such citizens. By the inter-war period, for many in Britain, the United States had come to epitomize classlessness and ambition. Such a characterization had its roots in the nineteenth century when British visitors to the United States, such as Charles Dickens, returned home with tales of an amorphous space where distinctions in social class were not made obvious by dress, behavior, and speech. The eminent British poet and literary critic Matthew Arnold noted in 1888, "In truth, everything is against distinction in America, and against the sense of elevation to be gained through admiring and respecting it. The glorification of 'the average man,' who is quite a religion with statesmen and publicists there, is against it."[18] As well as noting classlessness, Arnold commented that, due to a lack of strict social demarcation, "the great bulk of the community" found themselves able to "rise and make their fortune."[19]

In the 1930s, British commentators were still discussing American classlessness and social mobility, but were frequently using alarmist tones. America had come to Britain via Hollywood and those in power were uneasy with the influence American movies appeared to be having on the public. In 1931 British journalist Basil Maine commented in *The Radio Times*, "The American invasion of the entertainment world is responsible ... for changes of taste, for the blunting of dialect ... for new manners of thinking, for higher pressure of living, for discontent among normally contented people, for big ideas and for 'Oh, yeah!'"[20] In Maine's concern for the "blunting of dialect" can be detected some anxiety that the population was becoming as amorphous and unfathomable as that of the United States, and his citation of "discontent" and "big ideas" betray his fear that classless America encouraged in Britons a desire for social change. Maine and his ilk portrayed citizens that, corrupted by American influence, were ready to question the structure of their society with an exclamatory, quizzical "Oh, yeah!" The four films in question, then, are explorations not only of new kinds of British citizen, but also of the American influence that was widely regarded as a root cause of their novel behavior. They examine a Britain that was changing from within and, simultaneously, from without.

Leveled-Down Worlds: Secret Agent, Thunder in the City, Return of the Frog *and* Murder in Soho

In each film, the American is the poster child of the leveling-down process. He brings together the coarse and the refined, reducing a world of patrician quality to a more vulgar state. Inhabiting the middle ground between high and low culture, he insists on dragging others into this space with him. In *Secret Agent*, Robert Marvin (Robert Young) barges into the rarified world of two English spies, Edgar Ashenden (John Gielgud) and Elsa Carrington (Madeleine Carroll). Ashenden has traveled to Switzerland to kill a German agent, but his demeanor and that of Elsa, his British contact, is more appropriate to the drawing room than the killing fields of World War I Europe. The obviously upper class pair spend their time trading wry remarks and witticisms until the intervention of the American, Marvin. Though he sports the well-tailored suit of the upper class, his rudeness and lasciviousness suggests his affinity with a lower stratum of society. "Are those your teeth?" he asks Elsa, before going on to ask, "If you won't let me kiss you, do you mind if I bite your Adam's apple?" He refers to Ashenden, his rival for Elsa's affections, as "bow-legged" and says of a Swiss coachman, "Look at that nose, I bet you could squeeze it and get a quart of whisky out of it." Indeed, Marvin will define himself as a man who stands between barbarity and civilization by characterizing himself as a "caveman with a college education."

Thunder in the City's Dale Armstrong (Edward G. Robinson) also brings a certain degree of vulgarity to rarified environments. Armstrong is an American advertising man with all the subtlety of P.T. Barnum. He travels to Britain in an attempt to learn about dignity, yet his good intentions are soon put aside when he becomes obsessed with publicizing a new wonder-metal, magnalite. He does so by deploying every excessive marketing scheme at his disposal, thereby transforming the hushed chambers of London's financial district into a circus.

2. "But he's so kind and friendly!" 61

The American gains entry to formerly exclusive space. Dale Armstrong (Edward G. Robinson) and Lady Patricia (Luli Deste) in *Thunder in the City* **(1937).**

Like Robert Marvin, he blends together—and moves between—worlds that usually have heavily policed borders. For instance, he brings American-style ballyhoo to the more reserved environment of Britain's stock market, trying to convince his investors that they are Americans in embryo. "I've observed that you English don't appreciate your own ability as ballyhoo artists," he tells them. He brings white and blue-collar people together: while journeying by train, instead of riding in the comfort of a carriage, he joins the driver in the less glamorous environment of the locomotive. Later, he allows working-class friends access to the exclusive world of stock market trading by encouraging them to buy shares in magnalite. He also brings popular culture into an environment infused with high culture: befriending some street musicians, he asks them to bring their dilapidated piano up to his room in an expensive hotel. In reply to their protestation ("It wouldn't be right sir") he scoffs, "Who says it wouldn't be right?" He duly grabs one end of the instrument and wheels it through the hotel lobby, causing a rash of raised eyebrows. Armstrong downplays the divisiveness of class, culture, and nationality with utterances such as "the human race is a pretty decent club to belong to."

Dale Sandford (Hartley Power) of *The Return of the Frog* brings criminal tendencies into a law-abiding environment. He claims to be a Chicago policeman who has come to Scotland Yard to study foreign police methods, but his dress and deportment seem to betray a kinship with the underworld. British movies of the thirties tended to present policemen as soft-spoken, dour fellows sporting bowler hat, raincoat, and rolled-up umbrella. Since Sandford dresses like a hood—in loud pinstripes, fedora, and spats—he immediately demonstrates his willingness to straddle two worlds. He neither looks nor acts the part of lawman, poking fun at the British police at every opportunity. Flattering his mentor, Inspector Elk (Gordon Harker), by telling him that he is reputed to be the shrewdest brain in Scotland Yard, Sandford immediately undercuts this statement by saying that he has also heard he "mustn't go by appearances." After he is shown a demonstration of fingerprinting techniques, much to the consternation of those around him, the American pockets the fingerprinting kit, along with a nearby ashtray to which he takes a liking. Sandford is a liminal figure, not only because he is a hybrid of cop and criminal, but because he has no qualms about mixing with the criminal fraternity. His lusty pursuit of Lila (Renee Ray), a girl from a criminal family, confirms this.

In *Murder in Soho*, Steve Marco (Jack LaRue) is another representative of the leveling-down process. A Chicago mobster whose London nightclub is a front for all manner of criminal activity, he is able to slip between the persona of hardened criminal and that of gracious, gentlemanly host, effortlessly mixing with his simian henchmen and the dinner jackets out on the dance floor. It is not just the American who can journey between worlds. His presence encourages Britons to do the same. Marco's nightclub "The Cotton Club," is a liminal space that, like its American namesake, brings together races and classes that would not usually rub shoulders.

Murder in Soho is very concerned to point out that the club is a place where the upper classes are brought low by contact with the masses. Ruby Lane (Sandra Storme) is a "nice girl" with an aristocratic accent who descends to Marco's world because she has become mixed up with the wrong kind of guy: a British criminal in cahoots with Americans. Ruby's fall from grace is repeatedly noted by characters who comment that she is an incongruous presence in the club. A hostess tells her, "If you don't mind me saying, you look a bit out of place here." In Marco's world, nice girls become sullied and gentlemen throw aside their manners. Lola Matthews (Googie Withers), one of the club's entertainers, twice mentions that she has been forced into a clinch by one of the club's patrons. Each time, she ends her story with the line "he was always a perfect gentleman about it," thereby revealing the class to which her amorous assailant belonged.

"The Cotton Club" brings together different races as well as different classes. The music of choice in the club is jazz, an African American art form. Black bartenders serve drinks and minstrel-style henchmen "yowzer" in response to Marco's commands. The mingling of different classes and races is undoubtedly the reason the club is dubbed "a zoo" by British journalist Roy Barnes (Bernard Lee) who is, fittingly, both a society reporter and his newspaper's zoo correspondent.

To varying degrees, the American is responsible for a coarsening of British society because he brings together realms that are conventionally separated. He is the quintessential leveled-down man, neither truly barbaric nor truly civilized. As if to further stress the American's liminal nature, each film presents characters that the audience is supposed to regard as indisputably barbarous. For instance, in *Secret Agent*, the General (Peter Lorre) is defined by his crazed libidinous appetites, his readiness to commit murder, and a tendency to rant at the top of his voice. The first time we meet him he is attempting to molest a girl. Later, he flies into a rage when he mistakenly concludes that Ashenden has been given a beautiful female accomplice while his needs have been overlooked. Discovering that he has killed an innocent man instead of an enemy agent, he laughs heartily. The General is linked with 1930s notions of third world barbarism by his nickname, "The Hairless Mexican." Elsa highlights this connection when she tries to convince Ashenden that they should give up on espionage. She pleads with him, "No more killing, no more Mexicans," thereby suggesting an inherent link between the General and the wholly uncivilized act of murder. The General's bestial nature is further emphasized in moments when he refers to himself as a bloodhound and, instead of knocking on a door to gain entry, barks outside it.

The truly barbaric characters in *Murder in Soho* are Steve Marco's henchmen, Spike and Lefty. In contrast to Steve, they are unendingly stupid. "Two fives" says Lefty, noting his darts score. "How much is that?" Spike wonders. They are not comfortable in the evening clothes that Steve forces them to wear, or able to mask their background with refined speech. When Steve tells Lefty he should not cheat at darts, he replies, "You mean I have to be honest about it? What do you want to learn me a game like that for?" Spike and Lefty's barbarity is obvious to Inspector Hammond (Martin Walker), a British policeman, who refers to them as "gorillas."

In *The Return of the Frog* barbarity is much more obviously represented by the criminal fraternity than by the American, Dale Sandford. The accents, clothes, and mannerisms of underworld figures suggest that theirs is the antithesis of civilized society. A prominent member of the criminal community is a character called Dutch, a monocle wearing mid–European of indeterminate nationality who, like the General, is a glaring example of the barbarous foreigner.

In *Thunder in the City*, the barbaric characters are the disheveled, forgotten men and women of the Depression. This underclass are easily identifiable as such because they dress in rags, constantly refer to men of a higher class as "sir," and sing songs about the plight of the workers, containing lyrics such as, "She was poor but she was honest, victim of a rich man's whim."

American Go-Getters

Presented alongside these obviously "low" characters, the U.S. citizen becomes an even more obvious hybrid of the civilized and uncivilized, upper and lower class. As well as embodying the leveled-down society, the American is linked with that other inter-war development bemoaned by the British elite: the emergence of working and middle class citizens who demanded a better life. In each movie the American surprises and alarms those around him with his ambition and tenacity.

Steve Marco, the gangster lead of *Murder in Soho*, does his best to climb the social ladder. One of his conversations with dance hostess Ruby Lane makes clear that his rise to power has been swift and dramatic.

> MARCO: A few years ago I was washing dishes in a cheap café.
> RUBY: You're what the Americans call a go-getter aren't you?

Marco's desire for social advancement is insatiable. In a later scene, he makes clear that he intends to continue his rise until he is at the very top of the pile.

> MARCO: I've had a dozen places. Each one's been better than the last. Why one of these days I'll have one better than this.
> RUBY: You've come a long way since you first started, haven't you Steve?
> MARCO: Yeah, everything I've done I've made a success of. And I'm not through yet. I'm going clear to the top.

Marco assumes that if he attains something he refers to as "class" his rise will be unstoppable. He theorizes that women can embody this commodity. "You've got something which to me is the greatest thing in the world, and that's class," he tells Ruby. Later, he attempts to school his criminal associates in classy behavior, asking his chief henchman, Lefty, "How often do I have to tell you to wear your shoes with dinner clothes?" He surrounds himself with people he assumes represent the cream of upper class society and with objects that exude class. He covets "genuine antiques" and describes the contents of his home as "everything the best that money can buy." Marco's aggression and ruthlessness aid his rise. A few minutes into the movie he tells Ruby, "If anyone tries any rough stuff with you, just let me know. I'll tear 'em apart personally." Soon after, he guns down a British associate who tries to steal from him. His henchmen revel in attacking authority, one of their number learning to play darts so that he can "knock a cop's eye out at twenty feet." If establishment fears were encapsulated in one man, Steve Marco was he.

The American characters in the other three films may not openly profess a wish to climb the social ladder, but their energetic displays of ambition and desire are nevertheless an obvious challenge to a British establishment that asked citizens to be content with the status quo. In *Secret Agent*, Robert Marvin proves himself an aggressive go-getter in his romantic pursuit of a female British spy, Elsa. When we first encounter Marvin his direct approach to courtship is highlighted by this exchange:

ELSA: I've only known you twenty-four hours.
MARVIN: Sure, that means in forty-eight you'll know me twice as well.

Marvin is defined by desire, Hitchcock quickly establishing him as a man of Bacchanalian appetites. He is introduced to us languidly seated, head cocked backward, holding a bunch of grapes to his mouth. After a comic scene in which he helps ensure that a fellow gambler's dog is not ejected from a casino, he suggests the victory "calls for a celebration." It is fitting that this man who exists, it seems, merely to gratify his desires, presents himself as a naughty child. Entering a room in which Elsa is taking a lesson in German, he says, "Please ma'am, my mommy says 'have you room for a new boy in your class?'" He appears even to regard espionage as a form of play, asking Elsa, "You're in the spy racket too?"

Dan Armstrong of *Thunder in the City* refers to himself as "the last of the go-getters." We are left in no doubt that when Armstrong wants something, he becomes an unstoppable juggernaut: "It's no use trying to stop him. Ballyhoo's in his blood," argues one of his colleagues. His American boss complains, "You jump at everything without pausing for a sober second thought." After magnalite stock makes huge gains in the market, Armstrong's British rival Manningdale (Ralph Richardson) pays tribute to the

American's achievement: "Armstrong's done more in thirty days than we could have done with luck in thirty years." Like Robert Marvin, Armstrong is defined by desire and has no qualms about making public his ostentatious appetite for all forms of experience. Soon after meeting his street musician friends, he announces to passers-by that he loves their music and encourages strangers to donate money to them. He then buys a huge meal for the musicians and himself. Later he claims that his appetite for cigars is so immense that he alone keeps a Havana factory in business. As in *Secret Agent*, the appetitive American is linked with childhood. Described by Manningdale as "full of boyish enthusiasm, energy and innocence," Armstrong engineers a business deal sitting astride a toy horse on a fairground carousel.[21]

In *The Return of the Frog* Dale Sandford chases women and criminals so aggressively that it alarms Inspector Elk, the Scotland Yard policeman assigned to be his partner. Seeing a shapely young woman in Hyde Park, Sandford's opening gambit is, "Say, nobody told me they grew things like you over here or I'd have been over here a long time ago." Elk tries to curtail this brazen display of desire by saying, "That's the kind of look that gets men arrested in this park," adding "she's what my grandmother used to call a hussey." Sandford ignores him and soon demonstrates that his pursuit of criminals is no less lusty. His wish to "study foreign police methods" immediately identifies him as an ambitious man, and his gun-blazing, door-shouldering attitude also suggests that he will let nothing block his path to success. He establishes himself as a man who shoots first and asks questions later. The first scene involving Sandford ends with him firing his gun. Inspector Elk exclaims, "You can't do that wild-west stuff here! This is a respectable country this is!" The contrast between "wild-west stuff" and a less go-getting approach to police work is highlighted throughout the film. The movie's last scene is a race to rescue a damsel in distress. Approaching the door of the flat where the woman is held, Elk signals his presence by knocking. A second later he stands aside so that Sandford may blast the lock with a gun.

Dangerously Mobile U.S. Citizens

As well as embodying the elite's concerns about leveling-down and the behavior of the lower orders, the American also represents the dangers of a mobile populace. In each film, the U.S. citizen cannot be efficiently monitored because he is a traveler. His expatriate status obscures his background and causes great confusion among British authorities. In *The Return of the Frog*, Scotland Yard tries to check on Dale Sandford's record with the U.S. police, but the three thousand miles between London and Chicago makes this very difficult. If the British authorities in *Thunder in the City* had known about Dan Armstrong's reckless ways, perhaps they wouldn't have invested in his ultimately disastrous financial scheme. However, because his journey across the Atlantic allows him to shed his past, Britons suffer the consequences. Steve Marco of *Murder in Soho* would have undoubtedly been refused a license for his nightclub had the British police known about his criminal past, but the act of stepping onto a plane has wiped away all his misdeeds. *Secret Agent* makes clear that enemy spies like Robert Marvin are a disturbing reality because they use the continent of Europe as a violent playground, roaming freely across its borders.

Because the four American travelers cause such consternation, they justify the proliferation of passports and borders in inter-war Europe. They also suggest, as did other movies of their era, that travelers from the United States, and the travel technology upon which they relied, were especially harmful to the existing social order. Perhaps inspired by tabloid headlines such as, "U.S. Gunmen Loose in London,"[22] *Non-Stop New York* (Robert Stevenson, 1937) is largely set on board a transatlantic airliner (one year before such a plane existed) that allows American mobsters quick, easy access to Britain. As well as bringing to London an American brand of ruthless violence, the plane carries the leveled-down world of the United States to the British people. While in transit, one of the plane's passengers, a British child prodigy of the violin, becomes attracted to American jazz. Throwing away his violin, he picks up a saxophone and, to the consternation of his fellow Britons, composes a tune he calls "The Atlantic Love Call." In a world of effortless travel, the movie implies, low and high cultures are easily blurred.

The Avenging Hand (W. Victor Hanbury, 1936) also dramatizes the invasion of Britain by American criminals, and a challenge to the social hierarchy that results. Lee Barwell (Ben Welden), an American gangster, comes to London "for a rest." When a murder takes place at his hotel he decides to investigate it since "if there's anything about crime that's ever been done that I don't know about, then nobody knows." With scant regard for British authorities, he goes about solving the case, prompting a hotel detective to express concern over the gangster's intrusiveness. "I say, do you think that American could have been rummaging about in the rooms?" he wonders. In contrast to Hollywood's tendency to present travel as a pretext for adventure—in *It Happened One Night*, Claudette Colbert leaps from an ocean liner and meets the love of her life while criss-crossing the United States by foot, car, and bus—British movies often suggest that travel results, especially if Americans have anything to do with it, in a challenge to the status quo.

A Nation of Conmen

Having introduced the American as a man who refuses to be "placed" because he respects neither the establishment's class structure nor its attempts to control his movements, it is unsurprising that each film suggests he is not to be trusted. In *Secret Agent* Robert Marvin's slippery nature is made obvious by the fact that British characters cannot accurately recall his name. Elsa calls him Roger Martin and Ashenden twists the name Marvin into Larkin. We are further encouraged to distrust him when he displays a talent for elusive wordplay. "Do you understand German?' he is asked. His comical, confusing reply, "No, but I speak it fluently" is typically inscrutable. The factor that most strongly presents Marvin as untrustworthy is his choice of an American identity. As discussed in chapter one, the British were prone to associate America with Hollywood and, in turn, Hollywood with artifice. *Secret Agent* presents Ashenden as one such Briton. Finding himself on a train full of German soldiers, he is confronted by one of them.

> SOLDIER: You English?
> ASHENDEN: No, American.
> SOLDIER: I have lived in Chicago town for three year. Where you live?
> ASHENDEN: Hollywood.
> SOLDIER: Is that in America?
> ASHENDEN: Sure.
> SOLDIER: Fine baby.

Considering contemporary British opinion, it is fitting then that when Ashenden needs a fake identity he chooses that of an American from Hollywood. The very fact that Marvin too chooses to pose, not only as a foreigner, but as an American, confirms his untrustworthiness.

Dan Armstrong of *Thunder in the City* cannot be trusted because he is more attached to artifice than honesty. He cheerfully admits that the Snyderling straight-eight is a terrible car and only salable because it has glamorous looks. Though he offers the Duke of Glenavon a huge sum of money for his magnalite mines, he later admits to being penniless. Though he has no idea what magnalite is, he is satisfied that he can whip up a huge amount of interest in it. Initially, Armstrong has enormous success, but after Manningdale buys the rights to the method of refining raw magnalite, he is forced to admit defeat. He subsequently shocks his British acquaintances by revealing that he has no substantial business acumen to complement his skills as a barker. One of Manningdale's colleagues delivers a eulogy on Armstrong's efforts: "Typical American loudness with nothing to back it up." Though the movie ends with a parade to cheer up the deflated Armstrong, it consistently hints that its American star is little more than a confidence man.

The Return of the Frog repeatedly suggests that Dale Sandford is untrustworthy. In an early scene, a British policeman peruses a newspaper article warning of American gangsters flooding into Britain. He eyes Sandford suspiciously, his action suggesting that we should do the same. Soon afterward, Sandford makes the cryptic statement, "There's nothing you can tell me about cops," further arousing our suspicions. Like Peter Marvin, Sandford's American identity associates him with Hollywood artifice. Elk describes him as "from Chicago, place in America, near that there 'ollywood." Sandford's claim to be an American damns him a second time, since the United States was regarded as a center of violent crime. As Elk says, "When people come all the way from Chicago to see me and bullets start flying around I begin to think." Hollywood and crime aside, Elk later suggests than an American is inherently untrustworthy by telling Sandford, "When I want lessons in geography, I'll get 'em from England, not from you."

Gangster as social climber. Steve Marco (Jack La Rue) in *Murder in Soho* (1939).

Murder in Soho's Steve Marco cannot be trusted because, unbeknownst to his British clientele, he murders people in the back room of his club. Not only is he a killer, he is a two-faced killer. He mixes with guests at his nightclub, not because he genuinely values their custom or friendship, but because he wants them to believe this is so. "Never let a sucker think he isn't appreciated," he tells a henchman. His insincerity is made obvious when, seconds before he shoots a colleague who has betrayed him, he pretends to be the man's best friend.

British Authority: Effete and Ineffective

Each film presents the American as the British establishment's worst nightmare: a man who is instrumental in the leveling down process, refuses to support the status quo, and whose movements and identity are difficult to trace. To make matters worse, each film suggests that the forces ranged against this man—be they the aristocracy, the police, or the press—are weak and effete. For most of their running time, the films suggest that the American is an unstoppable force.

Secret Agent, as well as being an espionage movie, is a study of the wealthy Briton abroad. Much of the movie takes place in the hotels, resorts, and casinos favored by the rich in the 1930s. The Britons who populate these areas are not the kind who might save the world from the likes of Robert Marvin. As Elsa says of Mr. Caypor (Percy Marmont), a Briton whom Ashenden suspects of being an enemy spy, "But he's English. He looks so harmless." When Robert Marvin refers to "little old Europe," he is referring to the whole continent but, since the film's chief representatives of European power are British, it is they who embody enfeeblement. Indeed, Ashenden will prove himself a rather innocuous creature by twice failing to carry out his duty to kill an enemy agent. The only relatively purposeful act we see him perform is that of slapping Elsa. He does so in retaliation after she has struck him for referring to her as vain. Even this hardly heroic act of violence is performed with a distinct lack of passion. After a few such moments, we may agree with Marvin's nickname for Ashenden: "Mr. Ash-in-can."

The movie offers a thesis to explain Ashenden's frailty. It takes place during World War I, a conflict inextricably linked with imagery of a lost generation of British men, mentally and physically wounded. The story begins at a military memorial service for a novelist named Brodie. The service is just a façade, however, a smokescreen that will allow Brodie to take on a new, fictional identity, that of Ashenden, in order to perform espionage work. Although Brodie and Ashenden are the same person, the movie hints that the new identity is a shadow of the old. Compared to the exceptional Brodie, Ashenden is insubstantial. We learn that Brodie was a successful writer and an aristocrat, the room in which the service takes place reeking of power and lined with portraits of Ashenden and his illustrious family. Yet, the central image of this scene is a coffin and the mood is one of eulogy. The movie legitimizes the opinion, expressed by many commentators during and after the Great War, that "the flower of Britain's youth"—code for the male children of the upper classes—had been swept away or weakened by the conflict. Ashenden's frailty is the frailty of those men born to take over the reigns of British power, but now, apparently, unequipped to do so. Another aspect of the scene hints that the world of aristocratic power has changed. Brodie's butler oversees the service. His martial sacrifice is symbolized not only by his medals, but also by a stump where his arm used to be. The butler, perhaps the most potent symbol of a British aristocrat's power, is as symbolically weakened as his master. So, despite the fact that the memorial service is a sham, and we soon learn that Brodie and Ashenden are the same person, the movie begins with imagery suggesting that Britain's powerful have suffered a mortal blow.

Thunder in the City presents the British aristocracy as symbolic of a nation in decay. The British aristocrats Dan Armstrong meets are keen to portray the nation as strong. They claim that an integral component of Britain's strength is its age. For instance, Manningdale tells Armstrong that Lord and Lady Challoner's house has "been in the family for twenty generations." Armstrong, the American tourist, is amazed by this fact, responding with a comment that paints his own country as the antithesis of such a world: "Over in New York we begin to get restless after we've been in an apartment for as long as two weeks." However, the idea that the British past is a source of strength is quickly shattered by the revelation that Lord and Lady Challoner's ancestral home is not only decrepit but is soon to be sold to the highest bidder. The aristocracy is weak because it is no longer wealthy. Lady Patricia tells Armstrong, "We used to laugh at you [America] because you glorified money, but that was when we had so much we didn't need to worry about it. Now we have to go out and struggle for it, just as you did. And so we appreciate its value." Furthermore, we discover that these aristocrats are not the chivalric heroes and heroines of British myth. Rather, they are an inert breed who, instead of taking steps to better their situation, rely on others to save the day. The Duke of Glenavon, a visitor to the mansion, is a lovable but inept businessman who fails to realize, until he meets Armstrong, that his magnalite mines have any worth. The Duke's daughter, Lady Patricia, is planning to marry Manningdale, a banker, simply to have access to his money. Manningdale himself, though rich, is presented as passionless. His fortune has been accrued not by bold strokes but by sly, underhand schemes.

The force of order in *The Return of the Frog* is the British police. In tracing the partnership of Dale Sandford and Inspector Elk the film takes every opportunity to paint the Briton as outdated and effete. "Old man Elk" as a colleague refers to him, has a ready wit, but his jokes and anecdotes refer only to classical literature and history. At various moments he discusses The Battle of Hastings, Helen of Troy, Mohammed, and *The Count of Monte Cristo*. When Elk suggests that Hyde Park should be the first destination on a tour of London, Sandford asks why. Elk replies,

> Oh, I don't know, sentiment. I often go there. Brings back the days when I was a handsome policeman in uniform. Chaperoning labor demonstrations by day and loving couples by night.

Elk characterizes the past as a halcyon time when the people of Britain were easy to police. Whether he was charged with regulating the activities of labor demonstrators or young lovers, a simple act of chaperoning was all that was required since, it is implied, the working class were once relatively obedient and young people relatively chaste. The film makes it obvious that such days are gone by characterizing the Frog as a ruthless, well-organized, violent working-class gang. Even the gang members are aware that Elk represents a different age. In Hyde Park, one of them is giving a coded speech about the benefits of a vegetable-rich diet. Seeing Elk and Sandford approaching, he warns his comrades of their presence by altering the text of his speech from, "You're as out of date as the Great Orc," to, "You're as out of date as the great Elk."

In contrast to Elk, Sandford is the quintessential modern man. This is nowhere more obvious than when the pair stumble across a hideout used by the Frog. There they discover an audio-visual system used by the gang's leader to transmit orders. The system incorporates a television that Elk is unable to work, but Sandford deftly manipulates. The men's dialogue runs as follows:

> SANDFORD: It's simple. It's just a matter of pressing a button.
> ELK: That's what life is nowadays. You press a button in your car and the engine starts.

SANDFORD: You press a button in sing-sing and your engine stops.
ELK: I knew you'd come in useful.

Though the movie credits both Sandford and Elk with the eventual defeat of the Frog, it is Sandford's achievements that are stressed, while Elk must be satisfied with a job well done.

The ineffectual forces of order in *Murder in Soho* are the press (who have the power to expose the gangster) and the upper class. Roy Barnes is a journalist who competes with Steve Marco for the hand of dance hostess, Ruby Lane. Barnes is so enamored with the show business glitter of Marco's nightclub that he is blind to the American's underhand dealings. He would rather write awful comic routines for the club's performers and glowing reviews of their acts. The well-dressed patrons of the club epitomize a corrupt and effete aristocracy, too drunk or too lascivious to resist a man like Marco even if they wanted to. We return repeatedly to an aging, tuxedoed buffoon who performs various drunken turns. Unable to find his mouth with a forkful of spaghetti, he heads to the dance floor to perform a unique gavotte. We cut from his antics to view a dowager eyeing a good-looking gigolo. Many of these guests are the newly rich (they include a boxer and a beauty contest winner), a fact that makes them contemptible in the eyes of the film. Surveying the crowd at one of Steve's parties, Roy Barnes disdainfully comments, "The flower of London society." Their conversations betray their lack of sophistication. A raucous woman exclaims in reference to her watch, "Jimmy got me this on a boat train out of Waterloo." Her husband replies, "You're getting mixed up with that mink coat. I got your watch at Paddington." Another such vignette begins with a woman claiming, "I know how to behave myself." A man replies sarcastically, "Sure, you can see she's a lady." Finally, a food fight breaks out.

False Alarm: The American Exposed and Humbled

It might seem, then, that by portraying the forces of order as ineffectual, the movies challenge British cinematic convention. However, it is more likely that they do so to advance a conservative agenda. The forces of order may be weak, but they rally. Each film confirms their legitimacy by, eventually, demonstrating their capacity to defuse the American threat. The British authorities are temporarily portrayed as weak because each film is intent upon delineating the ways in which Americans are dangerous. The dangers posed by the U.S. can only be fully played out if the authorities are off their guard. Ultimately, the films reaffirm the power of the British establishment by suggesting that, while the authorities may be under siege, they are still able to triumph over adversity.

Britain's powerful regain their authority by exposing the American's true identity. Each film dramatically reveals the American's true nature—Marvin the killer, Marco the street punk, Armstrong the huckster, and Sandford the cop. In *Secret Agent*, after regarding Robert Marvin as a charming and friendly vacationer, Ashenden discovers that he is in fact a German agent. Even after this discovery, Elsa can hardly believe it, exclaiming incredulously, "But he's so kind and friendly!" *Murder in Soho* implies that even though Steve Marco is rich and surrounds himself with women and possessions that he thinks are "classy," he is transparently unsophisticated. He tries to bury his proletarian roots by hiding his henchmen—Lefty is forced to remain out of sight during a party for local business people because, as he puts it, "The boss says I ain't that class"—and by dumping Myrtle, a girl he considers not classy enough to adorn his arm. Yet, however hard he tries, he cannot hide the truth. *Thunder in the City* makes clear that Dan Armstrong is, at heart, an unsophisticated opportunist. Though he travels to Britain to learn about dignity, he cannot, try as he might, change his brassy ways. Indeed, his magnalite campaign is more excessive than any stunt he pulls in the United States. Armstrong's failure to change suggests that he is essentially a huckster, unable to grasp the nuances of modern business strategy. In *The Return of the Frog*, Dale Sandford is revealed to be a policeman, on the side of the establishment all along. He is unable to hide his true self because, despite his brash tendencies, when faced with a crisis situation law enforcement becomes his priority. For instance, when the Frog imprison his girlfriend, he throws aside his laconic, wisecracking attitude in order to save her.

The act of identifying the American's true nature means that his threat can be neutralized. In *Secret Agent*, soon after Marvin has been identified as a spy, he is killed in a train wreck. He is ejected from the narrative not only because he is an enemy of the state. His death represents the defeat of the leveled-down world. Marvin had attempted to join a rarefied club: the world of upper class European espionage, peopled by the likes of Ashenden and Elsa. The club's rightful members find certain of their duties, such as murder, distasteful, but they perform them anyway, driven by loyalty to their nation. The new breed of spy, personified by Marvin, though he moves within the same sphere as Ashenden, is unmistakably crass and capable of any atrocity. His lack of true refinement means that he can carry out cold-blooded and conscienceless murders, while Ashenden and Elsa, because they belong to the elite, find themselves repulsed at the prospect.

Even though Elsa had been initially thrilled by the prospect of involving herself in the darker responsibilities of espionage, she finally admits, "I don't like murder at close quarters as much as I expected." Indeed, she and Ashenden will send a telegram to their boss that reads, "Home safely, but never again." The telegram indicates that, having discovered the world of espionage is inhabited by the likes of Marvin, it is now anathema to them.

Murder in Soho also contains the American threat via homicide. Marco is gunned down by Myrtle, a woman he has wronged. Another major reason for his downfall is the diligence of a policeman, Inspector Hammond. Knowing all along that Marco and his crew are no gentlemen (he tells Lefty and Spike, "And the next time you come into a room, take your hats off"), he finally compiles enough evidence against them to arrive at the Cotton Club with an arrest warrant. If we were not sufficiently aware that the British forces of order have woken from their slumber, the movie forces the point home by having Hammond trip Lefty with that iconic British phallic symbol, the rolled-up umbrella. The symbology of the scene was not lost on the authors of the movie's press book: "The detective is rather fond of his umbrella, an accessory much in the public eye these days; in the hurly-burly of the closing scenes when the gang is collared by the boys from Vine Street, the umbrella is deftly used to bring one of the flying hoodlums to the ground. Perhaps the touch was also inspired by current international politics?"[23] Yet, despite the efforts of Myrtle and Inspector Hammond, the movie hints that the main agent of Marco's downfall is Marco himself. His defeat it seems has been inevitable because he dared to scale the social ladder. Early in the film the nightclub band plays a song, the lyrics of which constitute a warning: "Don't build your dream house 'til your dreams come true. It may fall down on you." At the moment of his arrest, Marco delivers a soliloquy confirming his realization that social mobility can only lead to disaster. "It's nobody's fault but my own. I tried to step out of my class. Tried to reach too high," he moans.

Thunder in the City contains the threat of Dan Armstrong by packing him off on the first plane back to the United States. "I'll come back to England sometime when I've got another big idea," he assures us. He must bow out of the sedate world of British business because he doesn't belong there. The movie concludes that his American ballyhoo, though it may succeed in the short term, will ultimately fail. As he tells Lady Patricia, "I was reaching for the moon, Pat, and all I've got is a handful of stars." Eager to force home its point, the movie has Armstrong characterize himself as the fabled Hare and Britain as his slow-moving nemesis: "We Americans are mighty good in the short sprints, but you English seem to be pretty good over the distance." The movie ends by placing the nation's financial future in Manningdale's sober hands rather than in the grasp of the admittedly more entertaining Armstrong.

The Return of the Frog defuses the American threat by revealing that Dale Sandford is, after all, a policeman and on the side of the law. Unlike the American characters in the other three films, he ends his movie unequivocally a hero. He is allowed this privilege because his job as policeman makes him an authority figure and, by extension, a representative of the elite. The movie offers Sandford as a blueprint for an acceptable modern citizen. He may represent the advent of a slow but inevitable leveling-down process, but at least he attempts to bring some form of order to society. Marco, Marvin, and Armstrong, on the other hand, are irredeemable because they are agents of chaos, obviously threatening to the social order. Sandford is further absorbed into the world of the establishment by promotion. He is given the job of Assistant to the Chief of Police of Chicago. Moreover, it is hinted that he will marry Lila, his love-interest throughout the film, an outcome that suggests his wild side will be tamed. Early in the film, when Lila suspects that Sandford is the leader of the Frog, she comments, "He doesn't understand that that sort of thing he can't get away with in this country. The police always win." Though Sandford may not be a villain, his thorough rehabilitation means that the police, and their establishment bosses, have indeed won.

Robert Marvin, Steve Marco, Dan Armstrong, and Dale Sandford embody the British elite's fear of a citizenry that was socially and spatially mobile and, therefore, increasingly enigmatic. The movies in which they appear are cautionary tales, portraying a nightmarish world in which the authorities seem ill equipped to deal with threats to the status quo. Yet, as well as dramatizing establishment fears, each film acts as a reassurance. Their final reels, in which the authorities rally, function both to confirm that the elite remain in control, and to warn the lower orders that any American-style behavior will not be tolerated.

It has become a commonplace of film study to note that American movies, especially in the first half of the twentieth century, tended to portray foreign citizens, or racial minorities residing within the nation's own borders, in reductive, symbolic ways. Mexicans, for instance, were portrayed as shiftless, while the Chinese were inscrutable. Hollywood, it is claimed, used "others" as shorthand for particular human qualities. Less frequently discussed is the manner in which cinematic images of Americans have been presented and utilized by the rest of the world. In this chapter, I have attempted to further this discussion by suggesting that in the 1930s, at least in Britain's film industry, citizens of the United States became symbols of a new society that was less controllable, less stratified and, therefore, more mysterious.

3

Johnny in the Clouds
Middle-Class Fantasies of the American G.I.

Despite great suffering, World War II also brought with it a sense of hope. As the fighting wore on, many in Britain began to detect an imminent sea change in the class system. In his aptly titled *The People's War*, Angus Calder notes that the conflict engendered a less deferential society: "the people increasingly led itself. Its nameless leaders in the bombed streets, on the factory floor, in the Home Guard drill hall, asserted a new and radical popular spirit."[1] Instead of looking to those in authority for guidance, Britons more often used their own judgment to shape daily life. Related to this development was a sense that the war, with its shared privations, had brought about a new sense of camaraderie among the classes. In a 1942 editorial *Picture Post's* Edward Hulton asserted, "Disraeli wrote about two nations in this country—the rich and the poor, who lived their lives apart and were utterly remote from one another. This war is making these two nations one nation."[2] Once again, as in the 1930s, the social structure of Britain was shifting. Though the extent of wartime social change is debatable, it is undeniable that the conflict provoked many Britons to envisage a less class-conscious nation.

The middle class was in the vanguard of those who called for, as columnist Charles Madge put it in 1943, "a reconstruction of the social contract."[3] Reformist sentiment is notable in their response to the Beveridge Report, a 1942 government document that inaugurated a new system of social welfare for all Britons. A Gallup Poll on the report revealed that not only were middle-class people eager to see its recommendations put in place, they were apparently quite selfless in their desire to see a more egalitarian Britain. As Angus Calder contends, "The new idealism emerged

78

most strongly in the response of the middle class to the Gallup Poll.... Under half the professional and white-collared section of the population thought they would gain—but nine out of ten supported the scheme."[4]

The middle-class zeal for social change is especially remarkable when we consider the privileged lifestyle to which its members were accustomed. Writing in 1949, *Picture Post* correspondent Ruth Bowley provides a flavor of pre-war middle-class existence: "Before the war, the middle-class shopped by phone, and had most things delivered at the door. The doctor called in his car, and was probably shown in by the maid. The children went to the nearby private school. There were occasional sherry and bridge parties.... And the housewife from the council flats might 'help' with the spring-cleaning."[5] Able to delegate troublesome tasks and enjoy rarified leisure activities, the bourgeoisie lived lives that, as far as possible, mimicked those of the upper class. As the above suggests, membership of the middle class was determined not only by material wealth, but also by adherence to a set of values and behavior patterns. Bowley outlines some of these, noting their preservation even in the face of postwar financial hardship: "middle-class standards are still somehow kept up. Meals are eaten in the dining-room, though it would be less work to eat in the kitchen. The children still go out for a walk in the afternoon.... Mothers ... believe that young children should go to bed early."[6] The middle class placed great store in their way of life, but as the Gallup Poll hinted, they had nonetheless become endowed with a social conscience and a desire to see Britain changed.

Large numbers of middle class people staffed the British film industry.[7] In the 1930s, these individuals had often made films that protected the status quo. However, in the war years and after, as the middle class began to express dissatisfaction with society as it stood, many of its members began to make slightly more subversive films. As Michael Balcon said of the Ealing studios team he worked with in the 1940s and 1950s: "We were middle-class people brought up with middle-class backgrounds and rather conventional educations.... We voted Labour for the first time after the war; this was our mild revolution."[8] Censorship codes were still in place and were, to a large degree, respected, but the mood of the industry had shifted slightly to the left.

Role Models for a Postwar Britain

The reformist sensibility of Britain's middle class can be traced in three movies about American servicemen stationed in Britain: *A Canterbury Tale* (Michael Powell and Emeric Pressburger, 1944), *I Live in Grosvenor*

Square (Herbert Wilcox, 1945), and *The Way to the Stars* (Anthony Asquith, 1945). In each film, the arrival of an American on British shores provides an opportunity to embark upon an investigation of the state of the nation. As an outsider, the American is naturally inquisitive and is able to ask questions of the system that would seem unnatural on the lips of a native. In *I Live in Grosvenor Square* he discovers that the working class are an ever more visible presence in British political life and that the aristocracy is increasingly out of step with the rest of the country. The American air force personnel of *The Way to the Stars* arrive in a Britain where class barriers have been weakened by war, but succeed in bringing an even more egalitarian tone to the nation. *A Canterbury Tale* finds an American soldier witnessing the passing of feudal society, and aiding this process by exposing the crimes of a "gentleman farmer."

As well as proving instrumental in the examination of society, the American provides a role model for Britain's future. The three movies reveal deep ambivalence regarding the classes as they stand. Though the working, middle, and upper classes are treated, at times, with great affection, no group seems fit to lead Britain into the future.

The American, on the other hand, is endowed with the best qualities of each social class and unencumbered by their faults. He is a fantasy figure, born of middle-class frustration with the perceived inadequacies of British society. For this reason, there is special poignancy in the decision to change the title of *The Way to the* Stars for its release in the United States. Its alternate title, *Johnny in the Clouds*, derives from the fact that the eponymous American is an aviator and a man who presumably goes to heaven after giving his life to save an English village. Yet, the title aptly describes the status and ability of the American hero in all three films. He is privileged with a bird's eye, almost omniscient, view of Britain, able to reveal the nation's faults and strengths as no native can. Moreover, his placement in the clouds is apt since he will be lauded by each film as an ideal man, almost celestial in his perfection.

Of course it can be claimed that, rather than studies of a changing class system, each film is simply a work of propaganda, carefully designed to send a message, primarily to British audiences, that Anglo-American relations are healthy. For instance, it might be argued that the class system is a prominent element in each film purely because authorities feared it would be a source of friction between the British and Americans. Alternatively, it may be said that American servicemen are lauded by each film merely because authorities required that the film industry provide positive images of an ally.

Certainly, the movies in question function as propaganda. Their press books—studio publications intended to aid theater managers and journalists in promoting films—boldly communicate this idea. The press book for *The Way to the Stars* contains a headline asking that the film be taken as, "The story of ourselves, the British, and our friends the Americans."[9] Each movie sends the propaganda message that American doughboys should be regarded as unthreatening. The fact that "John" is present in each hero's name suggests that their ordinariness was intended to appeal. John Patterson of *I Live in Grosvenor Square*, Johnny Hollis of *The Way to the Stars* and Bob Johnson of *A Canterbury Tale* were designed to reassure Britons that rather than "overpaid, oversexed, and over here," as the saying went, Americans, despite some bravado, could be polite, international ambassadors, derived from Anglo-Saxon stock (crucially, for traditionally xenophobic Britain, none of their names has a whiff of continental Europe about it). The Americans and the British, the movies imply, although they may find each other's customs and behavior strange, are linked by a common ancestry and common values.

However, I would take issue with those who claim that a film's propaganda aims preclude any examination of more subversive themes. British filmmaking during World War II may have been closely monitored by the Ministry of Information—the governmental body responsible for the control and dissemination of propaganda—but despite such nannying, many movies made during the war constituted far more than rousing homilies. Filmmakers, although required to follow propaganda directives, often used the official framework to explore challenging subject matter. For instance, while Humphrey Jennings's celebrated documentary *A Diary for Timothy* (1945) provides stirring images of a wounded but cheery R.A.F. pilot steadily regaining his health and returning to the cockpit of his Spitfire, it also suggests that Britain is tired of war and ready for a postwar world in which the working class are afforded better lives. Alberto Cavalcanti's officially sanctioned *Went the Day Well?* (1942) includes scenes of British civilians violently repelling the feared Nazi invasion, laughing and smiling as they mow down the enemy. Despite such jingoistic imagery, as Cavalcanti himself later pointed out, the film can also be read as a study of Britons who "as soon as war touches them, become absolute monsters."[10] British films of the war era often pursued a line of argument palatable to the authorities and another that expressed a more personal set of ideas. The three movies discussed in this chapter are very much part of this double-barreled approach.

Quasi-Documentary Narratives

Each film stresses that it represents a realistic account of the recent past. This narrative device functions both to fulfill official propaganda requirements—stressing that the success of the Anglo-American relationship is real—but also aligns the movies with the investigative traditions of the British documentary. *I Live in Grosvenor Square* begins with a voice-over stating that three million Americans were stationed in Britain before D–Day and that the following is a "a record of what happened to one of them, Sergeant John Patterson, United States Airforce, of Flagstaff Arizona." The film's press book is eager to point out that events and locales portrayed in the film are imbued with a high degree of realism. It notes that paratroopers who have fought at Arnhem "acted as technical advisers in order that the D-day sequences in the film should be just right," and that, "A complete reproduction of 'The Rainbow Corner,' the famous American servicemen's club in Shaftesbury Avenue London" was built for the film.[11] The producers of *The Way to the Stars* also stress the accuracy of their film. The movie opens with the following words appearing on screen: "Our thanks are due to both the RAF and the USAAF—with whom the idea of this film originated—for their full and enthusiastic cooperation." This expression of gratitude not only suggests that the film enjoys official approval, but also that it is based on the real experiences of pilots. The press book for *The Way to the Stars* builds on this suggestion by stating, "The people in [*The Way to the Stars*] are real people living real lives and depicting one of the really great stories of the war."[12] *I Live in Grosvenor Square* and *The Way to the Stars* seem yet more true to life since, for many in the 1940s audience, they surely brought to mind the recent heroism of an American bomber crew who sacrificed their lives rather than crash land onto an English village. In some ways, *A Canterbury Tale* makes the most convincing claim to realism by awarding its leading role to a serving American Sergeant, John Sweet. A contemporary review of the film suggests that, at least for one viewer, a realistic tone was achieved. Writing about the film's principle characters in *The Sunday Express*, critic Ernest Betts enthused, "You can see yourself in them. The mirror is held up to nature."[13]

Certainly, these quasi-documentary narratives serve the needs of propaganda. Since the effectiveness of propaganda rests on convincing an audience that it is seeing and hearing the truth, then each movie was well equipped to do this. However, the stress on realism takes the films well beyond the simple claim that they are telling the truth, and links them to the tradition of British investigative documentary. In thirties and forties

Britain, thanks to John Grierson and his stable of young filmmakers, the documentary had become an oft-used and respected genre, not just for disseminating truths, but for provoking thought about the state of the nation. Films like *Housing Problems* (Arthur Elton and Edgar Anstey, 1935), an investigation of slum conditions, although they may be accused of providing easy answers, are notable for their inquiry into British malaise. The three films discussed here appear highly influenced by the Griersonian tradition since they also suggest, through their quasi-documentary elements, that we are witnessing an investigation rather than a simple statement of fact.

I Live in Grosvenor Square

I Live in Grosvenor Square concerns the experiences of Sergeant John Patterson (Dean Jagger), an American flyer who finds himself billeted in a London mansion owned by a family of English aristocrats, the Exmoors. He befriends the Duke of Exmoor (Robert Morley), falls in love with his host's granddaughter, Lady Patricia Fairfax (Anna Neagle), and observes a shift in British society as the upper class David Bruce (Rex Harrison) loses a parliamentary seat to a commoner. The movie documents an apparently imminent transition of power from the aristocracy to "the people" and offers an opportunity for its middle class authors to express their ambivalent feelings about this change. On the one hand, the movie applauds a Britain in which ordinary men and women have a greater role to play, but it also reveals a certain distaste for the working class. This aversion, thinly disguised, can be detected in any number of magazine or newspaper articles of the time. *Picture Post*, for instance, even though it professed egalitarian views, could not hide an attitude of condescension toward "the ordinary people, that is the three-quarters of the nation who are not particularly clever."[14] Furthermore, while it endorses the passing of the rule of the landed gentry, the movie also constitutes an affectionate tribute to the aristocracy. We might say that the movie's dilemma—and its founding question—is "who is fit to wield power in modern Britain?"

The movie portrays a working class that grasped, albeit gradually, the necessity for total commitment to the war effort. A plot charting the movement of a group of characters from a position of ignorance to knowledge was a staple of wartime cinema. For example, *Went the Day Well?* shows how Britons of all classes who are not fully aware of the Nazi threat, rise to the occasion when an invasion occurs. In *I Live in Grosvenor Square* working-class characters go through a similar process of development but, in this case, realizing a duty to the war effort means accepting the American presence in Britain. Early sequences demonstrate the extent of working class reticence. Soon after Patterson has entered the Grosvenor Square mansion, he is confronted by its housekeeper, Mrs. Wilson. Angered that he has wandered into a part of the house off-limits to American servicemen, she snaps, "What are you doing here? This is private property." A later scene finds Patterson asking Mrs. Wilson why she behaves in such a way. The scene runs as follows:

> WILSON: I don't like strangers.
> PATTERSON: You don't like strangers or you just don't like Americans?
> W: Put it which way you like.
> P: Do you know anything about Americans?
> W: I believe they're supposed to have won the last war.
> P: Well, you must admit, we did help a bit.
> W: I lost my husband at Mons.

After this inauspicious beginning Mrs. Wilson will gradually be won over by Patterson's charm. In later scenes, she darns his socks, offers him money, and cries when he informs her of his impending departure. In a sense, then, the movie applauds the workers for eventually embracing America. However, at the same time, middle-class suspicions about the working class are evident. Their initially cold and aggressive demeanor does little to endear them to us. The very fact that the workers do not immediately embrace the Americans suggests that they are an ill-informed group unable to realize the truth without coercion. After suffering Mrs. Wilson's verbal assault, Patterson takes a ride in a taxi. The cabdriver asks him sarcastically, "Come over to win *this* war mate?" The stress on the word "this" suggests that he harbors the same resentments as Mrs. Wilson and that ignorance is widespread amongst the workers.

The workers seem even less likable when their behavior is contrasted with the polite and well-informed upper class. The Exmoors and their kind are never in any doubt that the American presence in England should be welcomed. Patterson's fellow passenger during his taxi ride is Major David Bruce (Rex Harrison), an obviously decent fellow, who offers to share the price of the cab, and entertains Patterson by explaining quaint British customs. After Patterson mentions that he could never understand why the British drive on the left, Bruce tells him that the tradition came about so that a man's sword arm would be unencumbered when driving a carriage. "Oh, that's not so dumb after all," Patterson notes sagely. As Patterson and Bruce proceed through London, a parade of American soldiers passes by, watched by a British crowd whose response is lukewarm at best. Bruce assures the American that their support for America is genuine, but not readily noticeable due to English restraint: "You may not believe it, but that from a London crowd is what they call a hysterical demonstration," he notes. An invitation to Bruce's club, and the convivial Britons that Patterson encounters there, confirm that members of the upper class are effective ambassadors for their country. A charming guide during the first minutes of the movie, Bruce could not provide more of a contrast to the angry and misinformed workers. The fact that upper-class characters display none of the rudeness or ignorance of the workers, suggests that these tendencies are confined to the lower orders.

The movie also implies that, as well as welcoming and wise, the British upper class is very tolerant. Patterson's sidekick, Benji (P.f.c. Elliot Arluck), bridles at official suggestions that American servicemen be polite around the British. Reading from a book of etiquette supplied by the American military containing the advice, "It is not a good idea to say 'bloody' in mixed company in Britain," he notes, "Anybody'd think we were an army of occupation of something." Patterson quickly points out that the British upper class are being exceedingly tolerant under the circumstances and that the American gentry might act very differently when faced with a similar situation. "Imagine Rockefeller being kicked out of his bedroom for a bunch of Limeys," he quips.

In the matter of romance, the upper class again appears more admirable than the workers. The relationship between the aristocratic Patricia Fairfax and the American John Patterson is shown to be one based on equality. They trade witticisms (each apologizing for "knowing all the wrong answers" about the other's nation), and when Patterson offers Fairfax a cigarette, she is able to return the favor. In so doing, she dispels any suspicion that their affair is based on exchange. The movie makes every effort to distance Fairfax from the popular notion that British women threw themselves at G.I.s for the sake of a few cigarettes, better rations, or nylon hose. Its press book stresses that the Fairfax/Patterson relationship "is not the casual boy meets girl affair." Indeed, the book's suggestions for publicity campaigns seem designed not only to attract an audience, but to legitimize Fairfax and Patterson's partnership by stressing the more salubrious elements of the Anglo-American relationship. For instance, "a competition to find the first girl in your town to become an American bride," stresses state-sanctioned, long-term commitment, and an appeal for "letters telling of any amusing Anglo-American incident that took place in the district," emphasizes innocent fun. Patterson and Fairfax's romance is further distanced from the sex-for-cigarettes cliché, as Fairfax takes a train back to the military base where she is a member of the Women's Auxiliary Air Force (W.A.A.F.). Two working-class women sitting nearby discuss their relationships with American men. They embody the stereotype of the "loose woman." Though they are slightly dissatisfied that their interactions with G.I.s are based on exchange ("Don't they expect a lot for a few cigarettes?"), they are happy to continue such arrangements, proudly showing each other their stockinged legs. Fairfax smiles to herself at this entertaining conversation, confirming for us that her desire for Patterson is of a higher character.

In many ways, then, the American presence in Britain reveals an upper class far superior to the workers. However, despite obvious affection for the aristocracy, *I Live in Grosvenor Square* also suggests that the upper class are out of touch with modern Britain and ripe for reassessment. Patterson is invited to the Exmoor's country seat and is shocked to discover that the family are largely concerned with topiaries, tea, and sports. He remarks, "So, this is the one hundred percent war effort we've heard so much about—peacocks, tennis—no wonder the folks back home thought this was a phony war." Explaining the concept of the baseball fan to the group, Patterson argues, "There's a big difference between a fan and a spectator." His line implies that a little well-placed fanaticism might benefit the British upper class in their war effort. It might be expected that the film will work to undermine this criticism yet, surprisingly, the narrative does very little to reverse the idea that the upper class are rather distracted from reality. David Bruce will drop by parachute into Arnhem, as his job as a paratrooper dictates, but most of the film's upper class will retain the image of lovable, undeniably patriotic, but rather ineffectual people, useful mainly for the accommodation they provide to American troops. Such an image is strengthened by a comment from Patterson's love interest, Patricia Fairfax, an aristocrat obviously dissatisfied with her class. After Patterson's meeting with the Exmoors, she admits: "You know in this country we're in deadly earnest about things that don't matter at all, and not at all in earnest about things that matter a great deal." Once again, the movie does little to undermine this statement and it remains an indictment of the upper class after the final credits roll.

It is however, the movie's major subplot, the Exmoor's attempt to win a local by-election, which most clearly expresses the film's ambivalence regarding the upper class. They choose fellow aristocrat David Bruce as their candidate. The Exmoors have held power for three hundred years, largely it seems because of a loyal working class. This element is represented by a pub landlord who refers to Bruce as "Master David" and has nothing

Sergeant John Patterson (Dean Jagger, left) takes tea with the Duke of Exmoor (Robert Morley) in *I Live in Grosvenor Square* (1945).

but forelock-tugging praise for the Exmoors. A new mood is perceptible in the village however. At a stump speech delivered by Bruce, an audience member complains that the aristocracy has held too much power. A man in the pub hints that the electorate thirst for change. "This government's alright for now, but what about later on?" he asks. This comment echoes a line of dialogue spoken earlier in the film. As Patterson hails a taxi, he finds that David Bruce has had the same idea. While the two men decide which of them should take the cab, the driver tells Patterson that he has decided to take the Englishman, remarking, "Irrespective of race, rank, color, or nationality. First come, first served, and I saw him first." The comment could be an excuse for this anti–American to accept the Englishman's fare over that of the foreigner, but it can also be read as a hint that Britain is becoming an increasingly egalitarian society where aristocratic privilege is less often tolerated.

Significantly, David Bruce loses the election to Merridrew, a man whose accent and demeanor identify him as a member of the lower orders. Not as handsome or as charismatic as his upper-class opponent, it is his status as man-of-the-people that fits him for office. Merridrew's victory signals the advent of a period in British history in which the ordinary man would enjoy a greater share of power. The British media charted this development, *Picture Post* offering the story of W.D. Kendal, a working-class Yorkshireman who spent some years in the United States before being elected to political office in England. Keen to point out that Kendal demands a voice ("I won't sit down and I won't shut up")[15], the magazine stresses that he represents a challenge to the old boy network: "When he says he intends to 'try and please the boys,' he means to question the right of any man to spend the country's money just because he had the right grandfather."[16] Merridrew obviously represents the emergence of men like W.D. Kendal, and their potential to reform a class-bound nation. The Duke of Exmoor delivers a darkly humorous comment on the election's outcome: "We need a jolt every three hundred years or so. Stops us getting in a rut." In uttering these words he expresses not only his personal feelings, but also the opinion of the film's authors that the upper class do indeed need a jolt and that politicians drawn from the rank and file may be the ones to administer it.

A scene played between Fairfax and Bruce sums up the transition of power. The pair have known each other since childhood and it has been generally agreed that they would one day marry. The arrival of Patterson has changed their plans however, since he and Fairfax have fallen in love. Breaking the news to Bruce, Fairfax tells him tearfully, "It's always been you David, always until now." With these words she not only acknowledges the end of their romantic partnership, but also implies the crumbling of Bruce's world of privilege. He has not only lost her, but the parliamentary seat his family has held for three hundred years, the seat's concomitant power and status, and the world of tradition that their arranged marriage epitomized. Her words also link the demise of aristocratic power with the ascendance of "the common man" to a position of political prominence.

Despite its desire to chart the transformation of British society, the film stops short of endorsing the election winner as an ideal man of the future. Its ambivalence about the working class hints that outright support of Merridrew is unlikely. The upper class may be better informed and more charismatic than the workers but, as the movie makes abundantly clear, in their present form they are not fit to wield power. It is in the American, Patterson, that the movie finds the type of man suitable to lead the nation into the future. This is because he embodies the best of each class. Like the working class, he demonstrates admirable commitment to the war effort, eventually making the ultimate sacrifice as he dies returning to base after a bombing run. Like the upper class David Bruce, he proves himself a gifted diplomat. For example, after Mrs. Wilson tells him that she lost her husband at Mons, he responds by telling her that his father also died in the First World War. Beginning a line of argument that will serve him throughout the movie, Patterson suggests, "What do you say, Ma'am, we bury the last war and concentrate on winning this one." Such behavior is duly noted by the film's senior member of the aristocracy, the Duke of Exmoor, who tells Patterson, "You know John, having you down there for our little flare-up [the election defeat], made me feel, made us all feel, that you were a sort of ambassador." "Makes me proud to have you say that," Patterson replies. "Well you were the right man for the job," concludes the Duke. In addition to being diplomatic, Patterson is the "right man for the job" because he demonstrates a tendency toward upper class modes of politeness. In the early stages of his relationship with Patricia Fairfax, he apologizes for being "fresh" and having "skipped formality." Because he combines commitment to the war effort with diplomacy and politeness, Patterson is a hybrid of the best working and upper-class attributes. Indeed, the movie stresses that he is in some sense the offspring of, Mrs. Wilson, the main working class character, and the Duke of Exmoor, the senior upper class character. As the film progresses, Patterson takes to calling the former "Mom" and the latter "Pop."

Patterson is an ideal man because he combines the best of each class, but also because he refuses to live up to certain ideas about G.I.s circulating in British society during the war. He is never loud, wisecracking, small-minded, or sexually predatory. The movie admits that such attributes are displayed by Americans, but only by a certain type. This certain type, the stereotypical "Yank," is embodied in the film not by Patterson, but by, as the voice-over comments, "his sidekick, Sergeant Benji MacGregor-Greenburgh of Brooklyn, New York." Benji is in the movie to provide comic relief (the British had an affection for the boisterous Yank, even if they preferred that he stay away from their daughters) and to make Patterson look good. Our introduction to Benji is accompanied by a passage of high-spirited, jazzy music, suggesting his knockabout personality. Benji is unapologetically working class, his surname intended to suggest that he is the child of recent immigrants. While Patterson is shown to possess a fundamental understanding of Britons and British life, Benji delivers an endless stream of wisecracks about the nation in which he finds himself. Entering the opulent Grosvenor square mansion, he jokes "So this is the army," and continues "makes you feel downright expensive, Johnny." Seeing a portrait of Lady Fairfax, Benji exclaims "Whew! What a dame!" Patterson's reply is the first of many utterances that suggest his innate understanding of Britain and, therefore, his difference from Benji. Looking around the room with respectful awe he answers, "Yeah, but its got something, Benji." In a later scene, as he views St. Paul's cathedral, Patterson muses on its apparent immunity to German bombs. "That kinda gets you, doesn't it?" he notes. Whereas Patterson is celebral, Benji celebrates the physical. For instance, whereas Patterson's recollections of America are of moonlit nights and engineering projects, Benji's include Brooklyn Dodgers baseball games at which, he proudly relates, Dodgers fans keep their empty Coke bottles in order to threaten the referee with airborne injury. Aside from Benji, the movie takes every opportunity to delineate the kind of American Patterson is not. When David Bruce makes fun of the cab driver for his anti–Americanism, Patterson lambastes anti–British attitudes in his own country, noting, "We got some of his kind at home, only ours are still talking about the war debts."

Patterson may be refined, but he is far from spineless. As the pressbook reminds us "he pulls no punches, he says and does what he honestly thinks is right." He is as forthright and demonstrative as the working class, but he expresses these tendencies in a more diplomatic fashion. This combination of traits is demonstrated at the Exmoor estate when Patterson observes, "This isn't exactly what I thought England would be like somehow…. Officers quitting the army to go into politics. I guess the war hasn't changed things so much over here, huh?" Even Benji is shocked at this suggestion of British apathy. "Hey, you know what it says in the little pink book about knocking the British," he scolds, referring to a United States government publication, bound in a pink cover, regarding overseas etiquette. When the situation calls for it, Patterson is combative, but since he repeatedly proves himself a sensitive and thoughtful man, we understand that his barbs are born of necessity rather than simple belligerence.

Patterson, then, represents an ideal man, combining the best of Britain's working and upper classes, while rejecting the attributes of the Yank. In essence, he manages to mix vigor with refinement. In the universe of *I Live in Grosvenor Square*, the place that combines these traits most successfully is "Arizona," ostensibly the American state, but more accurately a mythical, ideal space invented for the movie. Patterson, an Arizona native, describes the state in glowing terms during his courtship of Patricia Fairfax, telling her, for instance, how far a person can see on a clear day. Arizona is defined by its outdoorsy energy—Patterson rides horses, builds dams, and rolls his own cigarettes using the Arizona method—but the state is also home to an unexpected sophistication. Fairfax, like most Britons of her day, initially assumes that Arizona is, as she says, "wild and woolly," but the American disagrees, connoting the state's modernity and refinement by claiming "it's on the road to California." In a later scene, in which Patterson beats Fairfax in a horse race, she jokes "I bet you earn a living in rodeos." His reply, "I've never even seen a rodeo," again stresses that Arizona may be more refined than she thinks. When Fairfax admits, "I should like to see Arizona sometime," she is not only expressing her desire to be with Patterson, but also a yearning for its combination of energy and refinement. Her question, "We will get there sooner or later, won't we John, when there isn't a blackout any more?" suggests an aspiration for a postwar Britain more in line with "Arizona."

By the end of the movie "Arizona" has been reached. Patterson's tenure in Britain has encouraged its citizens to mix refinement with energy. At a party held at the Exmoor's castle, Patterson notes that Mrs. Catchpole, an aristocratic friend of the Exmoors, "has got a little hidden streak of boogie-woogie in her." Even the aesthetic strategies adopted by the movie are a mixture of energy and refinement. As its press book notes, the movie offers the exotic spectacle of "doughnut dunking, jitterbugging to the music of the G.I. band, and dance hostesses from 'Rainbow Corner,'" but also assures readers that such garish American attractions will be tempered by a more tasteful British approach: "[*I Live in Grosvenor Square* is a film] bridging the Atlantic in its sentiments, and yet essentially British in its portrayals."[17] When Patterson dies, Fairfax is distraught and her plan to travel to America left in ruins. She sits chatting with her old flame, David Bruce. "Funny it should all end like this," she muses. "Yes," replies Bruce. She responds "I know where Arizona is now," and immediately bursts into tears. She may not be able to reach America, but she will live in "Arizona" from now on.

The Way to the Stars

The Way to the Stars begins in the present, 1945, and then whisks us back in time to trace wartime events at a British aerodrome, Halfpenny Field. The present is a time of uncertainty. In the opening moments, the camera takes us on a tour of the aerodrome, now empty and desolate. A voice-over intones, "This was an airfield. Now not a soul is here. Empty. Empty hangers. The control tower, once the very nerve center of the airfield and now derelict. No more happy landings." Thus, the war years are presented as a time of energy and happiness, while the present is empty. The voice-over continues, "Now sheep are returning to this English field, once mentioned in the Domesday book." This line could be interpreted as an assurance of continuity, but the exhausted tone of the voice-over and its sense that life at Halfpenny Field was once more exciting, suggests a sense of disappointment with the inevitable return to a predictable way of life. We then flash back to 1940, a more tumultuous time, and for the rest of the movie trace how, via American intervention, Britain was transformed. Like *I Live in Grosvenor Square*, *The Way to the Stars* is told from a middle-class perspective. Yet instead of ignoring the middle class, as the former movie does, it is highly preoccupied with the value system and behavior of this group. It is a film of two parts, the first examining Britain before the United States entered the war, the second portraying the nation after the intervention.

In the first half of the movie, the section detailing the Battle of Britain, the class system is shown to be in flux. Undeniably, some aspects of the system are unchanged. Officers are drawn predominantly from the middle class and are tended by working-class "batmen," glorified butlers who care for their superior's every need. Jones (Johnnie Schofield) is a batman who has great affection for his officer, Flight Lieutenant Archdale (Michael Redgrave). "Ooh, the fuss he makes about his buttons in the evening," he coos. It could of course be claimed that the two men's unequal relationship is based on military rank alone, but Jones's comment "He's a nice gentleman, Mr. Archdale," would suggest otherwise. Working-class characters tend to adopt a "below stairs" manner when dealing with their superiors, acting like gossipy servants who must curtail their conversation when the master approaches. Chatting before a bombing mission, working-class Nobby Clarke (Bill Owen) complains that his new superior officer, Flight Officer Penrose (John Mills), is "Another one of these 15 hour sprogs." As Penrose approaches, Clarke is warned by one of the ground crew, "Look out, here he comes." With Penrose's arrival there is an immediate change of tone: "Port engine's not doing the revs she should, Sir. Careful not to overheat her," advises the mechanic. In such ways, the officers and men of Halfpenny Field effortlessly reproduce, within a military sphere, the class system they knew in civilian life.

However, several moments suggest that the war has brought with it a more egalitarian atmosphere. A class system based on rigid behavioral codes and the maintenance of hierarchies is disintegrating. For instance, Squadron Leader Carter (Trevor Howard) is annoyed by "fighter types" who insist on performing flamboyant victory rolls when returning from a mission and leaving their "top button undone." "Bad show I think" he notes, but a few seconds later concludes, "Mind you I'm not saying they're not doing a good job." Of course, Carter is bemoaning the lowering of military standards, but he is also annoyed by the way such behavior flouts middle-class ideals of restraint and order. His comment that the flamboyant and scruffy pilots are "doing a good job" is an admittance that adhering to middle-class behavioral codes does not necessarily make a person an effective warrior. It also suggests that "fighter types" are ever more tolerated. A sense that hierarchies are increasingly irrelevant in British life is suggested by a conversation between Flight Officer Penrose and Flight Lieutenant Archdale. Fresh out of flight school, Penrose admits, "I'm afraid I'm just an amateur." Archdale sagely replies, "There aren't any amateurs and professionals anymore. Just good pilots and bad pilots. The good pilots stay alive and the bad ones don't." Although it is still obvious from accents, demeanor, and rank which men are members of the working class and which belong to the middle class, another scene hints that an individual's class identity has become less important than his identity as an airman. After a landing that Archdale describes as "ruddy awful," the middle-class Penrose is comforted by working-class pilot Nobby Clarke.

The lines between the classes may be blurring, but some behavioral codes remain very much in place. The working class is defined by a tendency to speak their mind, while the middle class value emotional restraint, otherwise known as "stiff upper lip." Whereas the officers refuse to mention the hardships of war, the ground crew display refreshing honesty. Sheltering from an air raid on the aerodrome, a mechanic discusses the carnage wreaked by German planes at a nearby base: "over fifty dead and lots still buried." Another man bemoans the chore of filling in bomb craters: "More ruddy craters. Makes you sick."

Such openness in not displayed by middle-class characters, who tend to epitomize emotional repression. When Archdale hears of the death of Squadron Leader Carter his face subtly registers inner pain, but he refuses to break down. Toddy (Rosamund John), Archdale's girlfriend, later his wife, asks him "he was a great friend of yours, wasn't he?" "I knew him pretty well," comes the stoic reply. Archdale is a poet, but not in the tradition of Shelley or Keats. His poetry admonishes the reader to practice self-control, to "keep your head" instead of openly mourning dead comrades. The following is a typically stoical extract:

> Do not despair for Johnny head in air,
> He sleeps as sound as Johnny underground,
> Fetch out no shroud for Johnny in the cloud,
> And keep you tears for him in after years.
> Better by far for Johnny the bright star,
> To keep your head and see his children fed.

Archdale is ashamed that he is a poet, such is his level of discomfort with expressing emotion. Informing Toddy that he has never before divulged his poetic tendencies, he tells her, "You're the only one who knows, or who ever will." A similar character is Penrose. After Archdale dies, leaving behind his wife and child, Penrose breaks up with his girlfriend, Iris (Renee Asherson), reasoning that a love affair during the uncertainties of war is futile and unfair. Though his actions are understandable, they add to a sense that the middle class would rather repress than express their emotions.

Middle-class restraint is again displayed in the person of the movie's villain, Miss Winterton (Joyce Carey), who, as her name suggests, is an exponent of frigid moderation. A longtime resident of "The Golden Lion," a hotel near the aerodrome, she is attended by Iris, her niece, who patiently puts up with the older woman's stifling regime. A typical Winterton moment is her postprandial announcement, "I'm going to have my cigarette now," a piece of dialogue that perfectly sums up her restrained and regulated universe. She does not approve of anything out of the ordinary, holding forth on her dislike for "non-residents" at the hotel. Her rule is not without its dissenters. A regular at the hotel bar, Mr. Palmer (Stanley Holloway) observes Miss Winterton's behavior with distaste. Turning to Penrose he notes, "Now, if they'd just drop a bomb on Auntie instead of Halfpenny Field..." As the movie progresses, Auntie Winterton and middle-class repression in general will, albeit figuratively, have a bomb dropped on them. The bomb will be provided by America.

The arrival of the United States Airforce at Halfpenny Field spells the demise of Archdale and Winterton, the movie's chief representatives of repression. Archdale dies in a bombing raid over Germany just before a flag-raising ceremony at Halfpenny field signaling the American takeover. As the Union Jack is lowered and the Stars and Stripes run up in its place, we cut to a shot of Archdale's wife reading the telegram informing her of her husband's death. It might be expected that the Englishman's passing would be followed by a scene of his funeral, but significantly, all we are offered is the ceremony linking his death with the end of British jurisdiction at the airfield. Miss Winterton takes longer to disappear from the narrative, but her end is no less obviously linked to American intervention. Her niece begins a relationship with a particularly outspoken American airman, Joe Friselli (Bonar Colleano), who points out that Winterton is a selfish tyrant. When Winterton boasts that Friselli enjoys her company, Iris can wait no longer to drop the long-awaited bomb, pointing out that the American has opened her eyes. The dialogue runs as follows:

WINTERTON: I took a lot of trouble to become friends with that boy. Just by using politeness and charm, if you wish, I got him to like me very much indeed.
IRIS: So much so that he called you a selfish old gorgon who thinks only of her stomach.
WINTERTON: What?
IRIS: And if I had any sense I'd leave you to stew in your own juice. And what's more I believe every word he said.... I am going to leave you and I'm going to get a job, and I'm never coming back as long as I live. Goodbye.

The second half of the movie finds American airmen defining themselves as the antithesis of the understated British middle class. Verbal restraint is not their forte. They are forthright about their ability as warriors. Joe Friselli boasts, "Our bombs are going right where they're meant to, right on that little old target, Zonk, Zonk, Zonk every time." They are vociferous on the subject of their aircraft, so much so that the British lampoon them for it. As the American C.O. enters the R.A.F. barracks, a young British pilot performs his impression of a boastful American flyer: "The B-17, or the flying fortress as we call it, is surely the greatest bombing ship God ever made. Why, it cruises at six fifty, well, let's say six forty-five, we mustn't exaggerate, must we gentlemen." They are outspoken about their desire to see combat. An R.A.F. officer admits that they are as "keen as mustard," an opinion proved by Joe Friselli's frustrated question, "When are we gonna get started?" This lack of verbal restraint is combined with an irreverent approach to hierarchy. An American orderly brings a British officer a cup of tea, touches him on the arm and says, "There you go, bud." If this were not enough, the British must endure "Flying clothes in the mess." Indeed, the Americans display all the top-button-undone attitudes so disliked by Squadron Leader Carter.

Though the British officers are initially reticent about American behavior, the movie goes on to prove that these unrestrained men can effect productive change in British society, specifically a dismantling of middle-class behavioral codes. The first half of the movie gives the impression that the British are endowed with a sense of fun, but their contact with Americans in the second half helps them to fully express it. When the Americans join the British for a song at the piano, it is the first time in the movie that the British fully display their capacity for raucous behavior. The noise produced by the Anglo-American effort is enough to provoke Miss Winterton to ask, "What do you think this is, a speakeasy?" a question suggesting that having so much fun may be dangerously American. The British become so much less reserved by the end of the movie that, in the final scene, as American and British personnel drink together at "The Golden Lion," an employee good-naturedly scolds them with the words, "Ooh, you Americans!

And you R.A.F.! There's nothing to choose between you." The image of Americans as uninhibited is celebrated by the film's press book. Discussing one of the film's American stars, it tells how: "Douglass Montgomery, who at the age of sixteen took matters into his own hands to 'go on the stage,' inherits his 'up and doing' tactics from his grandfather, who at the age of fifteen had run off to get mixed up in the Gold Rush…"[18] Moreover, the book hints that American behavior may prove inspiring to the British. The American characters, it claims, provide an "inspiring picture of young America and a distinguished addition to this topical film."[19]

However, it is not an Americanized Briton that the movie chooses as its hero. This role is handed to the American who combines the most attractive aspects of working class and middle class culture. His name is Johnny Hollis (Douglass Montgomery). Like the middle-class Britons, he proves himself polite. His first words of dialogue are an apology for interruption: "Sorry to burst in." He also realizes that, at times, restraint is necessary. On hearing that he must fly a mission the next day, he cancels his plans to attend a movie. "No picture for us," he earnestly tells his companions. When Joe Friselli insists on disrupting the calm of The Golden Lion's restaurant, he responds by telling him to "pipe down." Friselli's questions, "Is this supposed to be a restaurant or a funeral parlor?" and, "What's the idea of talking in whispers when we eat?" are met with Hollis's reply, "It's kind of sort of a custom." However, like the British working class, Hollis is always forthright, his tendencies to restraint never stifling his emotions. Setting off on a bombing run, he tells his crew. "I love you, so get up them stairs."

In order to further champion Hollis, the movie stresses that he is no "Yank" by comparing him to boisterous Joe Friselli. Wisecracker par excellence, he makes no attempt to understand British customs and makes fun of his hosts at every opportunity. Entering his barracks on the day of his arrival in England, he greets his fellow Americans with the words, "Hello my jolly old fellow. Boy, these English slay me. There's an orderly in my room asks me if I want to be called with a cup of tea in the morning." Joe has two functions in the movie. Firstly, he is present to remind the British audience that Johnny Hollis is a far superior human being. Secondly, he proves that, just as the British can be fruitfully changed by Americanization, the Americans would do well to adopt some British manners. Joe will eventually be tamed, coming to respect the British. Referring to his earlier claim that all his bombs would "Zonk" onto their targets, he humbly apologizes to Penrose: "Say, listen Flight Lieutenant, I guess I owe you a bit of an apology. If I gave you or anybody else the idea that bombing targets over there was going to be easy, I'll eat my words right here and now." Another

American adds to this chorus of apology. Speaking of German pilots he remarks, "They're good alright. Like you said they were, only like some of us didn't believe." Because of the gradual softening of Friselli's personality, the movie will accept him up to a point. For instance, after Hollis dies, he takes over his post as entertainer at a child's birthday party. He can also be admired for encouraging Iris to leave Miss Winterton. But he will not be completely embraced by the film. Friselli is allowed to court Iris for a while, but fails to win her. "I suppose she'll turn out to be in love with some Englishman like all the rest," he laments. And indeed she is, the eminently more marriageable Penrose (John Mills). The Englishman gets the girl because the movie is not ready to accept the likes of Friselli, a man who has not managed to combine working and middle class traits to the same extent as Johnny Hollis, into British society. At a station dance Iris and Friselli listen to a song called "I'm Going to Marry a Far Nicer Boy." Prophetic words indeed.

Because Hollis is the ideal man of the future, the film awards him everything that Archdale forfeits in death. Hollis quickly begins a platonic romance with Archdale's widow, Toddy, and becomes a surrogate father figure to the Archdales' orphaned child. In terms of 1940s patriarchal culture, Hollis inherits the markers of Archdale's masculinity. After becoming a symbolic husband and father he acquires, via Toddy's hand, yet another talisman of Archdale's masculinity, his prized cigarette lighter. That Hollis is now the film's chief bearer of masculine power is made all the more obvious in a scene in which he nonchalantly takes part in a game of darts. He misses the board, but hits a pin-up of a glamorous woman. Amused, he uses chalk to ring the point at which his dart entered her body and then signs his handiwork. The last aspect of Archdale's life that Hollis acquires is his poetry. In the film's early sections, Archdale's poem about the death of a young aviator, "Johnny in the Clouds," seems to apply most readily to its author, since the Englishman dies before his time. Yet, at the climax of the film, when Hollis gives his life to save an English village, and we hear the poem in voice-over, it appears to have been written solely as an elegy for the American whose first name it invokes. As Joe Friselli comments, the poem "might've been written for him."

A Canterbury Tale

A Canterbury Tale is another movie in which an American serviceman examines the British scene, reveals a changing class structure, and symbolizes an ideal. He is U.S. Army Sergeant Bob Johnson (John Sweet). Headed for Canterbury, he mistakenly alights from his train in nearby Chillingbourne, where he immediately becomes embroiled in a local mystery, that of the "glue man," a criminal whose decidedly Freudian *modus operandi* is to throw "sticky stuff" into young women's hair. With the help of local Britons, Johnson discovers the glue man to be Thomas Colpepper (Eric Portman) a magistrate and "gentleman farmer."

As this synopsis might indicate, *A Canterbury Tale* was an unorthodox movie, a fact painfully obvious to its distributor, Eagle-Lion. Their press book informed theater managers that the movie would be a hard sell: "Certainly the film is of a kind to put showmen on their mettle; it is not easy, yet a long way from impossible to sell...."[20] A later comment, "There are no problems to this picture,"[21] suggests that Eagle-Lion were all too aware that the picture would prove problematic for its audiences. They were right. Audiences stayed away. The notoriously conservative British critical community veered back and forth between praise and anger. Reviewers considered the Bob Johnson character a boon to Anglo-American relations. For instance, Moore Raymond wrote in *The Sunday Dispatch*: "'I feel different about the Yanks now,' said a friend after the private show of *A Canterbury Tale*. 'I used to think they were a hell of a nuisance around town,' he added. 'But now I feel like going up to every American soldier and saying 'Hiya, pal. Can I help you?'"[22] Reviewers also appreciated the film as homage to Britain's landscape and history. An unnamed critic in the *Evening Standard* noted: "Through [the American's] wondering eyes you perceive the tranquil beauties and the unfading wonders of the British scene, and the endearing oddities of the British character."[23] Ernest Betts, writing in *The Sunday Express*, echoed such sentiments: "The film shows you, through the eyes of four pilgrims, how a typical American, visiting our pubs, farms, fields and teashops, meeting the vision which is Canterbury, meeting the girls, the villagers, the craftsmen and workers, comes to see that Britain isn't a bad place after all, that it is a glorious place, that it is, in fact, terrific."[24] However, several critics disliked the story of the glue man. A unnamed critic in *Lady* argued that since the film captured the British countryside so lovingly, it was, "All the more deplorable that it might hinge on a sort of detective plot, with a positively mischievous solution, suggesting as it does, that the sort of person who loves the country, its history and its crafts, is also liable to prove an unbalanced neurotic."[25] It seems the glue man story was troubling, not only because it was so bizarre, but because it makes clear that a magistrate, a member of the privileged classes, is mentally disturbed. "Lilian Duff wrote in *The Sunday*

A Canterbury Tale (1944). From left: Peter Gibbs (Dennis Price), Seven-Sisters Soldier (Esmond Knight), Sgt. John Sweet, U.S. Army (Bob Johnson), Alison Smith (Sheila Sim) and Sergeant "Stuffy" (Graham Moffatt).

Graphic: "Before and after the film came along, by the way, we heard much about its value as a means of interpreting Britain to America and vice-versa. What will Americans actually learn about Britain? Only that the scenery and architecture are lovely at their best and that magistrates are liable to mild forms of perversion."[26] Anthony Gibbs highlighted "the strange mentality of Mr. Michael Powell and Mr. Emeric Pressburger who have ... created and thrown away a thing of great beauty for this preposterous, this silly story of a simple British magistrate and his pot of gum."[27]

Critics were annoyed that the more pleasant aspects of the story—its sympathetic treatment of the British landscape and its characterization of Bob Johnson—should be marred by the strange tale of the glue man. They also grumbled that attempting to fuse several narrative threads rendered the movie loose and confused. Ernest Betts wondered: "Is this film about Anglo-American relations, is it a hymn to England, or what? I don't know, a film should know what it is about."[28] Moore Raymond echoed these words: "the interest drifts hither and thither, switching from the mystery of the glue man to the impact of the Yank on Canterbury."[29] I would argue that every one of its narrative threads is necessary for *A Canterbury Tale* to tell its story. If the film had limited its subject matter to, say, the beauty of rural England or the strength of Anglo-American relations, it would be a far lesser work. As it stands, the movie is a complex treatment of a class system many felt to be in flux. Rather than presenting a loose conglomeration of events, it demonstrates the interconnectedness of Bob Johnson's journey, Thomas Colpepper's mental crisis, and the glories of the British landscape. Take away any of these aspects and the story loses its impact. The film needs a Bob Johnson to ask questions of Britain's national identity and class system. It needs a Thomas Colpepper so that we may examine a ruling class many believed to be increasingly redundant. And it needs beautiful images of the landscape to suggest that Britain was worthy of such appraisals.

The film's ambition to examine the state of the nation is made obvious from its first moments. An opening sequence suggests that despite a great deal of continuity, Britain has changed in certain crucial ways. We begin in Chaucer's time, as medieval pilgrims make their way to Canterbury. The scene is one of carefree, bucolic fun. Moments later we are transported to the fields of wartime Britain. A voice-over informs us that "though so little's changed since Chaucer's day, another kind of pilgrim walks the way." At this, an armored personnel carrier bursts onto the screen. Serious travelers have replaced playful pilgrims. The continued existence of the pilgrim's road suggests that some aspects of British life are timeless and essential, yet the military presence hints that the war has changed the nation. The voice-over continues: "Six hundred years have passed. What would they see, Dan Chaucer and his goodly company, today?" Having posed this question, the movie suggests that an answer will be hard to come by. The war, it seems, has transformed Britain into an uncertain and confused society.

3. Johnny in the Clouds

The narrator intones, "Alas, when on our pilgrimage we wend, we modern pilgrims see no journey's end.... No genial host at the setting of the sun welcomes us in. Our journey's just begun." The idea that Britain's present and future are shrouded in mystery is exacerbated by a cut to a scene of inky darkness. We find ourselves in a blacked-out train station, only able to make out a few shapes in the murk and all too aware that the bright sunshine enjoyed by Chaucer's pilgrims has faded. Powell and Pressburger keep us in the dark for over five minutes, pressing home their metaphor about the state of modern-day Britain.

Starting by characterizing Britain as changed and uncertain about the future, the movie progresses by taking us on a tour of the film's present. Our guide is the American, Bob Johnson. His journey makes clear that Britain is a nation to feel ambivalent about. We join him on walks through undeniably beautiful landscape ("Sussex and Kent are like a garden fair," the voice-over confirms), magnificent architecture, and historic hamlets full of twinkling-eyed and friendly yeomen. We also accompany him as he learns how annoying some aspects of British life can be. Some of these seem trivial. "Limey mirror," he grouses at a malfunctioning piece of hotel furniture. Other problems are much more significant.

The movie's major grumble is with a working class that seems alternately obsessed with rules and positively lethargic. At the railway station where Johnson has disembarked by mistake, he encounters a guard who could not be more officious. After hearing a litany of rules and regulations, Johnson exclaims, "What kind of a place is this anyway?" He receives the haughty reply, "It's the kind of place where people sleep at night." After chasing the glue man, Johnson again comes face to face with working-class bureaucracy and torpor. He seeks help from a policeman, knowing that he has only seconds to spare before the glue man escapes, but is exasperated by the man's wish to see his identity card. "While you're looking us up in the Domesday Book, he's making his getaway," Johnson complains. The policeman replies in soporific tones, "We may be slow in Chillingbourne compared to London ways and we ain't no G-men neither." "Haven't you got a gun?" Johnson asks. The cop then makes clear something that the American has become all too aware of: "This is Chillingbourne, Sergeant, not Chicago."

The workers of Chillingbourne are locked into an almost feudal way of life in which they are conspicuously deferential to their "betters." The magistrate, Mr. Colpepper, has ordered a curfew for young women and it seems his wishes are respected to the letter. The station guard tells Alison Smith (Sheila Sim), just before she becomes the glue man's latest victim,

"No young lady must go alone at night. Mr. Colpepper's orders." The cap-doffing mentality of the lower classes means that, without the intervention of some outside force, in this case Bob Johnson and Alison, the glue man would go unpunished. Even though a man was seen running into Colpepper's offices immediately following the attack on Alison, not for a moment do the locals suspect that the magistrate could be a criminal.

It seems, however, that the deferential, officious, sluggish working class, although still very much a presence in Britain, might soon be a thing of the past. The future of working Britain is embodied by Alison Smith, a land girl (farm worker) defined by her irreverence and energy. Part of a new generation of mobile wartime women, she eagerly joins Bob Johnson in investigating the identity of her assailant. Just after the attack, an English soldier, Peter Gibbs (Dennis Price), asks her, "Can you run, Miss?" worried that her traumatic experience may have drained her of energy. "Just watch me!" she replies, darting down the street. Alison refuses to adopt the submissive role of her forbears. After she admits to a bartender that she does not know the identity of the Lord Mayor of London, he asks her, "Aren't you ashamed?" "Not a bit," she answers. Bureaucracy holds no attraction for her. She gleefully disregards official channels in the hunt for the glue man.

A Canterbury Tale expresses great hope for the future of the working class. By contrast, we meet no young members of the upper class, and the older member whom we do meet seems locked into a process of decline. Colpepper, it seems, has gone mad. His reasoning for throwing glue at young women is that, if disfigured, they will be less likely to spend time courting soldiers and more time attending his lectures on the glories of the English countryside. For the bulk of the movie it appears that Powell and Pressburger have little sympathy for this rather sinister man. Yet, when Colpepper delivers one of his lectures it is difficult not to warm to him. In a film so in love with English flora and fauna (Erwin Hillier's lush cinematography won a British Academy Award) he becomes a voice of reason rather than insanity. He even has wise words to say on the current state of the class system. When Alison uses the phrases "good family" to describe the well-to-do and "shop girl" to describe her position before the war, Colpepper responds, "Good family. Shop girl. Rather dilapidated phrases for wartime." He goes on to hint that the upper class is in decline while the workers are in the ascendant: "A shopgirl has a bigger chance of a miracle than a millionaire," he argues. An inscription over the door of the town hall where Colpepper delivers his lecture sums up the movie's ambivalent feelings about him. It reads, "Not heaven itself upon the past has power. But what has been has been and I have had my hour." These words could suggest that nothing can erase Colpepper's mark on history, but it can also be read as a kind of epitaph confirming that his day is done.

Unlike the other movies discussed in this chapter, *A Canterbury Tale* does not regard the American as the only role model for the future. Alison Smith is also regarded in this way. However, Johnson is the star of the picture because, like Hollis and Patterson, he combines the best of the working class (Alison's forthrightness and energy) with the best of the upper class (Colpepper's appreciation for history and culture). When he finds himself at the wrong train station, Johnson immediately confronts the guard: "Why don't you light up the names of your stations? How do you expect folks to read the signs?" Moments like this, reminiscent of Alison, are balanced by others that link Johnson to Colpepper: "I'm crazy about that old road and those Canterbury pilgrims."

Johnson's status as ideal American is made more obvious by his meeting with an American friend in a Canterbury café. Micky Rosinski, a typical "Yank," displays all the traits that Johnson refuses to adopt. He is loud, rude to the waitress ("Hey Babe! What's cooking?"), and reveals his love of nightclubs ("You know what you missed in London? Nightclubs like New York ... and girls and telephone numbers. Why, I got a million of 'em"). In contrast, Johnson is not loud and lascivious. He may be forthright, but he is sensitive to peoples' feelings. For example, as the station guard splutters an indignant response to Johnson's complaints, the American responds, "I didn't mean to hurt your civic pride, Pop." Johnson is consistently polite: "I hope you don't mind me calling you by your first name," he remarks to Alison. Unlike Rosinski, he is positively wholesome ("I've got to get to Canterbury. I promised Mom."). No over-sexed American, he pines only to hear from his girl back home, and is more interested in local carpentry techniques than raising hell in quiet English villages. Johnson's mixture of forthright, no-nonsense energy with respect and thoughtfulness endeared him to several British critics such as Ernest Betts, who wrote: "He has toughness with charm. He moves around slowly, in a detached, baffled, good-humoured way, never hurrying, never worrying, never losing his natural dignity. He is the best of America in battle-dress. I believe he will make tens of thousands of fans in this country."

The Ideal American in the British Press

It was not only in film that G.I.s were presented as role models for a new Britain. The popular British press offered them as the perfect antidote to stifling middle-class behavioral codes, many an article celebrating the G.I.'s open and boisterous display of emotion. For example, *Picture Post* ran a photo spread about a game of American football played in London to a crowd of quietly bemused Britons and ecstatic, bellowing Americans. The copy accompanying the photographs reveals, "It's polite to boo at an American football game, if you feel like it. No nonsense about 'well played, old man!' when the enemy—that is to say, your opponents—score a goal and you're gnashing your teeth behind that stiff upper lip."[30] *News Chronicle* was quick to defend American soldiers who openly celebrated more serious victories: "…when they wipe up the enemy they will feel good about it and utter various sorts of whoops, for that is the simple, honest, exuberant American way…. He will be a nitwit who builds a British grievance upon the Americans' lusty practice of exulting in his accomplishments."[31] The same newspaper carried an article whose headline—"Boy was I scared! Said U.S. Flier When His Plane Bounced"[32]—again stresses American honesty in the matter of emotion. It is impossible to imagine a British wartime newspaper reporting that one of its own countrymen had been scared in battle.

Journalists also presented the American armed services as refreshingly classless and, therefore, as attractive institutions to left-leaning, middle-class Britons. *Picture Post* underscored, "Americans are called up in this country not by classes but by the very flexible system laid down by the Selective Service Act…. Everybody, rich and poor, men with influence and men without influence, got a number…"[33] The G.I.s themselves were portrayed as intolerant of the deference and privilege they observed in British society. *News Chronicle* quoted "a soldier from Pittsburgh" who remarked, "Too much class distinction over here." … "Too much 'sirring' and too much scraping between one class and another."[34]

A popular press that presented G.I.s as unrestrained and egalitarian was also eager to point out that such attributes did not necessarily lead to anarchy. British journalists, like the nation's filmmakers, created an ideal G.I. who was irreverent but wholesome, boisterous but serious. An article describing a Halloween celebration for American servicemen notes, "There weren't any rules; there wasn't much attempt at organisation; and there was non-stop dancing" but also claims, "The strongest drink to be had was Coca-Cola."[35] *News Chronicle* reported the opinion of a British woman who emphasized that Americans were as interested in debate as they were in jitter-bugging. The article states, "while dances were the most popular feature of the U.S.O. program in her locality she had found that there was never any difficulty in filling a hall with soldiers and sailors whenever there was a lecturer who had something to say either on the war or on what is to come after the war."[36]

British films of the war years that centered upon Americans were very different from their predecessors. The films of the 1930s presented citizens of the United States largely as a malignant influence on British society and culture. By the latter stages of World War II, Americans—albeit of a certain stripe—had become role models. This transformation occurred because middle-class British filmmakers, observing the social changes wrought by war, harbored grave doubts about the state of their nation. Ambivalent about every section of British society, they looked to the United States to show the way forward. Of course, the creators of the three movies discussed in this chapter were not suggesting that Americans should be the leaders of Britain. Indeed, rather than a realistic representation of a U.S. citizen, each film's protagonist seems a fantastic impossibility, as cobbled together and unreal as Frankenstein's monster. John Patterson, Johnny Hollis, and Bob Johnson provide a positive picture of America and hint that Britain would do well to adopt some American attributes but, ultimately, they represent the best of Britain rather than the best of America.

4

"Funny thing about controls, suddenly they go haywire"
Debating the Necessity of Restraint in Postwar Britain

This chapter explores a period in British History—1945 to 1955—in which a nation that made a virtue of emotional and physical restraint reevaluated the place of these traits in the national culture. During World War II, the citizenry's ability to be stoical and calm in the face of devastation and privation was immortalized by journalists, among them an American, Ralph Ingersoll. As he was registering as an alien at a London police station, an air-raid siren began to whine:

> The sergeant in the middle of the counter chanted in a monotonous voice without looking up:
> "An air raid alarm has been sounded. There is a shelter underneath this building. The man at the door will show you the way to it. If you do not choose to go to the shelter we will carry on."
> Nobody went. The buzz of conversation resumed.[1]

Such anecdotes were legion and, whether they were all true or not, they reinforced the myth that to be British was to control oneself whatever the circumstances.

Wartime popular culture offered myriad images of Britons exercising emotional and physical restraint. For instance, songs and movies hinted that the citizenry could stave off sexual temptation. Britain's war was conducted to the strains of Vera Lynn's *We'll Meet Again*, a song that admonished citizens to "keep smiling through"—perhaps through gritted teeth?—until they were reunited with their lover. The conflict was also indelibly stamped with the image of Celia Johnson in the movie *Brief*

Encounter (David Lean, 1945) bravely waving goodbye to sexual passion as the man who embodies it takes the train out of her life.

The state also had a hand in restraining the populace. To live in Blitz-era Britain was to be subject to a sheaf of governmental rules and regulations. Householders were required to blackout their windows at night and endure the frequent officiousness of Air Raid Wardens.[2] The consumption of food was controlled by ration books, travel limited by petrol coupons, and conversation managed by warnings to avoid "careless talk." Limits placed on the individual by the state, added to those that citizens placed upon themselves, resulted in what might be termed a culture of restraint.

A Desire for Expression, an Attraction to Restraint

In the decade after World War II Britain embarked upon a reevaluation of this culture. Prominent Britons began to discuss emotional restraint as something that had hampered rather than helped them. For instance, in his autobiographical *Surprised by Joy*, British author and theologian C.S. Lewis notes that his parents "bred in me long before I was old enough to give it a name a certain distrust or dislike of emotion as something uncomfortable and embarrassing and even dangerous."[3] Popular British magazines, by repeatedly focusing on the subject of mental breakdown from the late 1940s to the mid–1950s, helped to normalize the idea of an individual abandoning emotional and physical restraint. "Is This Why Soldiers Break Down?" asked the headline of a sympathetic 1949 *Picture Post* article on battlefield psychosis.[4] The magazine's willingness to discuss mental instability in British soldiery was quite a step forward. Considering that after the Great War a soldier's mental illness was euphemistically described as "shellshock" and stigmatized as a "nervous" condition, the post–World War II era of more open discussion seems positively enlightened.

Articles admitting that servicemen might crack under the stress of battle appeared in tandem with those suggesting that civilians might be subject to the same degree of pressure. "Why Did the Salesman Really Die?" asked a late-forties article that attempted to catalogue the reasons Arthur Miller's well-known protagonist becomes exhausted and suicidal.[5] One of the main goals of the piece is to suggest that British workers suffer the same stresses as those in America and might reasonably react to such pressures by breaking down.

But the idea of expressing one's inner self was still tinged with horror. Other articles in *Picture Post* give the impression that the magazine was unsure whether it, or its readership, should delve into the subject. Four 1949 pages were devoted to a debate on whether the Hollywood movie *The Snake Pit* (Anatole Litvak, 1949) should be screened in Britain. The magazine muses that the film, about a woman's descent into madness and her incarceration in a mental institution, might be too troubling for British audiences. "Can it do more harm than good?" asked the headline of the piece.[6] Such squeamishness was also a feature of a 1954 essay entitled "This is Psychodrama." Reporting on the work of Dr. J. L. Moreno, an American psychiatrist who insists that patients discuss their problems in front of an audience, Jeffrey Mark presents one such meeting as a disturbing interaction between a bombastic, invasive interrogator and a timid, rather passive subject:

> At this point Moreno makes a direct appeal to his audience. Is there anyone in the hall suffering because of despair, fear, loneliness, or any problem of any sort? Anybody? Any problem?
> There is a silence…. A half-inaudible word comes from somewhere in the middle of the hall…. The hawk swoops! Moreno clambers down from the platform, walks towards a man in the audience and literally embraces his quarry. The psychodrama has begun! … He holds him by both arms. There is a barrage of questions. "What's your name? What's your age? What do you do?" and so on; almost ceaselessly.[7]

With such men in charge of the psychiatric profession, emotional restraint seems infinitely preferable to emotional expression.

The tension between a desire for expression and an attraction to restraint was especially notable in discussions of sexuality. The postwar popular press documented and encouraged a new age of sexual freedom. The end of the war heralded a slew of popular articles on sexual matters, from revelations about nudist colonies and bikinis, to more serious pieces on rape and pornography. So extensive was the press coverage that in 1955 a compilation of recent articles was published under the title *Morality Fair: Vagaries of Social Conduct as Reflected in the Press*. This book, which was intended to "illustrate the ever-changing attitude of the public and the growing tendency of the Press to deal frankly with all the facts of life, pleasant and unpleasant,"[8] was essentially a compendium of journalistic treatises on the sexual practices of the British.

Despite its openness, *Morality Fair* consistently hints that sexuality should be policed. Chapters on "Sex Crimes and Sadism" and "Sex in the Courts" are presented alongside those dealing with the thorny subject of homosexuality ("The Challenge of the Abnormal"). The spirit of the book is one of earnest, but rather squeamish, investigation. As its editor Geoffrey Williamson bravely claims, "It is always better to face up to unpleasant realities than to cultivate an ostrich mentality."⁹ While this may be sound advice, Williamson's book ultimately suggests that while it might be increasingly acceptable to discuss Britons as sexual creatures, matters should not be allowed to get out of hand.

Journalists also began to question not only the restraints that Britons imposed upon themselves, but those imposed upon them by the state. *Picture Post* often complained that Britons were hamstrung by their nation's petty bureaucracy. In a 1954 article entitled "The World Mocks London," Fyfe Robertson argues that "the world is quite right to snigger at London, to deride the…. British, who put innocent citizens in Sunday strait jackets, regulate drinking (for pub customers only) by the clock [and] inject a neat but not too lengthy dose of moral uplift into radio sound."¹⁰

Robertson was not alone in his suggestion that the ideals of order and restraint, imposed from above, were increasingly burdensome, if not ludicrous. A piece from 1955 suggests that, while British citizens had become more comfortable with cinematic sex and violence, the censor's scissors were as busy as ever. In "A Seat Beside the Censor," a profile of Arthur Watkins, Secretary of the British Board of Film Censors, Robert Muller muses: "To cut a lusty orgy scene from a French film, or a particularly bloody battle scene from an American film, is right and proper. For those are the things to which the paying British public is alleged to object. But does it—really?"¹¹ Thanks to such articles, a picture began to emerge of a populace that was outgrowing the nannying tactics of the state.

However, despite these hints that Britons might be clamoring for new freedoms, an attraction to state control runs through both articles. Robertson's piece goes on to demand that the authorities do something to regulate prostitution in London. The Muller article never questions that some form of governmental control of the nation's cinema screens is necessary. Indeed, the article can be read as an attempt to put a human face on the censor, thereby normalizing and legitimizing the authority of the state. *Picture Post*'s ambivalence over the question of freedom is nowhere more obvious than in a May 1955 article entitled "Are We Really Free?" Correspondent Charles Hamblett is apparently exasperated with restrictions on personal freedom. "If, after reading this, you feel like snatching a breath of free, fresh air in a public park, be sure to study the notice boards first. You may be committing an offence," he warns sarcastically.¹² Yet, elsewhere in the piece he suggests that the expansion of personal freedom remains a vexed question: "This question of censorship is troubling to conscientious people. Few of us can believe that there should be no restriction, but not many are agreed on where to draw the line."¹³

Though Britons may have been ready to contemplate a less restrained society, they were not prepared to see their nation spin out of control. Accordingly, individuals who embraced excess were demonized. Members of youth cults, for instance, were vilified in the popular press because they flaunted excess like a badge of honor. The "Spiv" was described by one journalist as "that grotesque figure in a zoot suit, flashy tie, snap-brimmed hat who talked the 'big time' in distorted American slang."[14] Spivs had become a familiar sight on Britain's streets during the war, but in the late-forties the popular press found time to devote more copy to them. By the mid-fifties the Teddy Boys—so called because of their long, flamboyant Edwardian jackets—had joined the pantheon of youth culture. They were regarded as excessive figures, not only because of their clothes, but because they could be exuberantly violent. For instance, in 1956, when London Teddy Boys heard Bill Haley's song *Rock Around the Clock* on the soundtrack of Richard Brook's movie *The Blackboard Jungle*, its anthemic spirit sparked off celebratory rioting.

Moral guardians claimed that the Spiv and the Teddy Boy had embraced excess to such a degree that they were now uncontrollable. Journalist Edward Hulton noted in 1954 that the old methods of control do not work on the new gangs. He runs through a number of options but finds them wanting:

> They need discipline or a good hiding perhaps? The two years national service should give them the first. But at the risk of denial by Forces authorities, it must be said that those two years are relished as "one long fiddle." ... Gaol perhaps? Many do indeed get gaol sentences, and, once inside, they behave themselves—but only to "fiddle" a good job.[15]

Youth cults were presented as living proof that if Britons discarded restraint entirely, the consequences would be both unpleasant and uncontrollable.

Postwar Britons were in a bind. A nation in which the populace had been heavily controlled, by individuals themselves and by the state, had begun to question the necessity of restraint. However, while they edged toward a freer society in which physical and emotional expression would be more acceptable, Britons remained attached to restraint and horrified by excess. This dualistic mindset found its way into four British movies released in the period from the end of the war to the mid-fifties: *Dead of Night* (Alberto Cavalcanti et al., 1945), *Mine Own Executioner* (Anthony Kimmins, 1947), *The Hidden Room* (Edward Dmytryk, 1949), and *The Quatermass Xperiment* (Val Guest, 1955). Each of these ponders the degree to which restraint should remain part of British life.

The four films debate the necessity of restraint by comparing two cultures: the culture of restraint marked as peculiarly British, and the culture of excess, unsurprisingly identified as American.[16] In each film, the two cultures clash, the conflict resulting in Britons losing control of themselves and/or their society. To some extent, then, the four movies are paeans to restraint, demonstrating the havoc that can be wrought when an individual is provoked to spin out of control. However, while the films are uncomfortable with excess, they do not present restraint as a satisfactory alternative. Indeed, they imply that the culture of restraint can lead to defeat, inertia, and madness. The American may be the catalyst to a British loss of control, but the overwhelming connotation of all four films is that the British, by clinging to restraint, have ensured their own downfall. Ultimately, the movies endorse a middle ground between riotous excess and suffocating restraint and, in doing so, reveal Britain's uncertainty about the cultural changes it was undergoing.

The Hidden Room

A young couple arrives home from a night on the town. They are Bill Kronin (Phil Brown), an American, and Storm Riordan (Sally Gray), the wife of a British doctor. In this scene, the movie's second, it is established that the pair are guiltlessly and recklessly helping to destroy the Riordan marriage. Although this destruction is a joint effort, it seems that the American is more reckless than his partner. As they enter the darkened living room of the Riordan household, Kronin makes no attempt to be furtive, asking, "How about some music?" before spinning Storm around the room. Noting that the Riordans' record collection is rather sedate, he jokes, "Brahms. Beethoven. Haven't you got any civilized music?" Obviously, he likes to jitter-bug. These hints that Kronin is rash and impulsive culminate in a line of dialogue that marks him as a kind of overgrown child. He tells Storm, "So that's why you love me. Maternal instinct coming out."

Presently the British cuckold, Clive Riordan (Robert Newton), reveals his presence in the room. His calm, reserved personality contrasts sharply with Kronin's. He holds a gun on the couple, but this is no crime of passion. His voice unwavering, his hand steady, he proceeds to coolly explain his desire to kill the American. His witty opening line, "Let me get the ice. We mustn't be inhospitable to our American cousins, must we?" establishes that he is from the "best served cold" school of revenge. Riordan is such an embodiment of restraint that, throughout the movie, Storm and Kronin will contend that he is not capable of the rash act of murder. The American mocks Riordan by telling him, "When it comes down to it, you won't kill me. You're not the type." Later, this sentiment is echoed by Storm who ridicules her husband. "You, kill a man? You, take a risk?" she scoffs. Indeed, Riordan's detractors are proven right since he fails to carry his murderous plans to fruition.

The scene in which Riordan confronts the adulterous couple implies that a controlled individual has been pushed too far by the excessive behavior of an American. Indeed, although Storm has engaged in many extramarital dalliances, as her husband points out, he has never responded to them in such a drastic fashion. It is only when she chooses a citizen of the U.S. for a lover that he snaps. "You've heard of the last straw, haven't you? Well, you're it," claims Riordan. Furthermore, his desire to kill only Kronin, leaving his wife unharmed, suggests that he reserves a special ire for the American.

More evidence that the excessive American has a special talent for making Riordan lose control is provided later in the movie. The Briton's plan to dispose of the American is a meticulous affair. Riordan imprisons Kronin in the basement of some bombed-out buildings, reasoning that, should the police accuse him of murder, he will be able to produce Kronin unharmed. When the investigation into the American's disappearance dies down, Riordan plans to kill his captive and dispose of the body in an acid bath. Blindfolded, the American is chained to a bed and fed at regular intervals. The circumference in which his chains allow him to move is marked out in chalk around the bed. All these safety measures are typical of Riordan, a man whose ordered sensibility is also demonstrated by his love of toy trains. He keeps a model railway in the basement of his house, a perfect symbol of his need for order and his desire to control. Yet, try as the Englishman might to remain in control, the American will foil his plans. Under investigation by Scotland Yard, in the form of Superintendent Finsbury (Naunton Wayne), Riordan keeps his cool but makes one mistake. In response to the Superintendent wishing him a good evening, he says, "Thanks pal." The Briton has been spending so much time with his American captive that his vocabulary has been affected. Finsbury notes Riordan's slip of the tongue by telling Storm, "Your husband's English vocabulary seems quite adequate, you know. I mean it did seem so odd to hear him borrow from our cousins across the sea." After all his care and planning, the Englishman loses control due to insidious American influence. Significantly, he loses control of his mouth, the part of his body that, through witty lines about "our American cousins" had most cogently expressed his reserved, English ways.

4. *"Funny thing about controls, suddenly they go haywire"*

It might seem, then, that this is a story about an ordinary, cool-headed Englishman pushed too far, and brought low, by America's influence in his life. The film encourages this response by encouraging us to sympathize with Riordan. After all, he has been betrayed and his underdog status naturally draws us to him. Moreover, because we wait with him in the darkened house for the adulterous pair, we might feel a sense of camaraderie with him. As he reveals his presence, a sense of being in on the joke lends the scene an added *frisson*. The fact that the movie is about taking revenge on an American may have elicited yet more sympathy from a British audience in 1949. It was obvious to many Britons that America had outstripped their nation's diplomatic power and influence. Therefore, to those who resented this development, the image of Riordan making an American suffer may have been a very attractive one. The moments when he redresses the romantic balance of power while referring to international affairs could have provided similar pleasures. "You will now see British diplomacy at its best," says Riordan, just before telephoning the Savoy Hotel in order to disprove the American's story that he had dined there with Storm. Also, the very fact that the film revolves around an American's love affair with a British wife suggests that it intends to mobilize residual resentment about the dalliances of wartime G.I.s with British women.[17]

Yet, while all these pleasures undoubtedly reside within the film, Riordan's restraint is shown to be a limitation. The movie begins in "The Liberal Club," an ironically titled watering hole peopled by the aged remnants of Britain's conservative elite. Three opinionated gentlemen, tended by the deferential manservant customary in such establishments, discuss the state of British foreign policy. According to one of their number, British inaction has caused the nation to squander the opportunity for economic self-sufficiency offered by the colonies. He argues:

> We change from a primarily agricultural country to an industrial one at the very time the colonies fall into our hands, and what do we do? Absolutely nothing. We pour money down the drain buying foodstuffs from all over the world instead of developing the empire. With the obvious result. When we have to pay for war, we can't pay for food.

The film invites us to make a connection between a nation that does "absolutely nothing" and the film's protagonist, Clive Riordan. How can Britain succeed in the international sphere, or any other sphere for that matter, if the fate of the nation rests in the hands of restrained men like Riordan?

A culture of restraint, in which "not doing" is valued over "doing," has resulted in disaster. Worse, it has placed the nation in a subordinate position to the United States. The same man continues, "Do you realize we're living on American dollars sir; that every mouthful of food we eat costs dollars?" He presents American currency as a murderous entity ("It's dollars all the time, sir. A stranglehold on the empire.") and U.S. culture as an overwhelming force of invasion ("We've only got to pick up a London newspaper, one of our own newspapers, and what do we read about? Americans, Americans, Americans."), but the fact remains that if Britain had taken appropriate action, America would not have become so powerful. Despite this energetic rhetoric, it seems that Britain will not change its ways. The man's companions are hardly listening to him and respond with irrelevant and inane *non sequiturs* ("Mmmm. We might get some decent coffee").

Like Britain, Riordan has failed to act, and consequently loses out to America. He has failed to act as a lover. Storm hints that he is restrained in the bedroom, telling him that Kronin "loves me as you've never loved me." Indeed, America's more aggressive approach to sexual matters is confirmed in a scene in which an American sailor tries to sell his buddy an address book filled with the names of available women. Riordan's reserve is again highlighted by his general attitude at the Liberal Club. He sits slumped in his chair, and says nothing in response to the other men's conversation. But, doesn't his plan to murder Kronin suggest he has finally decided to act? Certainly, but it seems he has waited too long. Since his action is so belated, he is not taken seriously. In the climactic moments of the movie, Kronin once again questions Riordan's ability to act: "When it comes down to it, you're nothing but a blowhard."

Restraint has meant that Britain has been defeated in the international sphere, in the romantic sphere, and is no longer taken seriously. *The Hidden Room* also suggests that restraint can be an extremely sinister commodity since it allows individuals to distance themselves from their actions, however heinous. Although he is engaged in a murder attempt, Riordan tries to make the procedure as civilized as possible. He brings Kronin a martini and asks him, "How about books to pass the time?" He consistently acts as if the American were a guest in his home, even though he knows he apparently intends to kill him. Riordan is so detached from his emotions that he appears inhuman. His talent for downplaying the monstrousness of his actions is underscored in a scene in which he transports acid—the substance in which he intends to dissolve Kronin's body—in a horribly inappropriate vessel: a child's hot water bottle.

Riordan's plans come to naught, and so we are left with the impression that the culture of restraint is counterproductive if not futile. Despite early scenes in which we are encouraged to side with Riordan, the film will make a hero of his enemy. Reveling in Riordan's defeat, the American tells him, "the joke's on you pal." Indeed, the film has steadily proven the redundancy of its British protagonist and his way of life.

Mine Own Executioner

Mine Own Executioner might seem a strange choice for discussion since its principle character is Canadian. However, I would like to contend that this man, Felix Milne, is a de facto American. The star that portrays him, Burgess Meredith, was by 1947, the year of the film's release, a well-known American actor who played staunchly American parts. British audiences had seen him in *Of Mice and Men* (1939) and *The Story of GI Joe* (1945). His character's Canadian citizenship is mentioned only briefly and seems motivated by plot requirements. Milne is a mental health specialist working in a British institution. It is therefore more plausible that he is Canadian, since a citizen of a commonwealth nation would have been more likely than an American to secure such a post. Furthermore, to most Britons, Canadians were virtually indistinguishable from Americans. As one of The Liberal Club's members says of Canadians in *The Hidden Room*, "Fantastic lingo. Same as Americans you know. Met a Canadian once. Couldn't understand a word he said. I said 'Look here young man, if you're going to stay in the empire, you're going to have to learn to speak English.' Took it quite well." But the most potent factor obscuring Milne's Canadian identity is his behavior. He acts in a way that British audiences expected of Americans—barely able to control himself.

Hints that Milne is out of control arise early in the movie. On a night out with his wife Patricia (Dulcie Gray), he thirstily drains his glass. "Knocking them back a bit aren't you?" she responds. "Who cares," comes the reply. He has little tolerance for his wife, angrily telling her "for heaven's sake don't fuss." His outbursts gradually increase in severity until, late in the film, he implores her "for heaven's sake shut up." His behavior is all the more disturbing because, while Milne is capable of showing affection toward Patricia, she can never be certain that his emotions won't take an opposite course. We learn that Milne has informed her of his intention to end their relationship but he soon reneges, noting, "That was last night and this is today." Milne is aware of his bipolar tendencies, yet he seems powerless to do anything to rectify them. "There's no excuse for me bullying you all the time," he tells Patricia, but he continues to do so. Since Milne is a mental health specialist, a question at the heart of the movie is, "How

The conundrum of restraint: Adam Lucian (Kieron Moore, left) under the care of Felix Milne (Burgess Meredith) in *Mine Own Executioner* (1947).

can this man, who is barely able to control himself, advise others about how to control themselves?" Indeed, the movie repeatedly makes clear that rather than being a qualified psychiatrist, Milne is simply an expert in the field.

The movie suggests that Milne acts this way because he has not mastered his inner self. Asked to perform a psychological examination of Barbara Edge (Christine Norden), a friend's wife whom he finds attractive, he reassures himself that he will be able to control his lust for her. But just as he says "can't be any harm, can there?" he accidentally snaps his pipe in half. The act of breaking the pipe suggests both that the liaison will be in some way destructive and, that Milne's subconscious is an extremely powerful force. He had not intended to break the pipe, but his inner demons—who know that he is attempting to hide the truth behind words—force him to do it, thereby demonstrating their jurisdiction over him. Later in the movie, after he has hurt his wife's feelings, Milne runs his finger through the flame of a cigarette lighter, apparently unaware that he is doing so. The moment invites us once again to read him as a slave to his subconscious, the inner self meting out masochistic punishment.

4. "Funny thing about controls, suddenly they go haywire"   117

As we learn more about Milne's personality, we may recall the film's first image after the title sequence, a quotation from the English metaphysical poet John Donne:

> There are too many Examples of men, that have been their own executioners, and that have made hard shrift to bee so ...... some have beat out their braines at the wal of their prison, and some have eate the fire out of their chimneys: but I do nothing upon myself, and yet am mine owne Executioner.

Like the unfortunate described by Donne, Milne is brought low from within, not by any outer, physical force. He is his own executioner because he has not mastered that part of himself that would destroy his marriage and injure his body with flame. He explains this part of himself to his wife:

> You see, there's a bit of me that's not quite grown up. It stays at the mental age of about fourteen. Of course most of me is very grown up indeed. If it weren't I couldn't do this job. But outside the job I run up against this thing. It takes all sorts of forms, teasing and bullying you for instance.... Yes, well now this business about Babs, the bit of me that finds her attractive is all part of this thing. It's kind of a deliberate, childish wantonness.

Milne's struggle with his inner demons infuses the movie with suspense since we can never be sure that he has conquered them or they him. His wife warns him about the predatory Barbara Edge. "She'll come at you, teeth bared," she argues, going on to ask, "You don't want her to, do you?" Milne ignores her. "You're not in love with her, are you?" she persists. Milne's reply, "Go to sleep.... I'll see you in the morning," might be taken as a sign that he regards her suggestions as ludicrous, but it could equally confirm their legitimacy. As the film progresses, Milne seems to have conquered his urges, refusing Barbara as a patient because "I'm a darn sight too interested." A few scenes later, he begins an affair with her. We may feel that he has regained control of himself when he puts himself in the psychiatric care of a colleague, Dr. James Garsten (John Laurie). However, after Milne leaves the doctor's office, a black look crosses Garsten's face betraying the continued seriousness of his patient's condition.

Several characters with whom Milne comes into contact place a premium on self-restraint, a talent that, try as he might, he fails to acquire. At a party Peter Edge (Michael Shepley), Barbara's boorish and boring husband, expresses his distaste for those he regards as taking undue advantage of the postwar welfare state. He points out "the utter lack of self-restraint we see all around, you know. Greed. Greed and selfishness. As much money as possible and do as little as you can. That's what these people want, you know." His attachment to restraint is again made clear when the conversation turns to psychiatry.

The science disturbs him because of what he sees as its invasive methodology. He asks Milne, "Do you find it does people good, I mean this digging about in their minds?" The psychiatrist's ability to expose what would otherwise remain hidden is also of concern to Peter ("seems to me a very embarrassing business"). Describing Milne's talent, he resorts to uneasy humor. "Takes one look and sees right through one," he jokes. Having established himself as a man who values restraint, Peter's horror of psychiatry can be seen to stem from its insistence that a patient hold nothing back.

A more significant character, Adam Lucian (Kieron Moore), is also terrified of opening up.[18] Lucian has become mentally unstable since being imprisoned and tortured by the Japanese during World War II. He becomes Milne's patient only because his wife insists upon it. Wary of confronting or talking about his wartime experiences, he is eventually coaxed into conversation by a drug administered to him by Milne. He proceeds to describe his crash-landing in enemy territory, interrogation, and eventual escape. As he comes around from the effects of the drug, he becomes agitated: "I've been talking. What about?" he asks excitedly. "Did I spill the beans?" he continues. He then refers to his interrogation—another situation in which he has been forced to open up—as a "disgraceful business." The drug Milne gave him was "a low trick," he concludes.

Lucian soon appears to warm to the treatment. He tells Milne, "I'm glad somebody knows," and expresses his new attitude by saying, "I just feel 'what the heck.'" However, Milne suspects, correctly, that Lucian may simply be trying to avoid further examination. He tells him that they have not yet tackled the root of his problem: "This thing inside you that's causing all the trouble is getting frightened. It can feel us moving the layers away from on top of it, and it's afraid that if we go on it will be found and kicked out. It wants you to stop the treatments before that happens." Just like Milne, Lucian is hampered by a "thing." Yet, whereas Milne's "thing" is an inability to control himself, Lucian's is an inability to relinquish self-control. In other words, Milne is too excessive, while Lucian is too restrained.

Milne attempts to help Lucian, but his undisciplined ways lead to his patient's losing control. Instead of monitoring his patient, Milne goes on a date with Barbara Edge. On another occasion, he nurses a headache instead of checking on Lucian's status. Left to his own devices, Lucian kills his wife and then himself. As Milne says of the tragedy, "If I hadn't let him go, this wouldn't have happened, don't you see?" Lucian's breakdown is partly Milne's fault, but it is also caused by the patient's obsession with self-restraint. It seems inevitable that this man's repressed memories and emotions will return in a monstrous form.

While the film never relieves Milne of the responsibility of Lucian's rampage, it does not condemn him either. It reserves its ire for the institution of self-restraint. Milne may be out of control and at the mercy of his subconscious, but at least he feels able to express himself. He rages, shouts, and gives in to his urges. This tendency, it seems, makes him a healthier man than his contemporaries. Peter Edge, who lives in fear of psychic exposure, is presented as a buffoon and, like Clive Riordan of *The Hidden Room*, a cuckold. Adam Lucian, who never fully confronts his demons, murders his wife and kills himself. Restraint forces men into precarious situations where they must constantly keep themselves in check. Indeed, precariousness is such a motif in Lucian's life that he becomes associated with the lullaby "Rock-a-bye Baby." During a flashback in which he flies over enemy territory he hums it to himself and, as he walks down the street on the way to murder his wife, the tune makes an extra-diegetic appearance on the soundtrack. Ironically, it is Lucian who voices the film's most insightful comment about the futility of restraint. Ostensibly referring to a malfunctioning light switch, he remarks, "Funny thing about controls. Suddenly, they go haywire." Controls cannot be relied upon, and if Lucian had taken his own words to heart, perhaps he would not have met such a tragic end.

At the conclusion of the movie, Milne's approach to life, though it is obviously by no means flawless, is held up as a possible way forward. In a rage, he contemplates leaving the world of psychiatry. "This job needs a god to do it properly," he tells his wife. However, he soon accepts that he, a mere human, may be able to help the mentally ill. Referring to his patients, he says wearily, "Sometimes I have headaches and I let them go away and shoot their wives, but at other times I treat them with skill and integrity and I cure them." *Mine Own Executioner* arrives at the conclusion that excessive individuals like Milne are a better influence on society than those who try to bottle up their urges and emotions.

The Quatermass Xperiment

Clive Riordan and Felix Milne are out of control, but the havoc they wreak affects only a few people. The chaos wrought by Dr. Bernard Quatermass (Brian Donlevy) could cause a nationwide disaster. Quatermass, the American protagonist of this science fiction cult movie, is head scientist of a space program. One of the program's rockets, returning from space, crash-lands in Britain. Of the three astronauts aboard, two have apparently disappeared and one has been rendered catatonic. It is soon discovered that the two missing astronauts were "absorbed" by an alien life form, and the body of the sole survivor has become a host for the same space-dwelling species. As the astronaut, Victor Carroon (Richard Wordsworth), gradually metamorphoses into a plant-like and then an octopus-like creature, he terrorizes the populace, absorbing several men and even the animals at London Zoo. The authorities race against the clock to stop the creature releasing its spores and consequently absorbing the whole nation.

Those who know him consider Quatermass a loose cannon. Carroon's wife, Julia (Margia Dean), understandably dismayed that her husband is turning into a plant, tells the American, "You've done this to him…. You've destroyed him like you've destroyed everything else you've touched." Quatermass's chief nemesis is Blake (Lionel Jeffries), an official of Britain's Ministry of Defense, who is constantly exasperated by the American's recklessness. Approaching the crash site, Blake suggests that the current crisis would not have occurred had the rocket been "brought … down by your own control." Blake is angered that Quatermass has allowed things to get out of hand and also that he refuses to do things by the book: "You deliberately launched that rocket without waiting for official sanction," he scolds. In response to Blake's protests, Quatermass grumbles, "You and your committee."

Once at the crash site, Quatermass strides about, tactlessly assuming that he should direct proceedings. "I'm Quatermass. I'll be in charge from here on out," he announces. Indeed, his actions suggest that Julia Carroon and Blake are correct in their bleak summation of his personality. Told that reporters are demanding "the facts" about the crash, the ever-cautious Blake responds, "They'll get some later." Quatermass immediately blusters, "They'll get some now. Bring them on." Like Felix Milne of *Mine Own Executioner*, Quatermass proves himself not only short-tempered, but erratic in his moods. He initially suggests that opening the hatch of the crashed spacecraft could prove lethal to any astronaut left inside. A minute later, he has changed his mind. In response, Blake asks him, "Are you mad? … But you said that would incinerate them." Quatermass delivers the rather weak rejoinder, "Don't tell me what I can and what I can't do." Like *Mine Own Executioner*, *The Quatermass Xperiment* asks, "Is this out-of- control man fit to be in control of others?"

Quatermass, then, is as out of control as his rocket. Indeed, the movie makes sure that we associate the two. The vehicle's code name is Q1 and, when a British official asserts that "it broke loose," we may associate its unrestrained behavior with that of its creator. There is another way that

4. "Funny thing about controls, suddenly they go haywire" 121

Quatermass is linked with his rocket. It is repeatedly suggested that both scientist and machine are inflicting some form of sexual penetration on Britain. In the opening scene, as the rocket falls to earth, two young lovers are embracing in a haystack. As their passion mounts, Quatermass's space projectile crashes into a nearby field. The idea of sexual penetration is revisited in a later scene in which Quatermass visits a British policeman, Inspector Lomax (Jack Warner). After the American has berated the cop's investigative methods, Lomax notes to a colleague, "Well, you might almost say we'd been given a rocket." In British slang, being "given a rocket" refers to the act of warning an individual about their unacceptable conduct, but it also, more literally, refers to a rocket entering some unnamed part of the individual's anatomy. Lomax, in discussing the "rocket" delivered by Quatermass, admits that the American has achieved a dominant position. This comes after an earlier scene when Lomax, hearing that Quatermass is on his way, had speculated, "Quatermass, eh? This is what's known as penetrating into enemy territory." The Briton who thought he would be penetrating an American, has actually been penetrated himself. Moments like these, built around the idea of sexual penetration as dominance, suggest that the American might be able to make the British lose control in more ways than one.

Another of Quatermass's creations, the ever more monstrous Victor Carroon, adds to the American's aura of recklessness. Carroon is a man physically and mentally out of control and, as his wife claims, it was Quatermass who made him that way. His body is no longer his own, and, as it becomes increasingly plant-like, he is reduced to communicating through whimpers. At the same time, his mind, once consumed with scientific data, becomes possessed by an irrational desire to kill. In creating the pathetic Carroon, Quatermass has become something of a Dr. Frankenstein. Like Mary Shelley's literary creation he is reckless and defiant. The film's debt to the Frankenstein legend is made even clearer by a scene in which Carroon meets a little girl by a river, reminding us of the similar moment in James Whale's film version of the novel.

The impulsive Quatermass barges into a Britain in which self-control is a way of life. Several moments suggest that the stiff upper lip is a highly prized attribute. For instance, when Carroon appears to be on the verge of tears, a British companion encourages him not to cry by saying "hey, steady, steady." In a similar moment, a man who suffered burns when Q1 crashed near his house is offered help by a medic. He refuses aid, displaying the requisite amount of restraint with the words, "Don't you start fussing, it was a singe that's all." As well as their emotions, the British also feel the

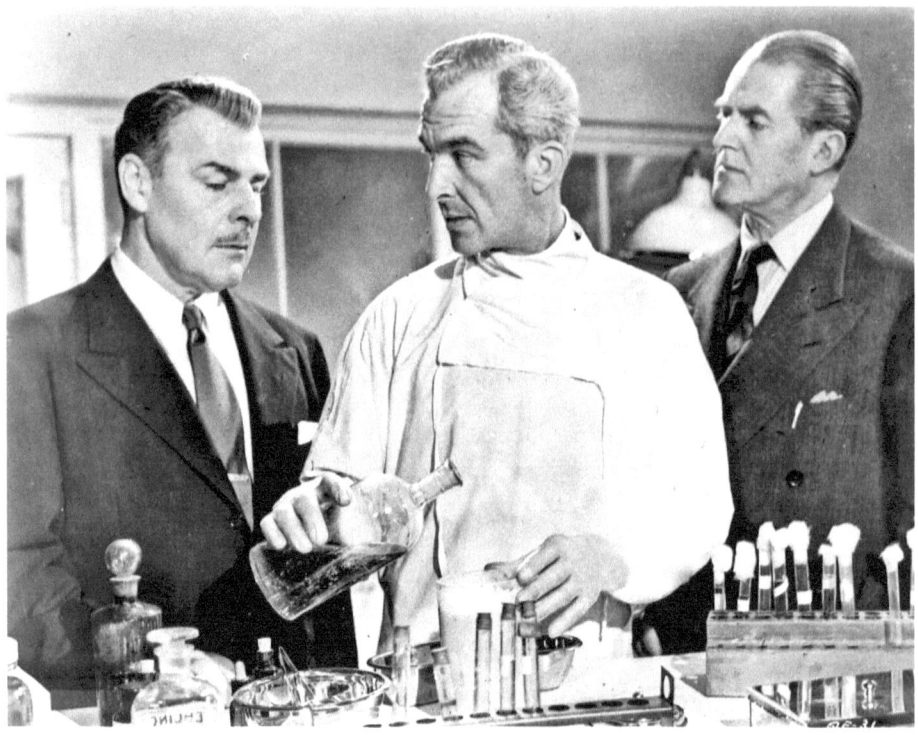

American science out of control. From left: Professor Bernard Quatermass (Brian Donlevy), Dr. Gordon Briscoe (David King-Wood), and Inspector Lomax (Jack Warner) in *The Quatermass Xperiment* (1955).

need to control the human body. It seems to be no coincidence that Inspector Lomax, who will soon find himself chasing an astronaut whose body is rebelling, is introduced to us as he shaves. The act of keeping the body in check will soon prove impossible as Carroon takes on an alien form and Lomax develops a prominent five o'clock shadow.

The emphasis that Lomax places on shaving suggests that this is a man who adheres to a set of behavioral codes. His proprietary nature is again obvious when he meets Quatermass for the first time, telling the American, "I wish you'd sit down. If I sit and you stand I'm being rude and I'm longing to sit down." The scene at the crash site emphasizes that behavioral codes are instituted by a society cordoned off both literally and figuratively. Ropes and policemen warning the attendant crowds to keep back surround the location of the rocket. We cut to a radio station where an announcer intones, "Members of the public are warned to stay away from the area. I will repeat that." Quatermass ignores all these entreaties. His disregard for the rules distinguishes him from the many minor characters in the film that, through apparently throwaway lines, contribute to the mood of a nation keeping to the rules. For instance, a photo-lab technician responds to a request for expedited prints by saying timidly, "Well, I don't know what the old man'll say."

Inspector Lomax's five o'clock shadow is not the only sign that America is making Britons lose control. When Carroon—Quatermass's creature—attacks his British prey, they don't just die, they metamorphose, going through a process of rapid decomposition until they are virtually unrecognizable as their old selves. Examining one of Carroon's British victims, an astonished doctor announces, "The whole tissue structure's been eaten away."

The Quatermass Xperiment dramatizes Britain's horror of losing control. Bodies that have been contained through emotional and physical restraint lose their integrity. Significantly, the film concentrates solely on the male body losing control. All Carroon's victims are men, their gender repeatedly stressed. Quatermass is astounded that, "Some fantastic invisible force turned two men into jelly." A doctor emphasizes that he is dealing with "a shell of a man." The masculine loss of control is emphasized almost certainly because, in mid-twentieth century Britain, men were expected to be more adept than women at restraining themselves.

Quatermass and Carroon may cause a few Britons to lose control, but it is their potential to affect the nation as a whole that causes the greatest alarm. A society that has been maintained though rules and regulations is plunged into chaos as the lead characters become aware that the alien life form may release spores into the atmosphere. To avoid this eventuality, Quatermass suggests that the authorities try to electrocute the beast.

Inspector Lomax exclaims that this plan will use so much electricity that it will "bring the city to a standstill." He is proven correct as we witness London's architectural icons plunged into darkness. Battersea power station, Big Ben, and the Trafalgar Square fountains are all drained of power. Just as America's influence has drained Britain's men of life, it will sap the strength from the symbols of Britain's power and prestige. The climactic scene occurs inside another iconic British building, Westminster Abbey, during the recording of a B.B.C. television show about its restoration. Even this space is sullied by excessive Americana, Quatermass's creature oozing its way across the rafters.

At the film's conclusion, disaster is averted, but we are left with no cosy notion that American excess has been contained. Inspector Lomax delivers a wry coda on the affair. Turning to Quatermass he says, "Well, this time you've won." Unchastened, Quatermass announces, "I'm gonna start again." An image of him stalking off into the night is followed by one of a new rocket, presumably code-named Q2, blasting off.

Certainly, Quatermass has caused Britain a great deal of death, destruction, and chaos, but the film does not condemn him utterly. Rather, the movie is ambivalent about the two world views it has presented: the world of British order and restraint and, as Julia Carroon says, "the world of Quatermass."

It must be remembered that Quatermass is the film's lead character, a fact that affords him a certain status. Moreover, he is something of a hero because he successfully clears up the mess he has made. But his most attractive attributes are his energy and tenacity. Quatermass has spent the entire movie running from place to place, formulating plans, and leaving the British authorities in his wake. Quite obviously, he and his fellow U.S. citizens let no setback stand in their way. He implies this by saying of the astronauts that disappeared on Q1, "They'll fire the imagination so that there'll be a hundred men begging for the privilege when we launch the second rocket."

British caution may ensure that the nation causes no Quatermass-size disasters, but restraint, it seems, has created an inert and hamstrung society. Inspector Lomax embodies his nation's outlook, saying, "I'm an old fashioned sort of chap. I don't know much about rockets or traveling into space. I don't read science fiction. I'm a plain, simple bible man. I have a routine mind and I like to do routine things." Undoubtedly, this level-headed cop will preserve the status quo, but he and his ilk will ensure that Britain is left behind by nations that are prepared to take chances. Though it is eager to point out the American's faults, the film also suggests that British society might benefit by adopting his energetic and optimistic ways.

The Quatermass Xperiment makes no final decision as to where our sympathies should lie. A conversation between Blake, a British stuffed shirt, and Quatermass, the American adventurer, confirms the movie's indecision. Quatermass argues, "If the whole world waited for official sanction, we'd be standing still." Blake interrupts him, grumbling about the American's readiness "to gamble with three men's lives." Quatermass barks back, "The unknown is always a risk." As the credits roll, the question remains: Should Britain cling to restraint and "stand still" or adopt the more excessive ways of Quatermass, plunging forward into a future that holds both triumph and disaster?

Dead of Night

Dead of Night is a horror movie made up of several stories of the supernatural. A group of guests at a country inn recount their otherworldly experiences to one another. As they do so, we flash back to the time and place of each occurrence, witnessing how it played out. One of these tales is very pertinent to this chapter. It concerns a British ventriloquist, Maxwell Frere (Michael Redgrave), and his dummy, Hugo. One night, performing in a Parisian cabaret, Frere meets American ventriloquist Sylvester Kee (Hartley Power). Hugo seems very enamored with Kee. "You interest me my man. You interest me quite a lot. We two could make beautiful music together," the dummy tells him. Of course, since we assume that Hugo's words are provided by Frere, it appears that the Briton finds the American attractive. However, after Hugo has made his advance, Frere—the man who is ostensibly controlling Hugo—begins to look shocked and worried. Is this all part of the act? Is Frere pretending to be upset because his dummy is attracted to another man? As the movie progresses, it seems that Frere is not acting. The film provides us with two possibilities regarding his mental state and keeps us guessing as to which is correct. Either Frere is insane and imagines that his dummy has a life of its own, or he is sane and Hugo is indeed alive.

There are three American characters in this tale. All have excessive qualities. Upon entering the nightclub where Frere performs, Sylvester Kee orders a whole bottle of champagne that he apparently intends to consume by himself. He quickly begins to chat with Beulah (Elisabeth Welch), an African American chanteuse dressed in a sparkling, painted-on gown. Beulah proceeds to sing a sexually suggestive song. The third American is Hugo, Maxwell Frere's dummy. Though Frere, the ventriloquist, has a distinctly British accent, the voice that emanates from Hugo is noticeably Americanized. For instance, when using the words "not" and "impossible" Hugo pronounces the letter "o" with an "ah" sound instead of the more British "oh." While Kee and Beulah help to establish an excessive American environment, it is Hugo who most fully represents his apparently out of control nation. For example, he refuses to sing when Frere commands him to, preferring instead to talk to his new friend Kee. Unable to keep a secret, he reveals to Kee and the nightclub audience that his relationship with Frere is troubled: "I'm just about through with that cheap ham," he admits. He plots behind his master's back, making plans to meet Kee after the show. Appearing from between the stage curtains after Frere has made his exit, the dummy tells Kee, "I'll be waiting for you in my dressing room."

Unlike the Americans who surround him, the British Frere appears to be a slave to restraint. He constantly scolds Hugo for his behavior, at one point holding his hand over Hugo's mouth to silence him. He is bitten in response. The spectacle provided by Frere's ventriloquist act is that of a reserved Briton trying and failing to control a mischievous, outspoken American. Like Adam Lucian of *Mine Own Executioner*, Frere's horror of psychiatry suggests a fear of exposing his inner self. "You want to psychoanalyze me, don't you? Want to look inside my brain and see how the wheels go round. Dissect me like a guinea pig and show me off to your distinguished colleagues," he tells a psychiatrist entrusted with his case.

However, because we suspect that Frere is the author of Hugo's words, it is very possible that excessive urges lie dormant within the Briton. At times it seems that Frere simply uses Hugo as a medium to express all the darker forces he usually holds in check. At a hotel bar two women and a man strike up a conversation with Frere because they recognize him as a performer. Even though he is inebriated, Frere cannot bring himself to tell the rather irritating trio to leave him alone. He lets Hugo speak for him. "This cheap bit of skirt's getting after me," Hugo announces as one of the women begins to speak to him. When the male in the group is angered by this comment, Frere protests innocence, blaming the dummy. Hugo proceeds to make matters worse. "Will you kick his teeth in, Maxwell, or shall I?" he asks Frere.

While at such times Frere seems to be in control of Hugo, using him for his own ends, there is a prevailing sense that the two are at war, constantly vying for control over each other. During their stage act Hugo tells Frere that a ventriloquist is "a chap who makes a voice come out of a stuffed dummy, the way I do out of you." This apparently innocent joke, a staple of ventriloquism, takes on a more sinister aspect as events progress. Whether Hugo is alive or not, it is undeniable that he eventually gains the upper hand over Frere. Ignoring Frere's obvious distress that Hugo has chosen another man, the dummy goes to Kee's room. How he arrives there remains a mystery, but Frere is so distressed when he finds him with Kee that he shoots and wounds his romantic rival.

Frere's mental breakdown can be interpreted as the fault of excessive America. Until he met Sylvester Kee, Frere was sane. After the American enters his life, chaos ensues. Another excessive American, Hugo the dummy, might also have caused Frere's mental collapse through disloyalty. However, it might also be reasonably argued that Frere loses control because he places such a high premium on self-restraint. Since he constantly holds himself and Hugo in check, it seems only a matter of time before his repressed urges manifest themselves in some monstrous form. Like Clive Riordan of *The Hidden Room* and Adam Lucian of *Mine Own Executioner*, his attachment to restraint is likely the cause of his murderous rampage; his eventual failure to control himself, or the excessive American forces in his life, can be taken as proof that restraint is a futile obsession.

Following World War II, Britain embarked upon a reevaluation of the culture of restraint. A society that placed many restrictions on the behavior of its citizens began to ask whether these limitations were still necessary. In cinema, this period saw the stiff upper lip, so pervasive in wartime popular culture, begin to wobble. By the 1960s, due to the phenomenon known as "Swinging London," Britain would become famous throughout the world as a nation that, in many ways, had divested itself of restraint. Accordingly, the sixties saw the arrival of a new breed of British cinematic male, dubbed "the angry young man." Loud, openly emotional, aggressive, and frequently bare-chested, he was the antithesis of his predecessors. I would like to suggest that the four movies discussed in this chapter, along with popular press articles similar to those cited, eased Britain through the transition from wartime repressiveness to sixties expressiveness.

5

"A well-intentioned but inexperienced colossus"
British Cinema, Picture Post and the Redefinition of National Identity in the Postwar Period

World War II left Britain destitute. The massive financial burden of fighting for over five years had emptied government coffers, and even after the instigation of America's Marshall Plan in 1949, Clement Atlee's government was forced to devalue the pound sterling against the dollar.[1] Postwar Britons soon realized that America had not only wrested the reins of world power from their grip, it had also snatched the purse strings. While America's economic tentacles reached into virtually every region of the globe, Britain's colonial system lay in ruins, and while America was visually defined by streamlined and chrome-plated plenitude, Britons woke each day, for several years after the war, to rationed food and a bomb-scarred landscape. Unsurprisingly, many Britons felt increasingly ineffectual. In his 1957 study of Anglo-American relations, British historian William Clark notes, "The Anglo-American habit of measuring themselves against each other is now producing in Britain that agonising feeling of inferiority which was the curse of Americans for at least the first fifty years of their national existence."[2] Yet the realization that Britain was a shadow of its former self not only created a sense of inferiority, it also instigated a crisis of identity. After hundreds of years in which Britain had defined itself as a "Great Power" and an "Empire Builder," such grandiose titles were now highly questionable, if not obsolete. With Britain's role in the world increasingly vague, how would the nation achieve a viable postwar identity? It would do so by defining itself less in terms of power and more in terms of experience, and it achieved this new identity by comparing itself to the supposedly inexperienced United States.

Shepherding America

British politicians reasoned that the United States was a novice in world affairs and, therefore, would benefit from the sober, steadying hand of British experience. This theory had been prevalent in political circles since the dawn of the twentieth century, but during World War II it took on new significance. As it became clear that the United States would not only win the war but also the peace, it was obvious that Britain's international stature would be fundamentally weakened. In order to save face, it was necessary for British politicians to create a new role for themselves and their nation. They achieved this feat by casting themselves as benevolent shepherds to a powerful but inexperienced America. For instance, Harold Macmillan, Prime Minister from 1956 to 1963, was supposed to have claimed when minister for Algiers in 1942: "These Americans represent the new Roman Empire and we Britons, like the Greeks of old, must teach them how to make it go."[3] After the war, such a mindset would become an integral part of British diplomacy. In 1951, British Foreign Secretary Ernest Bevin created a Permanent Under-Secretary's Committee that was largely entrusted with preserving the vestiges of Britain's international power. The committee came up with a rather patronizing strategy for dealing with the United States. It would "exert sufficient control over the policy of the well-intentioned but inexperienced colossus on whose cooperation our safety depends."[4] British politicians did their best to see that the world was remade, as far as possible, in accordance with their wishes.

The mood of Britain's political elite trickled down to the rest of the nation via the press. Many journalists were keen to portray Britain as a wise old shepherd. For instance, *The Times*, the nation's most prominent broadsheet newspaper, argued in 1948: "Britain has much to give, by way of counsel and initiation, to the shaping, still tentative and often uncertain, of a world policy, political and economic, 'at the summit' in America."[5] *Picture Post* also suggested that Britain should act as a guide. In a March 1954 article Edward Hulton claims, "If she is to survive, Britain must once more become big-hearted and clear-minded. Her influence is needed at American council tables."[6]

British pundits, like politicians, stressed that America needed guidance because it was inexperienced. "They seem to have no notion of the forces that shape events," Fyfe Robertson snorted in *Picture Post*, reinforcing an oft-repeated journalistic notion that America was woefully ignorant of geopolitical reality.[7] American inexperience was endlessly stressed, even in articles that, at first glance, seem to have nothing to do with international politics. An April 1954 article by Robert Muller on Marilyn Monroe's visit to Korea is exemplary. Muller stresses that America does not demand that its actors establish a pedigree or hone their craft.[8] Instead, instant fame, wealth, and influence are the order of the day. He notes, "Soldiers in Korea cheered ecstatically when they saw their favourite pin-up girl in the flesh for the first time. They saw Monroeism at its best. What is Monroeism?" Muller provides an answer: "Monroeism describes a now accepted method of becoming a successful film actress: the climb to fame, 1950s style." This climb to fame does not entail "the drag through drama school, the grind of small parts." Rather, it involves being noticed as a pin-up girl then, giving "a reasonably good performance in a reasonably good film. Pandemonium breaks loose. The critics wake up and start to wave flags. The public takes up the cry. She can act! She's great!" Muller notes that "in Britain the technique is making slow but steady progress." The hugely sarcastic tone of this short article stems from a suspicion that a rather unsophisticated American girl may not deserve the influence she enjoys. More broadly, it asks us to draw a comparison between an American actress who has not paid her dues, and a nation that lacks sufficient experience to properly understand its current role in the world.

An apparently dilettantish America was all the more alarming because it had recently come into possession of an atomic arsenal. Writing in *The Listener* in 1954, Richard Goold-Adams argues: "I think people here [in Britain] have every right to be extremely worried: not only because America might precipitate us all into a world war, but because it would be an atomic war, in which there could be little doubt about immediate retaliation against British targets if American atom bombers were flying from British bases."[9] The possibility of Atomic war was increased, according to Goold-Adams, because Americans placed so much power in the hands of their President: "the power to commit the United States to war has virtually passed from Congress into the President's own hands. This is a basic change of constitutional principle, and it is a terrifying power to rest in the hands of one man."[10] Even if the President were able to control his button finger, the weapons that America had created seemed terrifyingly unstable. O.R. Frisch, a correspondent of *The Listener*, reported in 1954, "There has been a feeling of alarm about the statement made by the President of the United

States, that the explosion of the hydrogen bomb on Bikini Island on March 1 was much more powerful than had been expected."[11] It seemed to many Britons that the U.S, its leader, and its weaponry might prove uncontrollable. Such claims, it should be remembered, emerged from a Britain that often portrayed America as the home of eccentricity and excessive behavior. Small wonder then that Britain was eager to shepherd its ally. William Clark ably sums up the mood of British politicians and journalists in the immediate postwar period: "No one doubted that America was stronger, few doubted that we were wiser."[12]

The idea that Americans needed guidance was reinforced by a popular notion that they did not understand the British. Harold Nicholson, writing in a 1954 edition of *The Listener*, points out that Americans are unable to fathom Europe's attachment to antiquity: "we in Europe are proud of being very old, whereas to many Americans the idea of not being new is as depressing as a Ford tractor of 1928."[13] Five years earlier, *Picture Post* published a collection of Britain-bashing cartoons from recent American newspapers and claimed that they presented a hopelessly skewed version of reality. One of these, from the *New York Daily News*, shows a lion (the well-known symbol of Britain) struggling to free itself from a ball of twine marked "Socialist Experiments." Commenting on the cartoon's inaccuracy, *Picture Post* claims that it "illustrates the current view that American dollars, spent by this country largely on raw materials and food, have been wasted to finance crazy Socialist projects."[14] Both articles imply that Anglo-American relations would be vastly improved if only the U.S. were better informed.

Picture Post *and British Opinions of the U.S.*

As the preceding paragraphs hint, *Picture Post* had much to say about Britain's new role in the world. A pioneer in the field of photojournalism, the magazine was one of the most popular publications in Britain from its launch in 1938 to its demise in 1957, and, at its zenith, sold around one and a half million copies per week. Its journalists offered a mixture of lighthearted and more serious commentary on many aspects of British life and often commented on Anglo-American relations. The magazine was not overly concerned with lauding the United States and provoked exasperation in at least one of that nation's citizens. An April 1954 letter from "an American who has read your publication for some years" asks "why is it that you usually portray America in terms of Hollywood, McCarthy, and crime [?]"[15]

The accusation is not far from the truth. A browse through 1950s issues of *Picture Post* suggests that, although the magazine delved into a variety of American subjects, it consistently associated the United States with reckless youth and unchecked modernity, while it linked Britain with the supposedly more admirable qualities of age, history, and moderation. In doing so, it provided a bevy of evidence that Britain was well qualified to act as guide to the U.S. Because of its large circulation many Britons were exposed to its editorial stance, and, therefore, it can be taken as a notable influence on public opinion. Moreover, *Picture Post* attempted to capture Britain's mood, regularly publishing articles that tried to encapsulate the spirit of the citizenry or recent changes in social structure. It can, then, be regarded, not only as influential, but as a fairly reliable barometer of the zeitgeist. Consequently, the magazine will be called upon to situate British cinema in a larger public discourse about Anglo-American relations.

Analysis of postwar editions of *Picture Post* reveals that Britain reinvented itself, not just as shepherd to America, but as a resilient underdog in the ongoing Anglo-American rivalry. No longer able to sustain the pretense that the two nations were equals in a struggle, the British opted to portray themselves as weakened but nonetheless feisty. The magazine made no secret of the fact that Britain was on the ropes, but suggested that it could still, on occasion, come out fighting. In 1948, Fyffe Robertson wrote an article entitled "The American Invasion" in which he comments on the large numbers of wealthy American travelers coming to Britain. After admitting that Europeans are the United States's "poor relations" and "supplicants for bounty," he reports with glee that the British Ocean Liner, Queen Elizabeth, impressed Americans with undreamt-of majesty. "They [the vessel's American passengers] knew it was big, but they didn't know it was as big as this," he gloats, and continues, "this is Clydebank's 83,000 ton rejoinder to Transatlantic condescension."[16] Similarly, a 1954 article on British pop singers is concerned to demonstrate that, although American stars may dominate the airwaves, their scrappy British counterparts are redressing the balance of power. Robert Muller argues, "Beating the Americans at their own game ... [British stars] are bringing prosperity back to our music halls" and continues, "The new singing idols are not, like their predecessors, Americans. They are British. But their records sell by the hundred thousands."[17]

Postwar malaise had instilled in the British a complexity of emotion. Feelings of emasculation were tempered by a conviction that the nation could enjoy continued relevance by acting as adviser to the inexperienced, unrestrained American colossus. Moreover, the realization that America was now undeniably the controlling partner in the Anglo-American relationship meant that it was easier for Britons to see their nation as a bloodied, plucky fighter than a dominant presence in the world. *Picture Post* explored these new aspects of British identity, but cinema would also provide a thoroughgoing examination.

Four British comedies of the 1950s—*The Maggie* (Alexander Mackendrick, 1954), *To Dorothy a Son* (Muriel Box, 1954), *The Sheriff of Fractured Jaw* (Raoul Walsh, 1959), and *The Battle of the Sexes* (Charles Chrichton, 1959)—facilitated the redefinition of Britain's self-image. In each, the U.S. is defined by its might, assertiveness, and modernity, while Britain seems emasculated, demure, and old-fashioned.[18] However, despite its flashy image, the American colossus is shown to be rash, lacking in a clear sense of identity, and obsessed with money to the exclusion of all else. In short, it is sorely in need of guidance. Britons are presented as wise enough to supply this commodity. As well as helping to characterize Britain as a shepherd, the films demonstrate that the nation, though weakened, is nonetheless still a force to be reckoned with.

Ugly Americans

A powerful United States is embodied in each movie by brash, dominating American characters. In *To Dorothy a Son* Myrtle La Mar (Shelley Winters) is introduced to us as she belts out a raucous torch song in an American nightclub. The song's lyrics leave us in no doubt that she is a woman who demands and receives what she wants. "Give me a man, any kind of man," she insists. La Mar is a singer who discovers that she is in line for a large inheritance, provided that her British ex-husband, Tony Rapallo (John Gregson), does not produce a male heir by a certain date. Needing Tony's signature to secure the money, she travels to Britain, and, to her horror, discovers that Tony's wife Dorothy (Peggy Cummins) is heavily pregnant. If Dorothy gives birth to a boy by the date stipulated in the will, the money goes to the British couple. If she fails to deliver, the American wins the day.

On her arrival in Britain, La Mar pursues her fortune with single-mindedtenacity. Though her English lawyer, Mr. Starke (Wilfrid Hyde-White), insists on the formality of wishing his client a good morning, she will have none of it, responding with a hurried "Yeah , yeah, yeah." Later, frustrated at her inability to acquire the two million dollar fortune in a timely fashion, she screams and roars her disapproval. At times, she resorts

Oversexed and over here: Myrtle La Mar (Shelley Winters) sits next to a harried Tony Rapallo (John Gregson) in *To Dorothy a Son* (1954).

to physical coercion in order to get her way. For instance, instead of inviting her British ex-husband, Tony, to sit beside her, she pulls him to the ground. The movie insists on a connection between La Mar's brash assertiveness and her nationality. Taking offence when a pub landlord looks askance at her dollar bills, she angrily responds, "I am an American citizen!" If we were not sufficiently aware that her forcefulness is a particularly American trait, the soundtrack augments this outburst with a brief rendition of "Stars and Stripes Forever."

American strength is personified by another brash, dominating woman in *The Sheriff of Fractured Jaw*. Kate (Jayne Mansfield) is an even more robust and raucous presence than Shelley Winters. Our introduction to the character occurs as she throws two men onto the street outside her saloon. She will fall in love with a British gun salesman, Jonathan Tibbs (Kenneth More), who has come to the titular old west town to ply his trade. Yet, when she meets Tibbs for the first time, the pair do not seem particularly compatible. Inside the saloon, she tells him to read the rules of the house posted on a nearby wall, adding, "Remember 'em, if you wanna stay out of trouble with me." Later she offers him some more down-home advice: "Sit there or I'll bend this gun barrel over your thick skull." Other representative Americans are outlaws who attempt to assert their dominance upon the endlessly polite Englishman. Tibbs clings to the idea that these men might be "sporting," but Kate relieves him of such illusions by asserting, "Nobody in Fractured Jaw ever heard of a sportin' thing."

The Battle of the Sexes concerns an attempt by an American businesswoman, Angela Barrows (Constance Cummings), to bring automated manufacturing methods to an ancient Scottish firm of tweed merchants, The House of MacPherson. Her aggressive campaign rouses the ire of conservative, longtime employee Mr. Martin (Peter Sellers).

No sooner has Barrows entered the MacPherson offices than she breaks the monastic silence by loudly detailing the changes she believes the company should implement. Throwing open a window, she causes a gust of wind to decimate the firm's elaborate filing system and shower the room with paper. On one level the movie concerns itself with the subject of assertive women, but an introductory voice-over suggests that assertive women are an especially American phenomenon. It begins, "The battle of the sexes. In this timeless struggle for supremacy between man and woman, man had held his own until that fateful day in 1492 when Christopher Columbus discovered America. Out of this world emerged a new type of woman, destined to turn man the hunter into man the hunted."[19] Barrows proves this point by completely dominating the weak-willed chairman of the board, Mr. MacPherson (Robert Morley). "You just relax and leave everything to me," she coos before methodically dismantling his company.

The only movie of the four to concentrate upon an American man,[20] *The Maggie*, introduces Calvin B. Marshall (Paul Douglas), the head of the European branch of World International Airlines, as a highly assertive, no-nonsense organizer. Attempting to transport a cargo of furniture across Scotland to his new house, he mistakenly entrusts his cargo to the disreputable crew of a decrepit puffer-boat, "The Maggie." Realizing his mistake, he pursues and catches up with the boat, but, instead of transferring his belongings to a more felicitous vessel, he is forced by circumstance to charter the hulk for the remainder of his trip. As soon as he discovers that his cargo has been mistakenly placed aboard "The Maggie" he confidently asserts, "We'll have this straightened out in an hour." Leaping aboard a plane, he heads off in hot-pursuit. As in *The Battle of the Sexes*, the American is identified as typical of his people. Marshall's Scottish nemesis and skipper of "The Maggie," Captain MacTaggart, wryly notes of the foreigner's constant need for a telephone: "I've never seen such a man for the telephoning."

It'll be the American way. Everything in a rush." This comment also suggests that Marshall is possessed of the frenetic energy that defines the Americans in the other three films. That Marshall is intended to represent not just a dominating America, but also America's dominance over Britain is, of course, suggested by his name.

In their presentation of dominating, brash characters the movies echo the representational strategies of *Picture Post*. Choosing to profile the most imposing, energetic American citizens, the magazine constructs an image of the United States as a nation of colossuses. For instance, Marlon Brando is characterized as "the wild and violent film hero" alongside a photographic still from *The Wild One*, in which he struggles with two policemen.[21] Ernest Hemingway is dubbed "the great adventurer from America," in a photo essay documenting one of his African safaris.[22] Other articles document the darker side of American assertiveness. "American industrialists are invading Scotland" begins a piece on increasing U.S. investment in the country.[23] A social climbing American, Pal Joey, the eponymous character of a new Rodgers and Hammerstein musical, is also considered worthy copy. "Pal Joey is not nice…. [He is] a nasty little opportunist from the upper underworld of Chicago," notes the article.[24] Though this is a statement of fact, the magazine's concentration on *Pal Joey* is significant since it appears alongside a sheaf of articles intent upon stressing American assertiveness. Trevor Philpott's description of Billy Graham represents the height of this tendency: "his voice persuasive, his stature imposing, his frame massive, his jaw thrusting, his shoulders square, his nose straight, his suits natty, his ties bright, his wife pretty, his children four in number."[25] Reading *Picture Post* and attending movies during the 1950s, how could Britons dispute the notion that Americans bestrode the world like giants?

Reserved Britons

The American's brash assertiveness is only exacerbated when it stands in contrast to the calm and quiet of Britons and their nation. Myrtle La Mar of *To Dorothy a Son* seems yet more huge and loud when she appears alongside a succession of small, demure Britons. The Amazonian Myrtle enlists the help of a diminutive private detective named Mr. Potts, a nervous man with an eye patch and uneven teeth. Sitting in London traffic she asks him "doesn't this traffic ever move?" Potts replies apologetically, "This is quite fast for London." A scene taking place at the House of MacPherson epitomizes the sedate world of *The Battle of the Sexes*. A collection of drab, aged scribes methodically go about their paperwork with fountain pens. One of these company men creates the only audible sound in the room, his pen scratching against paper more audibly than those of his colleagues. Mr. Martin looks up irritated and addresses the offender. "Mr. Meeky, could you not find a quieter nib?" he asks. Meeky, a man who makes a point of living up to his name, duly complies. Martin himself refuses to indulge in any activity that would allow temporary escape from this sedate world. He abstains from alcohol and cigarettes, provoking an aged member of the MacPherson clan to wryly comment, "Man is fallible, but Martin is not." In an echo of Myrtle La Mar's complaint about the pace of London traffic, Angela Barrows complains of Edinburgh, "If there's any night life in this dump I haven't found it yet." The crew of "The Maggie" are defined by their calm, easy-going approach to life and work. Much of the movie's humor derives from a comparison between the energetic, demanding Marshall and the laid-back Scotsmen. While the American strides about a dock, demanding that the crew hurry his cargo toward its destination, MacTaggart and company enjoy a drink at a quay-side pub and formulate clandestine plans to attend an imminent birthday party. A low-key approach to life also defines the hero of *The Sheriff of Fractured Jaw*. After arriving at Kate's saloon, Tibbs asks to be moved "to a quieter spot." Instead of solving his problems with violence, he would much rather talk his way out of trouble. "Mr Jonathan is never happy with a gun in his hand," a butler informs Tibbs's father in the first scene of the movie.

American Modernity, British Antiquity

The American colossus is not only defined by its stark contrast to quiet, sedate Britain. Another of its key components is its modernity, further highlighted by its presentation alongside British antiquity.[26] In *To Dorothy a Son* Myrtle La Mar is a thoroughly modern woman. Her nightclub act is built around the latest pop music, her car is a streamlined convertible, and she sports the latest styles. Her platinum hair and dangerous curves identify her as a blonde bombshell, a look that dominated the fashion world of the 1950s. In contrast, her British ex-husband, Tony, is a classical music composer who drives an aged, sensible car and wears worn, comfortable clothes. In a scene in which Tony temporarily gains the upper hand due to the time difference between England and the United States, he recognizes La Mar and her nation as representatives of modernity, noting:

"I know that it's difficult to appreciate that America can be behind us in anything, but in the little matter of time we are in point of fact five hours ahead."

Although *The Sheriff of Fractured Jaw* is set on the American frontier, Kate can still be regarded as a thoroughly modern American. Looking like she has dropped in from a 1950s burlesque show, this platinum blonde snubs Tibbs's guns as old-fashioned, asking him, "You're not going to try and sell that antique around here?" Tibbs & Co. are gunsmiths so anachronistic that they mistakenly regard the weapon as the height of murderous chic. Tibbs replies to her question with, "My dear Kate, it's absolutely brand new. A perfect gentleman's sporting gun." Britain is so far behind the times—approximately one hundred years in fact—that some of its citizens still regard America as a rebellious colony. A store manager at Tibbs & Co. proclaims, "Once a colony, always a colony. One of these days they'll realize their mistake and beg to be taken back."

The Battle of the Sexes soon makes clear that Americans value modernity. An early scene presents two American tourists buying tweed at MacPherson's and establishing themselves as up-to-date by asking if the firm makes any synthetic tweed. A sales representative, Mr. Robertson, bridles at the suggestion, telling them, "We've nothing to do with synthetic fiber here." But Angela Barrows will soon make certain that the House of MacPherson is smothered in such material. When Mr. MacPherson looks surprised at her plans, she responds, "Don't tell me you've never heard of mechanization." On her first visit to the company, she expresses her amazement at its antiquated appearance, shrieking, "This place is just not for real! It's like something out of Dickens!" After Martin expresses the sentiment that women should stick to "women's work," Barrows establishes herself as an up-to-the-minute businesswoman and the Scotsman as a stick-in-the-mud by replying, "Mr. Martin, you must join the twentieth-century." From this point on, the bulk of the narrative is concerned with Barrow's attempts to modernize offices filled with old men, teetering piles of paperwork, and choking quantities of dust.

An early scene in *The Maggie* sets up a dichotomy between British antiquity and American modernity. In pursuit of his cargo, the technologically advanced Marshall flies over the puffer-boat in a helicopter. As mentioned, he's "one for the telephoning," but his modernity is further stressed by the fact that his precious cargo is predominantly made up of advanced appliances such as a refrigerator. While the American is defined by his modern accouterments, the Scotsman is defined by his aged boat. It is left to a reporter from the Scottish newspaper, *The Evening News*, to explain to the American and to the movie audience the significance of boats like "The Maggie" in Scottish life.

> Well Mr. Marshall, these old puffers are public characters in Scotland. They're very popular.... They're not much to look at, I admit, but there's something kind of heartwarming about them. Now you're a big man in the transport world. You might not be able to see it. But they've got a touch of tradition, Mr. Marshall. Of the old, simple live-and-let-live, of human values....

At this point Marshall cuts him off, demonstrating that he is either unwilling or unable to understand the value of anything old-fashioned.

The pages of *Picture Post* provide more evidence that the British regarded America as a symbol of modernity and that, as in each movie, many looked upon American modernity with suspicion. Articles on the increasingly mechanized workplace identify the United States as the bringer of automation. While such articles point out that automation may free workers from drudgery, they also suggest that it may herald massive unemployment. A June 1956 article notes, "A seat reservation system at La Guardia airport replaces several hundred clerks."[27] Another, appearing in April 1955 under the heading, "Will the Americans show the way?" suggests, "They ... [Americans] have achieved the automatic factory and they have coined a new word with frightening social implications—automation."[28]

A Nation Feminized

To reinforce the idea of a dominant and modern America, each movie presents a demure, old-fashioned Britain. But they go one step further. Each presents Britain as feminized space where men are unable to live up to the masculine standards of their forebears. In all likelihood, the movies present so many images of emasculation because since the 1930s—as discussed in chapter one—Britain's idea of itself as a mighty patriarchy had been under threat from America. By the 1950s, Britain's position on the world stage was more weakened than ever, but the nation continued to place great store in images of powerful men performing heroic deeds. Lord Cardigan's charge of the Light Brigade, the Duke of Wellington's victory at Waterloo, and Lord Nelson's triumph at Trafalgar were a ubiquitous presence in the culture, immortalized in school books, mass-produced prints, commemorative plates, mugs, and greeting cards. For more than a hundred years three of the most potent British icons had been the very male institutions of the "thin red line," the Navy, and the cartoon embodiment of Britain, John Bull. In austere and desperate postwar Britain the disjunction between image and reality must have been especially poignant.

British films offered the nation images that were more in tune with the current international situation. Though movies still insisted on the reductive strategy of equating strength with masculinity, their comic images of emasculated British men crushed under the heel of dominating, usually female, Americans suggests that cinema was at least attempting to come to terms with the nation's weakened state. In poking fun at the British male, the films confront the idea of national fragility while simultaneously allowing audience members to distance themselves from the concept through laughter.

The Battle of the Sexes gently mocks British patriarchy by suggesting that men are more like women than they think. The film's opening voice-over makes a joke about the hallowed institution of the kilt. After we hear the words, "So destiny brought Mrs. Barrows to carry the sex war into one of the last bastions of male supremacy—Scotland—a man's world," there is a cut to a shot of men dancing in kilts. The voice-over continues, "A world in which the shortest skirts are worn by men." The movie makes repeated suggestions that its men fail to live up to their ancestors. We are told that the new head of the House of MacPherson is a shadow of his father. Angela Barrows also regards Mr. MacPherson as something less than masculine: "Oh, but you're so helpless. If only there were a man here," she laments. MacPherson's inadequacy as a Scottish patriarch is exacerbated by the fact that he is played by Robert Morley. The sight of this quintessentially English actor making no attempt to assume a Scottish accent, flustered and pouting like an exasperated codfish, confirms that he is a disgrace to the kilt. The anti-hero of the movie, Mr. Martin, fails to salvage any masculine dignity for his country. On the night he attempts to kill Barrows, he is so nervous that he only succeeds in breaking a number of objects in her apartment. Realizing that Martin poses no physical threat to her, Barrows ridicules him by dubbing him "Samson."

To Dorothy a Son repeatedly offers the supposedly humorous spectacle of a man performing "women's work." Tony makes breakfast for his wife and takes it to her as she lies in bed. Later, he vacuums the house while wearing an apron. Like Mr. Martin he is a klutz. Moments into the movie, he splashes himself with milk as he opens the bottle. The sense that the days of more heroic British men have passed is intensified by the presence of Myrtle La Mar's private detective, Livingstone Potts. This diminutive and seedy looking individual is the current chief of the "Holmes Detective Agency." He tells Myrtle, "Mr. Holmes, alas, is dead, but I am the head of the agency that bears his name." Amused by the incongruity between this detective and the illustrious name of Holmes, La Mar refers to him by the ironic title "Sherlock."

The Maggie's most obvious representative of emasculation is a bureaucrat from an organization called Clyde Shipping Services (C.S.S.). Not only does he bear the suggestive name Pusey, he spouts lines that identify him as the antithesis of Marshall's more adventurous American approach to life. For instance, finding himself caught up in a poaching expedition, he proves himself a prig, protesting, "I don't see anything amusing in breaking the law." No more in control of his physicality than Mr. Martin or Tony Rappelo, at various moments he falls over, runs afoul of a tree limb, and finds himself caught up in a telephone wire. To a lesser extent, the all-male crew of "The Maggie" can be regarded as symbolic of emasculation. Traditionally, Scotsmen have suggested a particularly rugged form of masculinity to the British. Captain MacTaggart attempts to live up to this image, claiming that he is his own man, unbound by the whims of an employer, since he does not work for the C.S.S. Drinking in a harbor-side pub, he makes fun of some sailors who do: "You're very smooth with your gold braid, and your pensions, and your five days a week. But you're no better than hirelings, standing like wee bairns there in front of Mr. Campbell's big desk down yonder. This moment is discussed by film historian Philip Kemp, who demonstrates that MacTaggart is no monument to rugged independence.[29] The captain plies his trade in a decrepit puffer and is just as controlled by the C.S.S. as the sailors on its payroll. As Kemp points out, as MacTaggart concludes his paean to independence, his cabin-boy, Dougie, warns him that C.S.S. men have arrived to inspect "The Maggie." As MacTaggart swiftly exits the pub, we realize that he's not only scared, he cannot pay for his drinks. MacTaggart's braggadocio seems all the more misplaced when, later in the movie, it is revealed that the boat he captains is owned by his sister.

Even though Tibbs becomes a successful lawman in *The Sheriff of Fractured Jaw*, he notes that his brand of masculinity is nothing compared to that of his ancestors. Tangling with some Indians, he invokes the memory of his grandfather, Digby, who "single-handedly put down a rebellion in Karachi." Tibbs resolves to face the Indian threat, but admits, "I don't suppose I'm half the man that my Grandfather Digby was." The scene draws a comparison between an age in which Britons were fearless and heroic colonists and the period in which the movie takes place, the late Victorian era. However, Tibbs's comments also hint that the 1950s British male may not be able to measure up to grandfather Digby. As well as questioning his

"Mr. Jonathan is never happy with a gun in his hand." In *The Sheriff of Fractured Jaw* (1959) Jonathan Tibbs (Kenneth More, left) is roped into being a lawman by Major Masters (Henry Hull).

martial skill, the movie suggests that Tibbs is a less adept inventor than previous Englishmen. Apart from colonialism, Britain's Victorian era was also defined by invention. Tibbs is introduced to us as an amateur inventor, but he is forced to flee one of his "contraptions" as it blows up and catches fire. Evidently, an era of Victorian gentlemen skilled in violence and able to invent world-changing machinery has come to an end.

In the pages of *Picture Post*, American male sex symbols stand in stark contrast to confused, emasculated British men. An April 1954 *Picture Post* article centers upon the confusion of a British man who feels his world spinning out of control. Significantly, it suggests the obsolescence of the popular images he once used to structure his identity:

> After a time, he succeeded in laying hands on two words. Frustration. Impotence ... it may have been those very things that used to make him want to steer a space-ship and glide under water like Hans Haas did in that picture, because, as he now suddenly saw, a space-ship pilot and Hans Haas couldn't be either frustrated or impotent, for they were in control of what was happening.[30]

Added to the idea of the confused and despairing British man were claims that, though he was emotionally restrained and polite, such tendencies stemmed from a crippling nervousness. For instance, in a February 1954 item entitled "The Englishman as Lover" Honor Tracy explains that "the young Englishman is nicely dressed and properly behaved.... He never gets himself up like something out of a carnival—or argues hotly over a bill.... [Because he] is terrified of appearing ridiculous."[31] In contrast to the confused, nervous British man, the article offers the virile, desirable American. Film stars of several nations—Rudolph Valentino representing Italy and Ramon Navarro representing Mexico—are profiled under the heading "The Lovers the World Thinks Greatest, Not a Britain in Sight."[32] Pride of place is given to the American lover represented by Gregory Peck. Described as the "American Adam" he is "the man most girls would like to be married to. (If not married to, kissed by)."[33]

Even when the magazine was not specifically referring to British and American masculinity, *Picture Post* repeatedly offered the thesis that Britain's strength was diminished and America's concomitantly enhanced. In Edward Hulton's piece entitled "The British Have Been the Best Travelers ever.... But their Freedom to Travel has been stolen," the author claims, "It is a commonplace of history that the people of this island must be adventurous and seafaring, or perish."[34] He goes on to argue that bureaucratic red tape is stifling this spirit of adventure, and that the United States is central to Britain's diminishing presence on the high seas. Under the subheading "When Britain's mastery of the sea protected America" Hulton romanticizes, "The gallant and beautiful China Clippers, of which now only the emasculated *Cutty Sark* remains as a memorial."[35] These ships he argues "were built to win the 'Tea Race' from American rivals," yet are "now outstripped in speed by the United States."[36] The article harkens back to halcyon days when "the infant United States was protected not so much by the oratory of its President, Monroe, as by the invincible British Navy."[37]

Although the movies and *Picture Post* highlight a variety of ways in which the United States is powerful and Britain weakened, their ultimate goal is to complicate such assertions. They admit that the United States is powerful, but also show Americans to be rash, greedy, and possessed of an unstable identity.

The Rash, Greedy Colossus

Each movie includes scenes that show Americans using their strength in rash and shortsighted ways. In *To Dorothy a Son*, the first time that

Myrtle assumes she has secured the inheritance, she immediately begins to squander money on fur coats and a sports car. In *The Battle of the Sexes* Angela Barrow's rashness is most noticeable in her attitude to progress. So determined is she to transform the way that the House of MacPherson does business, that she is prepared to destroy the lives and traditions of the company's employees. Her stated goal—to use automation to make cloth "for the millions, not for the privileged few"—is admirable, but she pursues this goal in a very myopic manner. Traveling to the Hebrides to view the tweed-weaving methods of the islanders, she is initially charmed by images of rural tranquility. Approaching a weaver's cottage, she coos, "Get that picture. Isn't that something." Moments later, she is planning to transport the islanders to a mainland factory where they will trade their looms for more efficient machines. *The Maggie* demonstrates Calvin Marshall's rashness in a scene in which he decides to walk to a telephone to call for help in transporting his cargo. Ignoring the fact that the telephone is several miles away, he takes off at a brisk pace. The Scotsman, MacTaggart, accompanies him, but instead of charging down the beach with Marshall, he strolls along behind him. On arrival, Marshall is completely exhausted. MacTaggart concludes his pleasant ramble as fresh as the moment he set out. The American's rash decision, to embark on a journey he is unfamiliar with, ensures disaster. *The Sheriff of Fractured Jaw* is replete with moments in which Americans shoot first and ask questions later. For instance, hearing that Indians are riding toward town, many townsfolk prepare to do battle, quickly assuming that the approaching tribe has hostile intentions. In fact, as Tibbs will discover, the Indians are coming to aid him in his conflict with warring ranchers.

America values money over all things, the films imply, while for Britain it is a secondary consideration. This is not to say that Britons would not like a little more cash. On several occasions in *To Dorothy a Son*, British characters joke about their financial difficulties and America's comparative wealth. Tony tells a nurse about his money troubles and asks her, "Why is it that banks never give overdrafts to people who really need them?" She answers, "I don't know. Something to do with the dollar gap I suppose." *The Battle of the Sexes* also makes no secret of the fact that the British enjoy money. Mr. MacPherson is initially eager to accept Angela Barrow's business plan because it will mean profits for his company. Similarly, in *The Maggie*, Captain MacTaggart's decision to transport Marshall's belongings is based on a desire to make money, as is Tibbs's decision to sell guns in *The Sheriff of Fractured Jaw*.

However, despite their claim that the British are as fond of money as any other nationality, each movie juxtaposes the American's love for cash with the Briton's relative indifference to it. *To Dorothy a Son* may portray a battle over an inheritance, but ultimately it suggests that the British value family over material wealth. The last two shots of the movie clearly demonstrate this idea. In the penultimate shot, the British Dorothy pulls her newborn twin babies to her side, telling them "you're mine, all mine." The final shot is of America's Myrtle La Mar pulling a pair of luxurious furs to her neck and repeating Dorothy's line. In *The Battle of the Sexes* Mr. MacPherson eventually chooses a happy, eccentric, if inefficient, staff over Angela Barrows's vision of a more lucrative, automated workforce. Barrows returns to America to continue her attempts to increase corporate wealth, but the House of MacPherson, rather than concentrating on productivity and earnings, chooses a return to traditional business practices. Family, represented by the family firm of MacPherson and by its staff, who interact in a very familial manner, wins out once again. The crew of "The Maggie" is also very like a family. MacTaggart is a father figure, the first mate acts like a wife, and the cabin-boy, Dougie, can be regarded as their child. It is this familial world that the movie values over Marshall's world of money. Significantly, Marshall has marital difficulties, suggesting that a preoccupation with money is incompatible with family.

The Maggie demonstrates its attitude to money in a scene in which Marshall chats to a young Scots girl, Sheena, about her two suitors. She must decide between a successful storekeeper and a rather shiftless fisherman. Marshall advises her to marry the storekeeper "if he really wants to be somebody, if he really wants to make something of himself." But Sheena disagrees. Admitting it would be pleasurable "to be given fine clothes and expensive presents," she chooses the fisherman because "he'll have more time for me."

The movie's heavy-handed message was not missed by a delighted British journalist, Thomas Spencer, writing in *The Daily Worker*. He lauds "the sense of human dignity and enjoyment of life which the American has lost. Before the voyage is over they have taught him that money cannot buy everything in Britain and that the individual in entitled to consideration."[38]

In *The Sheriff of Fractured Jaw* Americans are associated with money making, while the British are more interested in people. Kate is such an adept poker player that she claims to have invented the game, and is such a natural saleswoman that on one day hawking Tibbs's wares she outstrips all the Englishman's previous efforts. While Tibbs is no salesman, he is frequently successful in winning friends. Adopted by an Indian tribe and uniting warring ranchers, he seems much more at home with arbitration than acquisition. Indeed, the movie revives one of the sustaining myths of the British Empire: rather than seeking material wealth, British empire builders felt a duty to bring order and civilization to lesser men and savages.

1950s editions of *Picture Post* also make the point that Britain is a country where money is a secondary consideration. They often do so by comparing the British attitude toward money with that of Americans. In an April 1954 article on tourism a hypothetical American visits the London theatre and is amazed to discover that he will not be overcharged for his ticket and that the skilled actors in the show are not highly paid stars:

> As for the American he is bemused. The show he has chosen is a hit. Yet he still has to pay only the advertised price for his seat. The ticket scalpers haven't been at work, buying up the house, and re-selling it, at a hundred per cent profit.... Our visitor from Broadway is used to every major part being played by an accomplished star. But it is a total surprise to him to find the smaller parts filled to perfection too. Home was never like this.[39]

The magazine also reveals a deep-seated British suspicion of America's approach to business. The article on Billy Graham's visit to Britain notes:

> The British Press were so eager to get at Billy Graham that newspaper men went out in a tug-boat to meet the *United States*. It wasn't that they were bursting with eagerness to embrace a man of God. They were more eager to discover if he had come to rail against TUC-type socialism, in the name of God and American business interests.... So their eyes were wide-open for any sense of guile.[40]

The American way, the articles imply, is to value money over all else and to convince other nations to adopt their financial strategies.

An American Identity Crisis

The American colossus is further weakened by mental fragility. Each film hints that behind the American's brash self-confidence lurks an individual who may at any moment lose control. *The Maggie* takes Calvin Marshall from a position of supreme self-confidence to a state in which he is no longer sure who he is. This crisis of self occurs when a rising tide causes the puffer to destroy the pier to which it is moored. Marshall realizes that the destruction of the pier leaves his cargo inaccessible, and he slumps to the ground in despair. The camera lingers over this image of the mighty fallen. A C.S.S. officer approaches. "Are you Mr. Marshall, sir?" he asks. "I'm no longer absolutely sure," Marshall replies. Although this moment represents the height of Marshall's identity crisis, MacTaggart will provide further hints that the American has no clear sense of self. After remarking on Marshall's obsession with the telephone, he muses, "Aye, he's not a man that's at peace with himself."[41]

In the penultimate scene of *The Battle of the Sexes* Angela Barrows is reduced from hard-hearted businesswoman to stammering wreck. Realizing that Mr. MacPherson believes Mr. Martin's story and not hers, she babbles, "You're mad. You're crazy. Bagpipes." Her last significant act in the movie is to swipe at Martin with a sculpture as House of MacPherson employees carry her screaming from the room. Jonathan Tibbs of *The Sheriff of Fractured Jaw* is frequently amazed by the speed with which supposedly civilized Americans give in to primal urges. At the merest whiff of potential conflict, his American hosts rapidly arm themselves and charge off to find someone to shoot. On one of the many occasions in which he appears to be the sole voice of reason in the insane world of the Wild West, Tibbs asks, "Is everyone in America hostile"? In *To Dorothy a Son* Myrtle La Mar's identity wavers between that of an adult and a spoiled child. Repeatedly throwing tantrums, she howls if she doesn't get her way. When her loss of self-control affords her a victory, she gloats. Taunting the penniless Tony, she sings a repetitive schoolyard refrain: "I got two million dollars. I got two million dollars."

The British historian William Clark noted in 1957: "'I'd rather be poor and happy in England than rich and neurotic in America,' is a saying often to be heard."[42] If *Picture Post* can be regarded as a barometer of British thinking, then it seems Clark was accurate. The magazine frequently associates the United States with psychic trauma, taking particular pleasure in reporting instances in which mental instability is revealed in apparently mighty Americans. For example, Marlon Brando, who, Robert Muller reports, is as sexually alluring to British women as Marilyn Monroe is to British men, "is now in the care of a psychiatrist."[43] The March 1954 article may be justified on the grounds that British readers were interested in the private lives of Brando and other American stars, but the piece has a more ambitious agenda. Suggesting that Brando's mental crisis was brought on by playing too many rebels, *Picture Post* would have its readers regard him as a symbol of American anger and aggression. "The target of his anger and nonconformity is no longer the society he lives in but himself."[44] Muller goes on to claim Brando's aggression is a useful measure of the American zeitgeist: "We [the British] need Brando because he is a brilliant actor, and because he tells us something about America."[45] Specifically, Brando reveals that Americans may not be able to control themselves: "Brando, the actor, may win this battle with himself and come to terms with the seeds of his own violence. But will the new American rebel? And for that matter, will America?" This article was not an isolated example of the equation American Actor = American zeitgeist. In a June 1955 piece entitled "Brando or Beefcake?" Muller presents two types of American actor, "the Brando" (the tortured soul) and "the Beefcake" (the carefree strongman). Once again, the article would have its readers draw conclusions about American life from American movies, principally that the American actor and the American man are split personalities:

> A film hero is the dream image of his spectator, the kind of man he would like to be. The Beefcakes and the Brandos reflect the twin ideals of American manhood pushed to extremes: the magnificent, all-conquering physique and the tortured, self-searching thinker.... [They] present a Mr. America split down the middle. Both sides—complete as idols, incomplete as men—speak to us in their own language. In what they say and do they meet at one point only. Neither of them are adult.

Picture Post, like British movies, presented dramas of revelation in which the outwardly strong American is shown to have a highly unstable inner self.

By portraying America as rash, greedy, and lacking in a clear sense of identity, the four movies hint that if the U.S is not ill equipped to wield power, it is at least in need of guidance. Britain, the films suggest, is the nation best qualified to act as shepherd. This is because, as many a scene demonstrates, its people are wiser than Americans and able to teach them a lesson.

Canny British Diplomats

To Dorothy a Son includes moments in which Mytrle La Mar's intellectual inferiority is obvious. She refers to her legal representative as a "solicitator," mispronounces the county of Suffolk as "Suh-foke," and has trouble understanding the concept of the international dateline. At a British customs desk an official asks for her passport, but since she has no experience of the British pronunciation of this word, she has no idea what he means. Tony, her British ex-husband, may not win the battle for the inheritance, but he is able to demonstrate his intellectual superiority. When he

5. "A well-intentioned but inexperienced colossus"   149

and La Mar take a trip to the coast, she declares her happiness by saying, "You and me, sitting on the beach." Tony scolds her for using incorrect grammar, retorting, "You and I."

Near the end of the film it seems that the British couple have secured the fortune. Dorothy graciously offers La Mar half the cash. Amazed, the American replies, "Aren't you English funny about money." When it becomes clear that Myrtle is in fact the victor, our knowledge of her childish, money-obsessed character leads us to the conclusion that she will be selfish. However, it becomes clear she has learned from the British couple that, as Tony had put it earlier, "Money isn't everything." Myrtle gives them half the money.

The Battle of the Sexes implies that the British are skilled in subtle scheming and backroom diplomacy. Though Mr. Martin briefly responds to Angela Barrow's aggressive intrusion into his life by resorting to his own aggressive tactics (he briefly embarks on a half-hearted murder attempt) the movie makes clear that violence is not the British way. Martin's initial strategy is characterized by clever scheming in which he uses his experience to make Barrows look foolish. For instance, he wrecks her plan to have a clocking-in mechanism installed at MacPherson's by making sure many more clocks than necessary are delivered. He sneaks into the office after closing time and sabotages the new gadgets.

Martin's most successful scheme is hatched at the moment Barrows assumes she has unearthed his secret life as a drinker and smoker. She remarks, "What would they think at the office? They'd think I was out of my mind." At this, Martin gets an idea. He begins to make sexual advances toward her and she throws him out. Barrows reports the incident to Mr. MacPherson, claiming that Martin was drunk. Knowing that Martin is a strict teetotaler, MacPherson assumes she is lying. When MacPherson informs Barrows that he does not believe her, she throws the tantrum that will cause her to be dragged from the room. Martin has succeeded through wit, not violence, and, at the film's conclusion, delivers a homily to a small boy holding a toy gun: "There is no need to use violence. There is many a battle's been won without ever striking a blow." In a final, consummately diplomatic, gesture he gives Barrows a flower.

Of all the scenes in which *The Maggie* offers the spectacle of the American outwitted, the most ingenious involves a bluffing match between Marshall and MacTaggart. The American, following the puffer in an airborne plane, talks with the aircraft's pilot.

> MARSHALL: Tell me, if they thought I thought they were going to Inverkerran, where do you reckon they would make for then?

PILOT: Strathcathaigh, maybe.
MARSHALL: This sounds silly, but if they thought I'd think they were going to Strathcathaigh because it looked as if they're going to Inverkerran, where would they go then?
PILOT: My guess would be Pennymaddy.
MARSHALL: If there's such a thing as a triple bluff, I'll bet MacTaggart invented it. OK, Pennymaddy.

Onboard "The Maggie," MacTaggart demonstrates that he will not be mentally outmaneuvered.

MACTAGGART: Aye, he'll have guessed we're making for Inverkerran.
HAMISH: Will he not go there himself then?
MACTAGGART: Oh, no. He'll know we know he's seen us, so he'll be expecting us to make for Strathcathaigh instead.
HAMISH: Will I set her for Pennymaddy, then?
MACTAGGART: No. If it should occur to him that it's occurred to us that he's expecting us to go to Strathcathaigh, he would think we'll be making for Pennymaddy.
HAMISH: Well, shall I set her for Pinwhinnoich?
MACTAGGART: Och, no. We'll make for Inverkerran, just as we planned. It's the last thing he's likely to think of.

Marshall is right to be wary of MacTaggart's bluffing abilities, but a quadruple bluff is something even he could not have counted on.

The Sheriff of Fractured Jaw frequently delights in the spectacle of Americans outwitted by British diplomatic skill. On Tibbs's arrival in the west, Indians attack his stagecoach. After the fight, he approaches one of his attackers irately declaring, "Now listen to me, my good man. That coach was traveling at a legal rate on a public highway. Your interference is not only unjustified, it's positively dangerous." Having never encountered such a white man, the incredulous Indian is intrigued enough to make friends with Tibbs. This is only the first of the Englishman's diplomatic successes, his gift of the gab provoking a farmer to declare, "That Sheriff's a heap smarter than he looks." Tibbs is not a violent man, but is defined by the gun he introduces to the west—the derringer. "It might be small but, believe me, its highly dangerous," he argues. This characterization of the weapon as apparently ineffective but surprisingly devastating aptly describes Tibbs himself. When he goes on to note, "A gun like that was used to assassinate Abraham Lincoln," the implication that the American Goliath may be felled by a well-aimed pebble is hard to miss. The rough customers he meets sneer at his old-fashioned weapons, but Tibbs's polite self-confidence and ability to defuse violent situations win him the job of Sheriff. He succeeds in cleaning up the town, wooing a saloon-keeper, forging an alliance with an Indian tribe, and ending a range war by brokering a truce between the belligerents.

Wiser than Americans, able to teach and outwit them, the British seem ideal candidates for the job of shepherd. The four films also justify Britain's reinvention of itself, not just as a guiding hand, but as a resilient underdog. Time and again the British surprise us with their passion and fortitude.

The Secret Desires of the British Citizen

While American characters are obviously brimming with energy and desire, the British reveal hidden, but nonetheless significant, passions. Though the British characters of *To Dorothy a Son* may seem positively chaste in comparison to the overtly sexual Myrtle, the movie consistently hints that Britain is an inherently sexy place. Tony tells Myrtle that since the date Dorothy was expected to give birth, four babies have been born in the hospital bed reserved for her. A surprised Myrtle replies, "It must be this English air." Later she admits that her honeymoon with Tony was "the happiest I ever was," implying that Tony's pipe-and-slippers demeanor may mask more bacchanalian appetites. In an early, character defining, scene, Dorothy asks Tony to search their house for the novel she is reading. Describing it, she tells him that the cover displays "a woman with a dagger stuck in her bosom or somewhere." Immediately, then, we are faced with a woman whose prosaic appearance may have little to do with her inner life.

The Battle of the Sexes demonstrates that the employees of The House of MacPherson have more than business on their minds. The company boasts a well-stocked and highly revered whisky cabinet. The Scotsmen regularly give in to their quiet passion for liquor, leaving the American Barrows to grumble, "Liquor and business don't mix." As in *To Dorothy a Son*, inner passion is suggested by a Briton's choice of popular entertainment. Attending a screening of the crime melodrama *The Case of the Unknown Killer*, Mr. Martin is inspired to do away with his archenemy, Barrows. Indeed, *The Case of the Unknown Killer* and *The Battle of the Sexes* both turn on the idea that a quiet ordinary man may be the repository of murderous passion.

Keep Smiling Through: British Resilience

The British may not be an efficient people, the four movies suggest, but they are resilient. Indeed, they are most at home in a crisis. This affinity

America as bringer of modernity. Angela Barrows (Constance Cummings) explains the benefits of mechanization to a bewildered, kilt-clad Robert MacPherson (Robert Morley) in *The Battle of the Sexes* (1959).

with chaos is best described as "muddling through." Indeed, in *To Dorothy a Son* Myrtle La Mar specifically refers to Tony and Dorothy's approach to life by using this phrase. Speaking by telephone to her American boyfriend she says, "They had a daughter *and* a son. Well you know the British, they muddle through." Rather than attempting to rule out inefficiency, "muddling through" entails the embrace of disarray and chance as integral components of life. *The Battle of the Sexes* includes a scene in which Mr. Martin demonstrates a baroque and antiquated filing system that allows him to muddle through the business world. The crew of "The Maggie" uses a system for navigating in fog that they refer to as "radar." Instead of the automated system used by modern vessels, their radar is the muddled system of throwing rocks in front of the boat to check that it is not about to run aground. Jonathon Tibbs of *The Sheriff of Fractured Jaw* is just as muddled in his approach to keeping the peace. Surviving mainly by improvisation, he provokes an amused American to state, "The good Lord he looks after fools and Englishmen."

Perhaps the most compelling evidence of Britain's resilience is its success in resisting Americanization. Mr. Martin in *The Battle of the Sexes* saves himself and his company from the horrors of American takeover, and does so without adopting the attitudes and habits of a Hollywood hero. As the voice-over points out: "Mr. Martin may not be cast in the heroic mold, but he is a hero just the same." In *To Dorothy a Son*, after a litany of jokes about British poverty, and an offer from Myrtle to leave it all behind and live in the United States, Tony Rappelo chooses Britain, saying, "I don't want to go to America. I like it here." Marshall's invasion of Scotland is effectively resisted by the crew of "The Maggie." Indeed, the movie suggests that they have "Scottishized" the American. Near the end of the movie, when the puffer runs aground, Marshall is faced with the dilemma of saving his cargo or saving the boat. Having learned to appreciate "The Maggie" and its embodiment of timeless values over the more transient appeal of his possessions, the American elects to dump the cargo. In the process he becomes more "Scottish," yet the crew remain unchanged. Similarly, *The Sheriff of Fractured Jaw* portrays a Briton resisting Americanization and simultaneously affecting change in Americans. The last scene of the movie takes place in the Sheriff's office that Tibbs has made his own. Sipping tea from a dainty china cup he asks a Native American valet to pass judgement on a new waistcoat. "It fits you jolly well, Sir," the man replies, confirming that Tibbs has not only Anglicized his surroundings, but the populace too.

1950s issues of *Picture Post* connote that Americanization was perceived by some as a threat to British identity. A March 1954 article on the latest Elizabeth Taylor movie humorously, but also rather chillingly, paints a portrait of British women willingly enslaved to the dictates of Hollywood-inspired fashion.

> Every morning Elizabeth Taylor punches my tube ticket. At lunch Elizabeth Taylor serves me with a drink. In the afternoon Elizabeth Taylor comes to my office to model for a story.... If imitation is the sincerest form of flattery, Elizabeth Taylor is the most flattered girl in the world—apart from being the most beautiful. Not since the war, when every girl one saw was Veronica Lake, have the girls of this country striven so hard to look alike.[46]

Americanization may have been a frightening prospect, but the magazine often reassured readers that it could be overcome. Like the four films, *Picture Post* argued that, rather than America changing Britain, Britain could change America. An April 1955 article that discusses an "invasion" of Scotland by U.S. business interests reassures readers that the Scots have not started their own baseball teams. Instead, an American has become part of the British sports scene:

> And those who feared that a base-ball league would be founded by such teams as the Dundee Blue Bonnets, Glasgow Slashers and Greendock Dodgers have been reassured. Indeed, the general manager of a Vale of Levn factory, a thorough American with a rich Connecticut accent, was recently elected chairman of Dumbarton Football Club.[47]

In the years following World War II, Britain, though frail, was still an intensely proud nation. "Pride. Pride," scoffs Myrtle in *To Dorothy a Son*, "that's all you English ever talk about." "That's all we've got left to talk about," answers Tony. The British were too proud to resign themselves to irrelevance or defeat. To preserve their self-esteem they reinvented their image. Instead of a "Great Power," they would be a wise shepherd and a resilient underdog. They achieved this transformation by comparing themselves to the people of the United States. Cinema was an integral part of this process. Movies also suggested that British weakness and antiquity were far preferable to a modern, Americanized world in which individuals were rash, covetous, and unstable. By casting Britain as an experienced old hand capable of guiding and occasionally besting a potentially reckless United States, filmmakers and *Picture Post* journalists helped to provide their nation with a viable postwar identity.

6

A World Worth Saving?
Redefining National Identity in Margaret Thatcher's Britain

For decades, the British had been told by their movies that they were a people defined by a set of national characteristics. The ability to exercise emotional restraint was one such attribute repeatedly committed to celluloid. Another was the capacity to know one's place in the class system. And, as film after film would eagerly demonstrate, to be British was to be, categorically, *not American*. Throughout the 1980s and into the early 1990s, British films interrogated such essentialist notions as never before. *Local Hero* (Bill Forsyth, 1983), *84, Charing Cross Road* (David Jones, 1986), *Stormy Monday* (Mike Figgis, 1988) and *Shadowlands* (Richard Attenborough, 1993) all ask their audiences to take a second, highly skeptical, look at national belonging. In each, it is an encounter with America that is the catalyst for reevaluation.

Local Hero and *Stormy Monday* take place in a Britain whose physical and psychic borders are porous, allowing the traffic of ideas, people, and images. The two movies suggest Britishness, rather than a definable entity, is a mysterious, hybrid state of being, the result of varied and difficult to quantify transnational influences.[1] *84, Charing Cross Road* and *Shadowlands* contend that, even if there ever were a definable set of British national characteristics—and both movies harbor serious doubts—any adherence to them is highly inadvisable.

National identity is such a thorny subject in each of these films because, during the period of their creation, a very particular—and limited—version of Britishness had gained ground. The Conservative Party, under Prime Ministers Margaret Thatcher (1979–90) and John Major (1990–1994), was eager to define the nation in terms of its imperial past.

Thatcher's actions and rhetoric, especially during the period of the 1982 Falklands war, demonstrated an eagerness to return the nation to its pre–Cold War identity, in which political swagger and gunboat diplomacy were the order of the day. In a July 1982 speech to a Conservative Party rally in Cheltenham, England, she claimed that victory over Argentina's forces had allowed the British a renewed self-knowledge:

> We have ceased to be a nation in retreat. We have instead a new-found confidence—born in the economic battles at home and tested and found true 8,000 miles away. That confidence comes from the re-discovery of ourselves, and grows with the recovery of our self-respect. And so today, we can rejoice at our success in the Falklands and take pride in the achievement of the men and women of our Task Force. But we do so, not as at some last flickering of a flame which must soon be dead. No—we rejoice that Britain has re-kindled that spirit which has fired her for generations past and which today has begun to burn as brightly as before. Britain found herself again in the South Atlantic and will not look back from the victory she has won.[2]

Britain, according to Thatcher, should see itself as a formidable force in the world, and this sense of strength should be derived from the spirit of Empire. The link between the past and the present was further stressed by Thatcher's lauding of "Victorian Values." Historian Howard L. Malchow notes this development: "Early in 1983, the year of the second National Heritage Act, and a year after she mobilized the rhetoric of history and nostalgia in the Falklands War, Thatcher adopted and reiterated the phrase 'Victorian Values' as a leitmotif of that year's election campaign."[3] In a TV interview, she argued that Queen Victoria's reign was an era of strength and, above all, national cohesion:

> Those were the values when our country became great, but not only did our country become great internationally, also so much advance was made in this country.... Yes, I want to see one nation, as you go back to Victorian times, but I want everyone to have their own personal property stake. Property, every single one in this country, that's why we go so hard for owner-occupation, this is where we're going to get one nation.[4]

Thatcher cast herself as the herald of a new Victorian age in which Britishness meant military might, self-respect, and a cohesive citizenry.

The eagerness to define both a national character and a unified people was perpetuated by Thatcher's successor, John Major, who, in a now infamous 1993 speech, painted a picture of the nation as a gentle, pastoral idyll locked in a mythic past. He waxed:

> Fifty years from now Britain will still be the country of long shadows on county [Cricket] grounds, warm beer, invincible green suburbs, dog lovers and pools fillers and—as George Orwell said—"old maids bicycling to Holy Communion through the morning mist" and—if we get our way—Shakespeare still read even in school. Britain will survive unamendable in all essentials.[5]

A fondness for terms such as "invincible," "unamendable," and "essentials" reveal a politician and a party entirely ill at ease with any evolution in national identity.

The Conservatives again defined Britain in terms of the past by revitalizing the "special relationship." By the time Thatcher took office, the phrase was almost redundant. Unsatisfied to witness its demise, she resurrected it with the help of Ronald Reagan. As historians Michael Smith and Steve Smith contend, "Not only was the 'special relationship' reinstated as the centrepiece of British foreign policy, but it also seemed to become part of an intense ideological and personal alliance centred around the two leaders themselves."[6] The revivified special relationship was an integral part of the Conservative project to return Britain to what they perceived as the days of a halcyon past. Indeed, Smith and Smith go on to note that this "renewed intimacy" can be interpreted as "the triumph of nostalgia and sentiment over reality."[7]

Why did the Conservatives attempt to define the nation via a mythic history? They did so because, in modern Britain, national identity was increasingly influenced by division and change. The 1981 riots on the streets of Toxteth—an inner-city area of Liverpool—and Brixton, South London, demonstrated that the nation was split along the lines of race and class. The coal miners' strike, stretching from March 1984 to March 1985, ignited intense ideological and physical battles between Britain's political left and right. Thatcher's appeals for Britons to rally round images of the past were undercut by her social policies that stressed the individual over the communal. She promoted an entrepreneurial culture, weakened the welfare state, and her famous comment, "There is no such thing as society,"[8] seemed to encapsulate a vision of Britain in which individuals were cut off from each other and left to fend for themselves.

In the face of widespread division and change, Thatcher and Major's version of Britishness purported to offer unity and continuity. Imperial greatness and Victorian values proved to be powerful talismans in an uncertain time. Widely televised images of flag-waving crowds welcoming troops home from the Falklands attest to this. Many, however, rejected the Conservatives' simplistic, antiquated version of national identity. For example, the British cultural critic Stuart Hall lamented in 1982, "we seem to possess no other viable vocabulary in which to cast our sense of who the British people are and where they are going, except one drawn from the inventory of lost imperial greatness."[9] It is apparent that during the period of Conservative government that spanned the entirety of the 1980s and much of the 1990s, Britons were faced with a dilemma: Hide in the past—where national identity was, ostensibly, coherent—or acknowledge the realities of a present in which Britishness is clearly a more complex proposition.

Transnational Citizens: Local Hero *and* Stormy Monday

In *Local Hero* "Mac" MacIntyre (Peter Riegert) of the Texas-based Knox Oil Company is sent to Scotland to negotiate the sale of a pristine Scottish bay to be used as an oil refinery. Gradually he becomes enamored of the beauty of Scotland and of Stella Urquhart (Jennifer Black), the landlady of the inn where he lodges. After the intervention of the chairman of Knox Oil, Mr. Happer (Burt Lancaster), the bay is saved from use as a refinery, and plans are made to build an observatory and center for the study of marine life. *Stormy Monday* highlights the relationship between Brendan (Sean Bean), a down-on-his-luck Irishman living in England, and Kate (Melanie Griffith), a disenchanted American waitress. Together with Mr. Finney (Sting), a canny jazz club owner, they foil the plans of shady American businessman, Mr. Cosmo (Tommy Lee Jones), to obtain a controlling interest in the economy of Newcastle, England.

Bill Forsyth, the writer and director of *Local Hero*, not content to present the usual stereotype of the austere and unsophisticated Scot, created Gordon (Denis Lawson) and Stella, a sexually voracious Scottish couple who prefer a glass of wine to a dram of whisky. The Scotland that Forsyth creates is so lacking in stereotypical Scottishness that even some Scotsmen feel alien to it. For instance, Danny Oldsen (Peter Capaldi), MacIntryre's colleague from the Scottish branch of Knox Oil, is often as bewildered by his surroundings as the American. Unable to read road signs written in Gaelic, this Scottish sophisticate is able, he tells MacIntyre, to speak, "French, Italian, Spanish, Greek, Turkish, Russian, Swedish, German, Japanese, Dutch, and Polish." Another character particularly lacking in "Scottishness" is Ben (Fulton Mackay), the last Scot to hold out against the American purchase. Before going to Scotland, MacIntyre is told, "You won't be dealing with a bunch of Indians, " but the movie makes several suggestions that Ben is more akin to a Native American than a Scotsman. For instance, his tiny, one-room, beach dwelling resembles a teepee and, as do many American Indians, he scoffs at the notion that land can be bought and sold.

Stormy Monday also presents characters that challenge essentialist ideas about national character. Mike Figgis, the movie's writer and director, ensures this by bestowing American characters with stereotypically British traits and vice versa. For example, the American villain, Mr. Cosmo, repeatedly asks his henchmen to be polite and to act like gentlemen. He is annoyed at the idea that they should engage in gunplay. Of all the characters in the movie, it is an Englishman, Finney, who acts the most "American." Utilizing gangster tactics far more effectively than Cosmo, he runs the Americans out of town as if he were Wyatt Earp. Cosmo fails because, as Finney tells him, "you didn't do your homework." The line suggests that he should have researched the complex reality of British life instead of relying on national stereotypes.

Another way the films complicate received notions of national identity is by demonstrating that Britain is a veritable transnational terminus. The area of Scotland in which most of *Local Hero* takes place is a meeting place for American businessmen, Russian fishermen, and a great variety of Scotsmen who spend the movie exchanging ideas and demonstrating shared cultural affinities. The locality is visited by N.A.T.O. jets on training exercises—whose pilots are likely to visit several nations over the course of a mission—and is presided over by a black vicar who, though originally from Africa, sports the quintessentially Scottish name of Murdo MacPherson. Much is made of the American interloper's transnational identity. To the Scots, MacIntyre is simply an American, to his colleagues in Texas he is "Scottish," and to himself he is a Hungarian-American whose family he explains, "changed their name when they got off the boat from Hungary. They thought MacIntyre was American." Even the water that fills the bay is symbolic of transnational interaction. A character comments that it is not really Scottish at all, much of it coming from the Bahamas, brought in by the North Atlantic Drift.

Both movies utilize music to demonstrate that national belonging is a complicated matter. Mark Knopfler, a British rock musician who specializes in blending aesthetic traditions, created the musical score for *Local Hero*. The name of one of his bands, The Notting Hillbillies, simultaneously invokes the Notting Hill region of London and the musical traditions and people of Appalachia. Knopfler's soundtrack mixes the sounds of Scottish folk music with those of rock, demonstrating the vibrant potential of transnational interaction. *Local Hero* also makes clear that the melding of musical styles may not always be so compelling. In the offices of the oil magnate, Mr. Happer, the iconographic Scottish song "Danny Boy" is piped in as Muzak. Stripped of all its grandeur and passion, the song is reduced to background or elevator music. The point remains, however, that culture—whatever its fate may be—is ever on the move. The movie also presents a Russian sailor performing a karaoke rendition of the American country song "I've Always Been a Rover." The scene suggests that aesthetic blending will occur whatever the odds, as the thick-accented Russian repeats the quintessentially American lyric "lonesome for a lone star man like me."

In *Stormy Monday*, Mr. Finney embodies national hybridity because he is an Englishman who owns a jazz club. The movie insists that jazz itself—though often considered a particularly American art form—is a transnational genre. The Kraków Jazz Ensemble, an outfit from Poland, provides most of the diegetic music in the film. Significantly, they perform in a style known as free jazz, suggesting not only that their music will not be tied down by the tyranny of conventional rhythm and meter, but also that it is unbound by national affiliation.

Both movies are about Americanization, yet neither presents a simplistic invasion narrative of dollar-obsessed Americans exploiting helpless Europeans. There is no villain in *Local Hero*. The man we might expect to embody American greed and insensitivity is Mr. Happer, the chairman of Knox Oil. Yet, Happer is a lovable eccentric and astronomer, far more concerned with the movements of the heavens than with business matters. MacIntyre certainly does not fit the stereotype of corporate raider. He begins the movie as somewhat cold and self-centered, but his Scottish experience transforms him into a man who would rather collect shells on the beach than hunt corporate heads. The movie never loses sight of the fact that turning the bay into an oil refinery would be an ecological disaster but, in a scene in which MacIntyre and Danny Oldsen wander down the beach, discussing the many products that are manufactured from oil, the film also makes clear that, for better or worse, contemporary life is inextricably bound up with fossil fuels. Rather than exploitative, the oilmen simply appear to be pragmatic.

The Scots who make their living from the bay are not simple country folk, ready to sell the farm for a handful of beans. The decision to let America into their lives is always theirs, and their toughness belies any victim status. MacIntyre's pet rabbit disappears, only to turn up as a meal served at the inn. In response to his dismay, Stella tells him simply, "We eat rabbits here." As a group of seals bask on bayside rocks, a Scot remarks that salmon fishermen would shoot the animals on sight. If there are any tough guys in *Local Hero*, they are the locals, not the Americans.

Stormy Monday certainly presents some tough, exploitative Americans. Mr. Cosmo, a cigar-puffing fat cat surrounded by slimy henchmen, is a caricature that could have been torn from Pravda. However, as in *Local*

Hero, the British are not portrayed as helpless in the face of corporate ambition. To a certain extent, they can choose whether they embrace or reject America. The U.S. provides Britain with popular culture products, such as jazz, which become transformed by their contact with Europe, enhancing the lives of British citizens. After all, the Kraków Jazz Ensemble, their leader stresses, is from Kraków, Poland, *not* Kraków, Pennsylvania. Quintessentially American foods, such as steak, are adopted and changed by British tastes. Kate, waitressing at Weegee's, an American-style restaurant named after the storied New York photojournalist, asks Brendan if he would like his steak cooked "English style." When he responds with puzzlement, she explains that she means "burnt." *Stormy Monday* repeatedly insists that the British can enjoy American products and images without "going American." Mr. Finney confidently claims that he can resist Americanization, even though he owns two establishments, his jazz club and The Precinct—the latter decorated with the paraphernalia of the New York Police Department—that many would regard as already wholly iconographic of the United States.

Despite these claims of autonomy, *Stormy Monday* casts doubt on Britain's capacity to appropriate and transform American products and styles. The proliferation of Americana, the movie claims, can limit choice. In Weegee's, Brendan is offered an array of U.S. beers but is unable to buy what he really wants, a Guinness. Other scenes point out that, at its worst, America's incursion into British culture is simply a land grab. Mr. Cosmo's aggressive acquisition of Newcastle property clearly demonstrates this. As his goons evict a British businessman from his premises, a voice-over reports that Newcastle citizens are accusing U.S. property developers of a "callous disregard for local heritage." Later, an American accented radio D.J. lists the Hollywood movies that will be shown as part of Newcastle's "America Week." The titles are read in quick succession, becoming a deluge of sound that transforms the film festival into something approaching a threat rather than an attraction.

A sequence near the movie's climax sums up its ambivalence on Anglo-American relations. A parade winds its way through the center of Newcastle. The celebration is pure Americana, the stars and stripes waving from every window as marching bands thrill the crowds. British people are willing participants in the attraction that, at first glance, appears to be a great deal of fun. However, it soon becomes clear that the British are taking part in a New Orleans–style funeral parade. Intercut with the footage of the parade is the lovemaking of Kate and Brendan, an American woman and a British man whose loving relationship demonstrates the possibilities of transatlantic partnership. But, just as the hopeful image of the parade gives way to the darker image of the funeral, the lovemaking scene gives way to images of a ticking time-bomb and of realtor's signs reading "acquired for development."

Fittingly for movies that refuse essentialism, those individuals who adhere to simplistic notions of national identity are presented as absurd. Right-wing politicians are afforded short shrift. For instance, in *Local Hero*, Margaret Thatcher telephones the chairman of Knox Oil. As she chats with his secretary about recipes and is subsequently put on hold, the so-called Iron Lady is reduced to a somewhat inconsequential figure. *Stormy Monday* parodies the alliance forged between Thatcher and Ronald Reagan, and references their rhetoric on transatlantic unity. The Lady Mayoress of Newcastle, sporting blue suit, pearls, and iron coiffure—Thatcher's standard wardrobe—standing in a room decorated with giant photographs of Thatcher and Reagan, tells Mr. Cosmo that their meeting is "ushering in a new era of transatlantic cooperation and friendship." She goes on to say that she wants the American visit to "contribute to the reemergence of this once great nation." The transatlantic summit is presented as farce, an English delegate groping an American counterpart, and the Kraków Jazz Ensemble memorably mauling the U.S. national anthem.

Shadowlands *and* 84, Charing Cross Road: *Celebrating and Rejecting the Thatcherite Vision of British History*

Shadowlands traces the bond between two writers, the Briton C.S. Lewis (Anthony Hopkins) and American Joy Gresham (Debra Winger). When Lewis first encounters Gresham, he is emotionally repressed and unadventurous, but, as her influence upon him increases, he finds himself more able to embrace life. *84, Charing Cross Road* tells the story of forthright American bibliophile, Helene Hanff (Anne Bancroft), and her two-decade relationship with an unassuming English bookseller, Frank Doel (Anthony Hopkins). Answering an advertisement from Doel's bookstore, Hanff orders antique volumes and corresponds with Doel. Although the pair never meet, their letters represent a love affair.

At first glance, both movies seem eager to bolster the Conservative Party project of defining Britain in particularly limited ways and linking the nation to the past. *Shadowlands* opens with a beautifully lit tracking shot of a church choir, singing amongst the ancient relics of a Norman cathedral. C.S. Lewis's daily life is one of wood-paneled interiors and cups of tea sipped from china cups. As an Oxford don, the man himself is an embodiment of British heritage. Joy Gresham surveys the dreaming spires of Oxford and sighs, "Now there's a world worth saving." Apparently, we are being invited to share her opinion.

In the second sequence of *84, Charing Cross Road*, Hanff is in a London Taxi, almost swooning as she admires the statues and monuments to Britain's past. Frank Doel's bookstore, "Marks and Co." is another environment reeking of British History. "It's like something out of Dickens," an American visitor enthuses. The film makes much of the fact that the bookstore, already aged, continues to exist into the 1980s. Undoubtedly, the store is meant to represent a "great" Britain of the past, tenaciously holding on, though threatened with extinction. Hanff tells us, "Marks and Co. is still there, though there's some talk it might be demolished." Perhaps we are to infer from this line of dialogue that, as the Conservatives would frequently opine, to do away with Britain's past would be disastrous.

Shadowlands and *84, Charing Cross Road* can seem particularly essentialist in tone since, unlike *Local Hero* and *Stormy Monday*, they tell the standard tale—beloved of mid-century British cinema—of the restrained Briton and the excessive American. In *84, Charing Cross Road*, while Frank Doel goes about his day in an ordered, time-honored fashion, Hanff lives her life in a much more haphazard way. Scenes of Doel carefully polishing his shoes and putting out empty milk bottles are contrasted with Hanff sleeping through her alarm and rushing off to work. Like many a cinematic American before her, Hanff is an energetic, exuberant person. She takes dance classes and is especially vigorous in her enjoyment of British English. "Imagine, a whole country says 'raahhsperies,'" she notes with awe and delight. Revelling in the way the word sounds, she repeats it: "raahhsperries, raahhsperies, raahhsperies." When Doel goes dancing with his wife, he is soon out of breath and must be persuaded to continue. "Oh, I can't dance. Oh, alright, just once more," he wheezes. His approach to language is much more low-key than that of Hanff. Revealing a conventionally dry British wit, he informs her that he has consulted his bookstore colleagues, by writing, "I have talked to the inmates here." While Doel sips cups of tea, or sits at a blustery seaside with his family, Hanff enjoys the more excessive recreations of smoking and drinking. Doel is the soul of propriety. He begins letters with "Dear Madame" (reading these words, Hanff muses, "I hope Madame doesn't mean over there what it means over here"), and stands to attention while the national anthem plays on television. Hanff is the American rebel. Sweeping out of a bookstore in disgust, she loudly asks its patrons, "Doesn't anybody read English literature in New York?"

Shadowlands is similarly dichotomous in its approach to national identity. As scholar W.M. Hagen says of Joy Gresham's entrance into the narrative, "Into the world of muted colors and gray-white tones that mark English life, into that 'safe' English institution, the tea room, comes a loud woman with a scarlet (well, maroon) hat."[10] Commenting on the energetic wording of Joy Gresham's letters, Lewis concludes, "I expect it's just the American style. Americans don't understand about inhibition." The Englishman is frequently stifled by propriety ("Does one wait for the train to leave?" he frets as he watches Joy depart) and prone to coin aphorisms on the subject of restraint, such as "The most intense joy lies not in the having but in the desire" and "Personal experience isn't everything."

The transatlantic romance detailed in both movies can be regarded as a demonstration of the strength of the special relationship, that institution beloved of Conservative political strategists. Each movie strongly suggests that the citizens of Britain and the United States are enhanced by contact with one another. *Shadowlands*, at least in its first half, presents Lewis and Gresham's relationship in terms that many a 1950s British diplomat would have warmed to: British age, experience, and sophistication, in the form of C.S. Lewis, interacts with youthful ingenuousness, embodied by Joy Gresham.[11] "I'm rather in awe of you," she informs him. *84, Charing Cross Road* pledges its allegiance to the special relationship by proclaiming that Britain and the U.S. share a unique bond. Toward the end of the movie, it appears, despite the three thousand miles that separate the Englishman and the American anglophile, the pair can communicate almost telepathically. Each addresses the camera, speaking aloud the words of a letter. A sequence of crosscutting, transporting us instantaneously back and forth across the Atlantic, gives the impression that the couple are talking to each other in the same room rather than communicating via letter. The closeness of their relationship is stressed repeatedly by lines of dialogue such as, "You know Frankie, you're the only one that understands me." Hanff's last words in the movie—"If you happen to pass by 84, Charing Cross Road, kiss it for me. I owe it so much"—suggest, as would many a British Foreign Office denizen, that America gained most from the transatlantic relationship.

Despite the several moments that are Thatcherite in tone, there are just as many that broaden and diversify antiquated conceptions of national identity. Both American women are notably complex characters. Joy Gresham is not just an American but, according to Lewis's brother, Warnie (Edward Hardwicke), she is a "Jewish, Communist, Christian American."

Gresham herself notes, "I'm a Christian, but I was brought up to be a good atheist." Helene Hanff continues this trend by identifying herself as a Jewish woman who enjoys reading the bible.

Flying in the face of decades of British films that insisted on presenting Americans as unsophisticated, these movies defiantly make room for the American intellectual. *Shadowlands* throws Joy Gresham to the academic lions in order that she may triumph. As throngs of Oxford University dons, clad in academic regalia, champagne in hand, make polite conversation in a historic dining hall, Gresham enters their midst, causing a riot of curious whispers. She is fascinating, not only because she is romantically linked to C.S. Lewis, but because she is an American. Sensing an easy target, a scholar swoops in for the kill, attempting to belittle her intellectual abilities. He is shocked to discover that he is not dealing with the crass and easily outwitted American of British lore, but a witty and sophisticated woman who is also a renowned poet. The predatory don claims to be amazed that there exists a market for her books in the U.S. Gresham's rejoinder to this condescending remark is, "We're not all cowboys."

In *84, Charing Cross Road*, Hanff initially succumbs to a cultural inferiority complex, feeling guilty about owning an antique British book which she notes, "should be read by the fire in a gentleman's leather chair, not in some secondhand overstuffed seat in a broken down brownstone front." However, she soon decides that her apartment in New York is just as fitting an environment for the book and, by implication, that she will not be controlled by condescending and essentialist notions regarding American culture.

The protagonist of *84, Charing Cross Road* may be highly enamored of British literature and historical iconography, but she can be a surprisingly pragmatic Anglophile. Not for her the easily identifiable Britain of the Conservative Party's mythos. Halfway through the movie, Hanff poses the question, "Does the England of English literature exist?" Her voiceover tells us that an American friend has informed her, "Tourists go to England with preconceived notions, so they always find what they're looking for." Accepting this maxim, she states that, if she ever goes there, she will "go looking for the England of English literature." Her friend replies, "It's there." By the end of the film, following her long correspondence with Frank Doel, she is no longer certain of this. "Maybe it is, maybe it isn't," she muses. "One things for sure, it's here [in her book-filled New York apartment]." Hanff's words suggest, firstly, that there can be more than one conception of a nation. If there is an "England of English literature" then there can be an England of English music or an England of English workers. Indeed, myriad Englands. Secondly, her conclusion that her favored version of England is with her in New York makes clear that nationality is a fluid entity, able to travel. Thirdly, her endorsement of the idea that tourists "find what they go looking for" connotes that national identity is highly subjective. It doesn't matter whether the England of English literature ever really existed. Because she wants it to exist, it does: in her apartment, and in her mind.

The Tragedy of Restraint

There is one other way that both movies question monolithic definitions of nationality. They demonstrate that emotional restraint, one of the most storied tenets of British national identity, can have tragic consequences.

Shadowlands portrays Lewis, before he falls in love with Joy Gresham, as completely ill at ease with all forms of emotional life. He and his brother Warnie cut themselves off from any experience that might arouse passion. After Joy remarks on the beauty of an Oxford landscape, Lewis replies, "I don't really go in for seeing the sights." Even the simple drama of the night sky is too much for Warnie. "Too many stars. It confuses me," he says. Both seek the safety found in routine. Warnie suggests that his brother's first meeting with Joy take place in the manageable environment of a hotel tearoom. "Tea is safe," he says. "A hotel is safe." Through daily ritual, these Britons render life predictable and unchallenging. Lewis and his brother climb the stairs to their rooms at the same time every night, even shutting the doors to their bedrooms with clockwork timing and efficiency. *Shadowlands* points out that, in holding passion at bay, Lewis exists in a state of arrested development. The first night he sleeps with Joy, she observes his nightly routine of putting on his pajamas by noting that he is "just like a little boy."

Hiding from emotion, Lewis scoffs at any mention of inner life. His Oxford colleagues quiz him about the sexual and Christian subtexts of his book *The Lion, the Witch and the Wardrobe*. Ridiculing their "Hand-me-down-Freud," he tells the group, "the imagery is what it is." A similar moment occurs as he discusses Aristotle with his students. Summarizing the philosopher's approach to narrative, he tells them, "Plot is character. Forget Psychology. Forget the inside of men's heads. Judge them by their actions." He then notices that one of his students, Peter Whistler (James Frain), is sleeping. Applying Aristotelian theory to the young man's actions, he continues, "He comes. He sleeps. The next question is not 'why?' but 'what is he going to do next?'"

Having witnessed such behavior, Joy informs Lewis, "You've arranged a life for yourself where no-one can touch you." In the course of their relationship, she introduces Lewis to the world around him. Eventually, he is able to see that having lived such an emotionally blinkered life has resulted in many missed opportunities. Toward the end of the movie, he happens once again upon Whistler, the sleeping student. Completely reversing the attitude he displayed in the early sections of the film, Lewis advises the young man to be honest and open with his feelings, commenting, "One has to say things. The moment passes. And then you're alone again." Lewis may be a changed man by the end of the film, but the bulk of the narrative contends that those who engage in emotional restraint are never truly alive.

84, Charing Cross Road also details the process whereby a restrained Briton "loosens up" due to the influence of a more exuberant American. Helene Hanff confides to a friend that, in her dealings with Frank Doel, "I keep trying to puncture that proper British reserve." However, like *Shadowlands*, the movie catalogues the somewhat tragic existence of the emotionally reserved Briton. In an excruciating scene, Doel visits a dying colleague. Instead of telling the man how much he is missed at the bookstore or offering any substantial words of comfort, he can only offer platitudes. Unable to find anything to say, he reads to his workmate from a letter he has recently received from Hanff. The American's forthright and honest words stand in stark contrast to Doel's verbal fumbling.

As the relationship between Hanff and Doel develops, so does his thirst for a more exciting life. During the period in which Hanff writes scripts for television, Doel admits, "I wish we could see one of your Ellery Queen scripts over here. Our [British] TV wants livening up a bit." This desire for the "livening up" of British culture is echoed in Doel's longing for a more fulfilling emotional life. For him, the correspondence with Hanff is more than platonic. In one particularly moving scene, the camera lingers on his face in close-up as, thinking of her, he reads aloud a John Donne sonnet.

Doel may have a rich inner life, but he does not express any passion, in word or deed. He is one of life's spectators, Hanff one of its doers. Although she admonishes him, "Don't just sit there," one of the last scenes in the movie finds Doel sitting on a park bench and warily passing comment on the social changes of the 1960s. As a mini-skirted young woman passes by, he tells Hanff, "We watch it all from a safe distance." In contrast, Hanff embraces the moment in which she finds herself. She becomes a political activist during the Columbia University sit-ins. Her comment that she is a "great lover of 'I was there' books," reiterates her passion for involvement. At the moment Hanff, through her activism, becomes part of history, Doel dies.

Though Joy Gresham and Helene Hanff disrupt and vivify the restrained worlds of their respective Englishmen, *Shadowlands* and *84, Charing Cross Road* make clear the midcentury period, in which the two movies are set, was a time when the lives of many British citizens were marked by an emotional torpor. Both movies suggest that the era the Conservatives harkened back to, in which notions of Empire and Victorian Values were still very much in evidence, would be better left in the past.

Local Hero, *84, Charing Cross Road*, *Stormy Monday*, and *Shadowlands* call for an end to dichotomous conceptions of national identity. In these films, America is not simply the malignant, invasive influence that British cinema has so frequently portrayed, and British national characteristics are unusually varied, complex, and problematic. This deconstruction of British cinema's traditional approach to the "special relationship" is also a rebuke to the comforting, simplistic world of the Thatcherite mythos.

The appearance of such movies was due in large part to the changed landscape of British cinema in the 1980s. Since the demise of the studio system in the early 1960s, and the radical loosening of censorship strictures that occurred around the same time, British films have been freed from their duty to support the status quo. The more positive depiction of the U.S. since 1960 was also spurred by a change in cinematic personnel. Britain's baby boom generation, including its filmmakers, were markedly less anti–American than their forbears. In 1961, an article by Professor H.C. Allen in *The Contemporary Review*, a British journal of social and political commentary, pointed out that anti–Americanism in Britain was dying away: "It might well be claimed that British youth today is in essentials less Anti-American than any generation which has preceded it. These young men and women have been born into a world in which the Anglo-American alliance is an existing, well-established, continuing fact."[12]

Films of the studio era had emerged from a nation in which an influential section of the populace was greatly concerned that Britain was losing out to an American rival. This concern was repeatedly registered on celluloid. Many Britons who came of age in the sixties, irrespective of social class, did not regard the U.S. as an opponent. According to Professor Allen's article, they thought "of Britain only as a partner, and not the dominant one at that, in the affairs of the free world."[13] Moreover, as Allen points out, by 1961 the majority of Britain's youth were possessed of "positive ideals which they share with their American contemporaries" such as "racial and social equality."[14] These youths, by the 1980s, had become the scriptwriters, producers, and directors of British Cinema. They began to question and dismantle the previous generation's opinions regarding the U.S. and U.K., the very ideas that Margaret Thatcher was attempting to resurrect.

7

"You're his little English bitch and you don't even know it"
Gendering Anglo-American Relations in Post-9/11 British Cinema

In the months following 9/11, as British Prime Minister Tony Blair became an eager member of George Bush's "coalition of the willing," political cartoonists around the world began to characterize the relationship between the two men as decidedly unequal. South African cartoonist Zapiro presents the British leader as Mini-me (the diminutive henchman of the *Austin Powers* movies) toadying to Bush's Dr. Evil[1]; American satirist Taylor Jones gives us Blair the monkey dancing to a tune played by Bush the organ grinder[2]; and Gado, a West African artist, shows a grinning, naked Prime Minister following behind Bush, gripping the hem of the President's regal cloak.[3] Blair is routinely depicted as a small, submissive lackey, while the U.S. premier tends to tower over him. But by far the most popular way to satirize the Anglo-American dyad was to portray Blair as Bush's pet dog. Canadian Cam Cardow draws Blair as a small, panting mutt perched on Bush's knee and restrained by a leash.[4] In a cartoon entitled "Allowed on the Couch," Britain's Steve Bell depicts the P.M. as a slightly more ferocious, but still tiny, hound whose bared teeth gnaw at a bone, while Bush scratches him behind the ear.[5] Such cartoons were a response to the seemingly ubiquitous opinion that Blair was "Bush's poodle."[6]

For the British, the idea that their leader was popularly conceived as an obedient and lowly creature, ready to do the bidding of an American master, had become a matter of urgent concern. In 2002, *Guardian* journalist Hugo Young debated the extent of Blair's "poodleism." He gives the Prime Minister the benefit of the doubt, noting, "thus far Tony Blair's contribution to events has been less poodle-like than the British left have assumed. That is not to say poodleism does not beckon, if Bush does plunge to war."[7] But, in 2007, the *Financial Times* was not so charitable, quoting a former U.S. official who reveals of Blair: "In private conversation with George Bush he was as quiet as a mouse."[8]

Widespread discussion of Blair's apparent submissiveness led many to view him as conventionally feminine, and Bush as conventionally masculine. For example, in an illustration captioned with "Doo Naht Fer-sake Me, Oh Mah Dah-lin,'" Alan de la Nougerede offers a reimagining of a scene from the movie *High Noon* (Fred Zinnemann, 1952) with Bush as Gary Cooper, and Blair, complete with gingham frock and bonnet, essaying the role of Grace Kelly.[9]

Gendered perceptions of "the special relationship" were given credence by the marked contrast in the political strategies of Blair and Bush. British scholar Rebecca Carpenter notes, "Blair's position, with its greater emphasis on humanitarian concerns rather than morally policing the world, helped the United States define itself by contrast: the British position was constructed as soft, naïve, idealistic, and utopian as compared to the clear-sighted, hard-headed, rational, truly masculine position of the United States, a nation which understood the need for overwhelming force and the value of shock and awe."[10]

The body language employed by Bush and Blair also helped to differentiate them along gendered lines. Vicki Woods of the *Daily Telegraph*, discussing a theory already propounded by the chief economic commentator of the *Financial Times*, contends, "Blair's government is feminine, of course," and points to the leader's "fluttery, unresolved hand gestures when speaking."[11] Professor of cultural studies Richard Johnson suggests that the P.M.'s version of masculinity is of a very different stripe than that of the President, contending that Bush's voice is "very masculine, clipped, brutal even, holding the emotion aroused by events in quite a tense and rigid body, close-set eyes almost hidden."[12] Blair, on the other hand, relies on "wide-eyed, 'winning' appeals."[13] Noting that Bush's "baseball 'performances' and fanship are part of his self-presentation as a very North American kind of *man*,"[14] Johnson muses, "Perhaps Bush's sport-related repertoire is not so easy to match from inside an English middle-class masculinity which deplores 'laddishness' and is centred on 'reason' and intellectuality."[15]

With Blair cemented in the popular and academic imagination as submissive and feminine, and Bush filling the role of dominant male, it was perhaps inevitable that homophobic depictions of the pair as gay lovers became widespread. Cartoonists led the way in this regard. Steve Bell draws

Bush at a White House press briefing declaring, "My coalition is enormous. I can keep it up all day. All nite [*sic*]. Just as long as it takes." Meanwhile a tiny Blair, buttocks conveniently level with the Bush's crotch, peeks out from behind the President's lectern.[16] Perhaps inspired by such images, Samuel Preston, lead-singer of English rock band The Ordinary Boys, argued in 2006, "Tony Blair is ... just George Bush's fluffer."[17]

For many Britons, the emasculation of the Prime Minister meant that the nation itself was feminized. Carpenter notes, "the widespread belief that Blair has failed to assert British sovereignty and has transformed the 'special relationship' into one of assertive superpower and submissive devotee has frequently been depicted as a feminization of the nation."[18] This depiction is given florid life by Steve Williams, a hospital porter from Liverpool, who pointed out in 2003, "Britain has become America's tart. We just lie down and get screwed."[19]

Post 9/11 British cinema regularly responded to this gendering of the transatlantic partnership. *Love Actually* (Richard Curtis, 2003), *28 Weeks Later* (Juan Carlos Fresnadillo, 2007), *In the Loop* (Armando Iannucci, 2009), and *The Special Relationship* (Richard Loncraine, 2010)[20] all pit American and British men against each other, and demonstrate the ways in which male virility is associated with national strength. Each film presents Britain as the underdog, but clearly demonstrates that if the nation's men are able to show courage and vigor at the crucial moment, they may regain some level of independence.

Love Actually

Love Actually offers an enjoyable fantasy to those Britons exasperated by Blair's perceived submissiveness. David (Hugh Grant), the British Prime Minister, is initially satisfied to take a back seat in his dealings with the U.S. President (Billy Bob Thornton), but becomes considerably emboldened after the American premier attempts to seduce Natalie (Martine McCutcheon), a member of the Downing Street staff. Since the Prime Minister has established a flirtatious rapport with this young woman, he obviously regards the President's designs upon her as an incursion into territory already claimed. At a press conference designed to summarize the state of Anglo-American relations, the President smarmily hints that Britain is a nation to be plundered, stating, "We got what we came for, and our special relationship is still very special." In the wake of the President's wolfish advance on Natalie, his use of the term "special relationship" takes on a particularly unctuous quality. David—fittingly named after a giant-slayer—responds by calmly making clear that Britain will no longer be taken advantage of:

> I love that word relationship. Covers all manner of sins, doesn't it? ... I fear that this has become a bad relationship. A relationship based on the President taking exactly what he wants and casually ignoring all those things that really matter to Britain. We may be a small country, but we're a great one too: the country of Shakespeare, Churchill, The Beatles, Sean Connery, Harry Potter, David Beckham's right foot. David Beckham's left foot, come to that. And a friend who bullies us is no longer a friend. And since bullies only respond to strength, from now onward I will be prepared to be much stronger.

As the non-diegetic music rises to a crescendo, the Prime Minister's enraptured aides and cabinet colleagues burst into applause. It is the kind of off-message, unscripted, diplomatically inadvisable speech that could only exist in a movie. Soon after, a pop music radio station dedicates a song to the P.M., signaling that his tough new stance has found an appreciative audience far beyond his inner circle. The song's title, "Jump (For My Love)" suggests that David's rhetorical exertions have won him the love of his people.

The scene is an obvious critique of Blair's apparent submissiveness and clearly implies that "Bush's Poodle"—still ensconced in Downing Street when the movie was released—would be well advised to display some of the derring-do of his cinematic counterpart. And if we are not sufficiently aware that David's speech is a rebuke to Blairism, the movie makes explicit reference to the then Prime Minister. Introducing himself to the staff at Number 10, David attempts to ingratiate himself with the group by noting that he brings with him "no teenagers, no scary wife." His words are an uncharitable reference to Blair's older children—Euan, Nicholas, and Kathryn—and wife, Cherie, a forthright political spouse whom the British press tended to portray as disturbingly eccentric.[21] Since *Love Actually* clearly establishes that David is Blair's successor, any reference to the shortcomings of "the last government" can be interpreted as criticisms of the Labour Party leader and his policies. For example, a cabinet meeting finds one of David's advisers warning him, "we mustn't allow ourselves to be bullied from pillar to post like the last government."

David's diplomatic strength is entwined with his masculine potency. His transformation into a tough, forthright politician is triggered as much by stirrings in his loins as an urge to defend his country. He spends the rest of the movie torn between his desire for Natalie and his awareness that pursuing a lowly employee might seem highly inappropriate. Managing to slough off his doubts, he pursues and wins the girl. In a movie brimming with romantic partnerships, this pairing is given particular emphasis by the fact that the P.M. and Natalie are the last major characters glimpsed before the closing credits. It is as though their coupling is the climactic event that each moment in the movie has been leading up to. David and Natalie's relationship is given such importance because it demonstrates the British male's diplomatic and sexual potency in comparison with his American rival. If Blair was considered emasculated in contrast to Bush, then *Love Actually* offers a British premier who can beat America is any contest of masculine one-upmanship.

Further proof of the British man's virility vis-à-vis the United States is offered by a parade of British males who find romantic success with American women. The film tells the enjoyably improbable tale of Colin Frissell (Kris Marshall), a young man so unsuccessful with "stuck up" English girls that he hatches a ludicrous plan to travel to the United States where the girls, "will seriously dig me with my cute British accent." Colin dreams, "any bar, anywhere in America, contains ten girls more beautiful and more likely to have sex with me than the whole United Kingdom." Amazingly, Colin's crackpot scheme is wildly successful and, on his first foray into an American bar—in unglamorous Wisconsin—immediately meets three lithesome beauties who are quickly atwitter over his accent and his "cute" good looks. Inviting him to sleep overnight at their house, they solemnly confess that, due to straightened circumstances, they possess only one bed that Colin must share with them. Their poverty is such that they cannot even afford pajamas.

Another successful Anglo-American coupling is achieved in the tale of Sam (Thomas Sangster) a boyish-looking teenager who pines after Joanna (Olivia Olson), a seemingly unattainable American girl. Concerned that she will never notice him, and all too aware of her imminent return to the U.S., Sam resolves to impress her by learning to play the drums. Coached in the ways of romance by his stepfather, Daniel (Liam Neeson), he, like Wisconsin-bound Colin, achieves success against the odds. Joanna is notably beautiful, a gifted singer, and the lead performer in the school band. Sam, a suitor fighting against notable odds, has the look of a Dickensian waif, must struggle mightily to learn his instrument, and, as a drummer, is very much in the background while the American star enjoys the spotlight. "How," the movie asks, "will the Briton step out of the shadows?" Sam acquits himself admirably as a drummer, but fails to tell his beloved how he feels about her. With Daniel, he races to Heathrow airport, where he slips through the security barriers and wins a kiss from Joanna. The triumph of the British masculine project is sealed by a bear hug between Sam and his stepfather.

Scenes in which Americans fail to satiate their desires further highlight the romantic successes of David, Colin, and Sam. Sarah (Laura Linney), an American graphic designer, pines after Karl (Rodrigo Santoro). After a romantic evening, they repair to her flat, but their relationship remains unconsummated due to a phone call from Sarah's mentally ill brother, Michael (Michael Fitzgerald). Karl quickly loses interest and leaves the frustrated Sarah crying on her bed. Sarah, like the American President before her, has, in romantic terms, struck out.

From its opening moments, *Love Actually* signals its profound interest in the Anglo-American relationship and its intention to present a newly viable form of British masculinity. The movie begins in the Heathrow Airport arrivals area, with a montage of loving families, fond embraces, and passionate kisses, augmented by a voiceover from David, the British Prime Minister. Hugh Grant's unmistakable and quintessentially English voice intones: "When the planes hit the twin towers, as far as I know, none of the phone calls from the people onboard were messages of hate or revenge. They were all messages of love." His mention of 9/11 immediately brings to mind the United States, contemporary political realities and, since the speaker is the British premier, the Anglo-American relationship. David manages to reinterpret 9/11, a defining event in American history, couching it in terms of love rather than the warlike and vengeful emotions that emanated from Bush's Whitehouse in the aftermath of the attack.[22] This is the movie's first suggestion that British men are adept in matters of the heart and unsullied by the aggression associated with America. As the film progresses, we will meet David, Colin, and Sam who, though romantically successful, are all endearingly gentle and ingenuous.

Having established Heathrow as an important space for contemplating the subject of love, the movie returns to the airport in its final scenes, showcasing the triumph of British manhood. Sam greets Joanna after her return to the UK. We glimpse David and Natalie, their romance now a matter of public knowledge. Colin, the British stud, strides through Heathrow, returning from American shores with a bevy of Wisconsinite beauties.

The Special Relationship

Like *Love Actually*, *The Special Relationship* revels in the spectacle of a British Prime Minister finding his feet and standing up to his American counterpart. This brave and redoubtable leader is Tony Blair himself. The movie tells the story of Blair (Michael Sheen) and Bill Clinton (Dennis Quaid) as they develop a close, often fraught, diplomatic affiliation. The film makes the claim that Blair was, for a significant period, the dominant party in this particular transatlantic double-act.

And an act it most certainly was, the movie contends. The opening titles comprise of archival footage of successive British Prime Ministers and American Presidents presenting themselves in tandem for the news cameras. These images of Winston Churchill and Franklin D. Roosevelt; John Kennedy and Harold Macmillan; Harold Wilson and Lyndon Johnson; Ronald Reagan and Margaret Thatcher, to name a few, are given jaunty accompaniment by the Cole Porter song "Friendship." In this upbeat number, a man and a woman pledge their allegiance to one another. "If you're ever in a jam, here I am," the male singer offers. "If you ever catch on fire, send a wire," replies the chanteuse. This vaudevillian ditty stresses that the "special relationship" is a performance, but also hints at the gendered aspects of the partnership. By comparing Anglo-American diplomacy to a love affair between a man and a woman, the opening titles beg the question, "Which of these nations and national figureheads is the most feminine and which more masculine?"

The film traces Blair's ascendancy from timid, junior partner in the Anglo-American dyad to a position as dominant powerbroker. We encounter him first in 1992, four years before his general election victory, emerging, tired and tousled, from an airport in Washington, D.C. A car and driver are waiting for him—a fact that seems to surprise him—but there is no pomp surrounding his arrival. He has traveled to the U.S. alone in order to attend a lecture given by Clinton's advisers. He earnestly takes notes and sagely nods at the advice he receives on making Britain's political left newly relevant. Blair has the air of a man who wants to be told what to do, and the American lecturer to whom he listens is abundantly self-confident and authoritative.

After Blair ascends to the leadership of the Labour Party, the movie repeatedly suggests that, despite his newfound political power, he is hardly in control of his life. The house he shares with his wife, Cherie (Helen McCrory), is cramped, claustrophobic, and festooned with laundry that gives it the appearance of a tenement rather than a political leader's residence. Hurriedly digging through a basket of clothes, he asks Cherie, "Where's my blue shirt?" She is pointedly unhelpful and sarcastic. In conventional terms, Blair is an emasculated figure, relegated to the domestic sphere, hemmed in by piles of dirty clothes and a wife who is the very caricature of shrewishness.

The next scene finds Blair and two male advisers sitting in the back seat of a limousine, on their way to the White House for an audience with President Clinton. As their motorcade nears its destination, Blair's Chief of Staff, Jonathan Powell (Adam Godley), announces in awed tones, "Good God. They're bringing us in through the northwest gate.... It's the front door, the heads-of-state entrance. As if you were already Prime Minister." In stark contrast to the slick diplomatic choreography that surrounds them, the Britons engage in a hurried and ungainly struggle to rearrange their seating positions so that Blair can be the first to emerge from the car. "I hope nobody saw that," he remarks ruefully. During their visit, the British delegation discovers that a security computer tracks the geographical position of the President at all times. "Will we have one of those?" Blair asks an aide. His hopes are dashed by a solemn shake of the head.

Much of this first encounter with Clinton will clearly establish Blair's position as diplomatic inferior. As Blair enters the oval office, the President is not there to greet him, using the telephone in a nearby room. After making the Briton wait, Clinton greets him warmly, but treats him in an avuncular fashion, rather than as a peer. Positioning himself on the arm of a sofa, he hovers over Blair and dispenses nuggets of homespun advice such as, "We all just got to chill a little." Despite these hints at his lowly status, Blair seems wholly satisfied and genuinely excited that he merits any attention from Clinton.

Even when he becomes Prime Minister, Blair must still contend with Clinton's tendency to belittle him. When Blair brings up the "special relationship," Clinton all but dismisses it, saying, "Every country on earth claims it, although—in terms of actual effect on U.S. foreign policy—Israel, China, Saudi Arabia, and the Irish Republic are the ones who merit it."

Though he is subject to Clinton's high-handedness, Blair remains very impressed by his American counterpart. Indeed, the movie suggests that Blair's infatuation is subconsciously homoerotic in nature. Soaping himself in the bathtub while chatting to his wife, Blair waxes lyrical about his "visionary" colleague. After listening to this ode, Cherie suggests that Tony harbors "a crush" on the President. Clinton too, seems somewhat smitten, repeatedly describing Blair in terms of his attractiveness. "He's quite a catch," he tells his wife, Hillary (Hope Davis), and goes on to describe the Blairs as "a couple where the husband is more attractive than the wife." "He is handsome," Clinton concludes. But, if these men are, in some sense, a romantic pairing, it is Blair who is the most emotionally needy and fragile. While Cherie sleeps, Blair seeks Clinton's council on the Northern Ireland situation, looking for all intents and purposes like a man cheating on his wife. During another midnight tryst, Clinton abruptly ends a phone conversation, causing Blair to look crushed.

Events conspire to humble Clinton and propel Blair to a position of dominance. The Monica Lewinsky affair results in Clinton's political fall from grace and it is Blair who comes to his rescue. Delivering a speech in which he pledges unswerving loyalty to the President, Blair looks, for the first time, unambiguously statesmanlike. Seemingly emboldened by the fact that Clinton is now deeply indebted to him, Blair becomes highly assertive. During the Kosovo War, as the Americans broker a ceasefire agreement with Slobodan Milošević, Blair is sufficiently emboldened to say, "It isn't enough, Bill." Clinton, somewhat annoyed, sarcastically responds, "Well, look at you baby brother, stepping up to the big roulette table."

If a traditional marker of masculine strength is aggression, then Blair will turn out to be far manlier than Clinton. "Unless we back up the threat of airstrikes with willingness to put men on the ground, I just don't see how he can take us seriously," Blair says of Milošević. The P.M.'s sudden warrior-like stance is allied to a newly minted streak of individualism. Sitting with Cherie in an American-style motorcade, he contends, "If Bill won't, it's up to me, isn't it?" Blair's emotional reliance upon Clinton has faded. In the House of Commons, the British leader makes a convincing case for increased military intervention in the Balkans. His words are given urgency by dramatic non-diegetic music, footage of bombers releasing their payload, and the voice of a newscaster describing the "massive force" of the airstrikes. The montage of sound and image is a celebration of military might. As his parliamentary colleagues receive his speech rapturously, Blair's advisers look at each other approvingly.

Blair's dominance of Clinton is complete after he travels to the U.S. to deliver his famed "Chicago speech."[23] Calling on the President to reject isolationism, he discusses the necessity of committing ground troops to the Kosovo campaign. Subsequently, *The New York Times* asks, "Why don't we have a President like Tony Blair?" while the *Wall Street Journal* dubs his speech, "Churchillian." An advisor informs him, "You're the number one leader in the world right now."

Clinton insists on regarding their relationship in terms of a masculine contest. At one moment, he declares grudging admiration of Blair's aggressive tendencies and regards them as evidence that the Briton possesses the requisite male attributes: "Who would have guessed what a tough little son-of a bitch you'd turn out to be. Stabbing me in the back, right in my own front yard. Now, that takes balls." At another juncture, the President characterizes Blair's request for American troops in the Balkans as distinctly unmanly. "What kind of a king begs others to do his fighting for him?" he scoffs.

Other characters in the movie echo Clinton's insistence that political power and masculinity are intertwined. During the Lewinsky scandal, when Clinton's premiership hangs by a thread, there is much discussion and mirth regarding the presidential penis. Blair's Chief of Staff, Jonathan Powell, comments, "They're discussing his penis in public now. Five-and-a-half inches, with a curve in the middle when erect." The Prime Minister's Director of Communications, Alastair Campbell (Mark Bazeley), derisively replies, "It's hardly Errol Flynn, is it? I wonder who's angrier with him now. His wife for his betrayal, or his press secretary for his modest endowment?" This is not the only scene to concentrate on Clinton's genitalia. Jacques Chirac (Marc Rioufol), the French President, asks Blair "exactly how many centimeters is five-and-a-half inches?" As the American's humiliation is ever more complete, it is a British member that is worthy of praise. Briton Alastair Campbell cannot help but point out that if he were placed under the same scrutiny as Clinton, "I'd have been eight inches long and as thick as a baguette."

Decisively outmanned by Britain, Clinton shuffles through the final scenes of the movie a figure of impotence. George Bush has won the American election, essentially consigning the Clinton presidency to the history books. Blair, in contrast, is still the leader of his country. Finally acknowledging that the P.M. is his political equal, Clinton declares that, were the Briton able to run for President, he would win by a landslide. While staying with the Blairs at Chequers, the country house retreat of the Prime Minister, Clinton scarfs a late night snack straight from the refrigerator, and tells his host not to wake him in the morning. "I'm tired, I need the rest," he admits. Blair's response, "Sleep as long as you like," suggests that Clinton is now a spent and irrelevant force.

In the Loop

In the Loop is another movie that paints Anglo-American diplomacy as a highly gendered game of dominance and submission, in which an initially weaker Britain will eventually stand up to the American overlord. Utilizing fictional characters, the movie satirizes the lead-up to the 2003 invasion of Iraq by the United States and its allies. At the outset, Britain is clearly identified as the underdog in the allied partnership. The U.K.'s most prominent voice in pre-war planning committees, Simon Foster (Tom

Hollander), the Secretary of State for International Development, is a small, timid man and a completely inept communicator with no opinions of his own. Always eager to deliver a pat and inoffensive statement, he informs a radio interviewer "war is unforeseeable." This apparently dovish sentiment ingratiates him with an anti-war contingent inside the American administration led by Karen Clark (Mimi Kennedy), U.S. Assistant Secretary of State for Diplomacy. When Foster is called upon during a British Foreign Office meeting to clarify his position, he flounders and fudges hopelessly: "I stick to what I said. Uh, that doesn't mean that what I said won't change in the future." After the meeting, his handlers reveal to him, much to his chagrin, his lowly diplomatic status: "You were just meat in the room, Simon."

Foster's chief aide is Toby Wright, a boyish-looking twenty-something almost as bumbling and ineffectual as his boss. Seemingly able to attract the ire of anyone he meets, he is at various times, insultingly referred to as "Ron Weasley" (a schoolboy from the Harry Potter novels) and "Frodo" (Tolkien's hobbit). An angry British government press officer silences Wright by bellowing, "Shut it, Love Actually!" apparently because the lad embodies something of that movie's admittedly soppy, bourgeois essence. During a visit to Washington, D.C., traveling in a limousine flanked by two police motorcyclists, the pathetic Wright phones a friend to exclaim, "I'm in a fucking motorcade!" This is hardly the case, since his is the only car being escorted. Nevertheless, he continues to bubble with childish enthusiasm, taking pictures of Washington scenery with his cell phone.

During their Washington sojourn, Foster and Wright are presented as boys in a world of men. In their limo, they giggle about the possibility of hiring prostitutes. When their driver offers to help them do so, they are suddenly embarrassed and apologetic. After arriving at their hotel, another awkward moment transpires as they realize they have brought no money to tip the bellboy. Wright has failed to arrange any entertainment for his boss, so the pair sit forlornly in their shared room, watching a documentary about sharks because Foster is worried about any embarrassing repercussions should he "watch a porno." Foster, it seems, regards the realm of women and sexuality as a disturbing one. Witness his wary, shark-related comment, "You can definitely spot the female ones can't you."

Foster and Wright make no claim to conventional manhood, either physically or verbally. The former sits primly on his hotel bed, knees bent and feet pointing off to one side like a 1940s pinup model. A visiting colleague is so amused by this sight that he invites Foster to "slip into your negligee." Wright is so lacking in confidence regarding his masculine credentials that he makes a sexual advance to an American colleague by meekly stating, "You're a woman. I'm not a woman."

The movie's American males are contrastingly self-assured and macho. For example, American Lieutenant-General George Miller (James Gandolfini), Senior Military Assistant to the U.S. Secretary of State, is a hulking presence, a man-mountain in comparison to the physically diminutive Foster and Wright. His first appearance in the movie, patted affectionately on the buttocks by his former lover, Assistant Secretary of State Karen Clark, establishes him as a desirable and sexual being. Almost immediately, his genitals become a topic of conversation. After telling Clark that his allergy to dogs makes him wake every morning with a swollen face that looks "like a giant ball sack," she remarks nostalgically that he has "a beautiful ball sack." General Miller proclaims his masculinity with verbal and physical aggression. When Secretary of State Linton Barwick (David Rasche) fails to meet with him at the appointed time, Miller snorts, "What the fuck…. I'm gonna take a nice big shit on his desk, just to let him know that I was here." He proceeds to kick an office chair and jabs one of Barwick's aides in the chest with a rolled-up magazine.

The overt masculinity of General Miller is a fitting reflection of America's diplomatic dominance. Washington is, as Simon Foster admits, "the political powerhouse of the western world," while everything about the British political scene bespeaks weakness. The first scene of the film shows Number 10, Downing Street shrouded in a web of scaffolding that connotes a distinctly precarious institution. Foster's constituency work in England is dominated by concerns over a teetering brick wall adjacent to his offices. The architecture of Washington is so contrastingly solid and impressive that, on his return to Foster's shabby workplace, Toby Wright wryly observes, "From Whitehouse to shitehouse."

Americans set the agenda, while Britons struggle to keep up with developments. Foster anxiously observes Karen Clark conversing with an assistant. "What's going on down there? That looks important," he frets. But no nugget of vital information will be gleaned from this interaction, since it centers on Clark's ailing dental health.

U.S. politicos flex their diplomatic muscles by disciplining their British colleagues. Karen Clark, though she has no formal jurisdiction over the U.K.'s Simon Foster, sees fit to rebuke him after he fails to support her anti-war position. "You sat there like a dumb sack of shit," she tells him. Foster is horrified at this breach of protocol, but is not brave enough to tell her of his dissatisfaction. Only after she has left the room does he impotently respond, "You're not my boss. Fuck off."

The only major British character able to stand up to the Americans is Malcolm Tucker (Peter Capaldi), the U.K. government's Director of Communications and fearsome enforcer, whose quick temper and flair for profanity-laced insults suggest that he is modeled after Tony Blair's notoriously short-fused spin-doctor, Alastair Campbell. Due to Tucker's influence, London's corridors of power are filled with frightened men. He and his deputy, Jamie McDonald (Paul Higgins)—"the crossest man in Scotland"—ensure that cabinet ministers, ambassadors, journalists, and political operatives of every stripe are humiliated, cajoled, and threatened into toeing the party line. And he is just as ready to sink his fangs into an American antagonist as a British one. At a Foreign Office meeting, Tucker grumbles, "We've got enough Pentagon goons here to stage a fucking *coup d'état*." At the White House, angered that a youthful-looking staff member has been sent to brief him, Tucker fumes, "We burned this tight-arsed city to the ground in 1814, and I'm all for doing it again." He defines his strength in terms of masculine competition, with frequent references to his genitals and his sexual prowess. Late for a meeting and swearing loudly, he attracts the ire of a family of American tourists. "Enough with the curse words, already," intones the father of the mortified clan. "Kiss my sweaty balls, you fat fuck!" is Tucker's rejoinder.

Tucker goes toe-to-toe with the two most powerful American males in the movie, General George Miller and Secretary of State, Linton Barwick. His confrontation with Miller is instigated by a suspicion that the General has leaked an anti-war, American government paper entitled "Post-War Planning, Parameters, Implications, and Possibilities" (known throughout the movie by the preposterous acronym PWiP PIP). Their sparring is quoted here at length since it epitomizes the kind of heavily sexualized masculine posturing that is central to the movie's conception of the Anglo-American diplomatic relationship.

> TUCKER: General Flintstone, was it you? Did you leak PWiP PIP? I mean you can't fire a gun, but can you use a fax?
> MILLER: No, I didn't leak PWiP PIP. I do everything up front. Not like some creepy little gay mercenary that sneaks around doing other people's dirty work.
> TUCKER: Hey, I am doing my own work. I'm doing my job.
> MILLER : No, you're doing Linton's dirty work. You're his little English bitch and you don't even know it. I bet if I went to your hotel room tonight I'd see you with little fishnets on and him hanging out the back of you.
> TUCKER : Oh, that's nice. That's nice. That's tough talk coming from a fucking armchair general. Why don't you put your feet up on the poof and go back to sleep, why don't you?
> MILLER : Now Tucker, you might be a scary little poodle-fucker back there in London, but here you're nothing. You know what you look like? A squeezed dick.

> You got a little blue vein running up the side of your head. See, that's where I'd put the bullet. But I'd have to stand back because you look like you'd be a squirter.
> TUCKER : Have you even actually killed anybody. I mean really?
> MILLER : Yeah.
> TUCKER : What? I mean falling asleep on someone, that doesn't count.
> MILLER : Hah. That's good. How about you, pussy drip? Ever kill anybody?
> TUCKER : Maiming is what I prefer. Psychologically.
> MILLER: Why don't you try to maim me? I'll hit you so hard in the face you'll be shitting teeth.

Tucker brings the conversation to a close by suggesting that the General's career would be irreparably damaged should he choose to follow through on his threat. He also gets the last word. "Don't ever fucking call me English again," demands the Scotsman, before striding away. The scene ends with a shot of a bemused General Miller, obviously not sure why the word "English" has caused such offense.

In his verbal sparring with Linton Barwick, Tucker again acquits himself admirably. The Briton is obviously annoyed that he must serve the American diplomatic agenda by collecting and massaging intelligence data that will stoke the fires of war. He is apoplectic that this work should be done for Barwick, a hawk whose saber-rattling recklessness is encapsulated in the live hand-grenade he keeps on his desk. Barwick—an obvious parody of Donald Rumsfeld, prone to senseless idioms such as "In the land of truth, my friend, the man with one fact is the king"—tells Tucker that he is dissatisfied with his intelligence gathering skills. Tucker barks back, "Quick reality check here, J. Edgar-fucking-Hoover, you don't tell me what to do." Despite this riposte, Barwick manages to humiliate Tucker in front of Toby Wright and Simon Foster, calling him a "useless piece of S star star T" (The puritanical Barwick refuses to pronounce the word 'shit' even though he is happy to deploy it as an insult). The scene ends with a close-up of Tucker's face, a truly frightening mask of rage that clearly portends a terrible revenge. The Briton will indeed achieve a verbal excoriation of Barwick. "I've come across a lot of psychos, but none as fucking boring as you," Tucker tells him. "You're a real boring fuck. Sorry, I know that you disapprove of swearing, so I'll sort that out. You are a boring F star star cunt." Tucker's characterization of Barwick as the latest embodiment of the banality of evil once again demonstrates that he is the lone Briton who has what it takes to stand up to America.

It is, though, highly debatable whether he has scored the decisive victory enjoyed by David in *Love Actually* and Blair in *The Special Relationship*. Tucker, despite his claim to the contrary, is as much a servant of the American political machine as he is of the British. At the movie's end, in large part due to Tucker's efficiency, the Americans have got their war and Barwick remains the conflict's most prominent architect. Britons Simon Foster and Toby Wright remain as dithering and ineffectual as ever. The former is fired and the latter, bereft of the standing he enjoyed through association with a cabinet minister, finds himself cast adrift, a political irrelevancy.

The only American to be truly humbled is General Miller. However, it is not Tucker who will deliver his chastening, but fellow American Karen Clark. Miller informs her that he will not resign in protest at the march to war, as he had previously pledged to do. Angered that he has reneged on his promise, she takes the opportunity to thoroughly question his masculinity. "You're not a soldier," she tells him. Like Tucker, she equates true soldiery with the act of killing. "When did you shoot a guy last?" she taunts. The *coup de grace* is a verbal jab at the General's genitalia, the testicles that Clark had previously heaped praise upon: "If you were a good General, you'd have some balls." We last see Miller, seated at the right hand of Linton Barwick, taking orders from the very warmonger he had tried to stop.

28 Weeks Later

Another film that pits the men of the U.S. and the U.K. against each other, *28 Weeks Later* is no celebration of resurgent British masculinity. Rather, it seems to have fully internalized the notion, inherent in depictions of Blair-as-poodle, that British manhood is no longer a worthy institution. This horror movie about the aftermath of a pandemic is, at heart, a movie about fitness for fatherhood. Its main British character, Don (Robert Carlyle), is a cowardly, mendacious man who abandons his wife and, transformed by the "rage virus" into a form of zombie, attempts to kill his children. Don's complete failure as a patriarch is compared to the success of a trio of Americans who struggle to protect his family.

Twenty-eight weeks after the outbreak of the rage virus, Britain has been transformed into a wasteland of corpses and zombie-like carriers of the disease. Authority now resides in an American-led NATO force housed within a heavily fortified and carefully quarantined section of London known as the "green zone." Completely lacking in authority is a small band of British survivors whom we meet in the movie's opening scenes. At a historic rural cottage, they feebly attempt to perpetuate a sense of the familial and the domestic. Preparing dinner and exchanging a kiss, we find married couple Don and Alice (Catherine McCormack). They sit down to a meager repast ("the last of the chickpeas") and engage in strained conversation with a group of relative strangers united only by their success in evading the contagion. This dingy parody of family life is made more pathetic by the absence of Don and Alice's children, currently in Spain, due to a recent school trip.

A child appears at the cottage, on the run, and screaming to be let in. Don is wary of acceding to his pleas, but the entreaties of his wife convince him to slide open the lock and let the desperate boy inside. Before and after the child's arrival, dialogue is concerned with those who fail in their responsibility to others. "Your boyfriend ran out on us," are the bitter words of one survivor to another. Asked about the identity of his pursuers, the boy responds, "my Mum and Dad, they were trying to kill me." In the bleakest of ironies, Don's decision to help this needy child results in the invasion of the cottage by the infected, and his own momentous failure of responsibility: He decides to flee to safety, rather than attempt to save his wife from the ravenous mob. "Don! Help us!" Alice cries in bewilderment as her husband darts out of the cottage, sprints across neighboring fields, and fights for control of a motorboat before disappearing downriver.

Presently, the bucolic chaos endured by the British survivors is left behind for the ordered, urban streets of the American green zone. Here is a vision of London as Baghdad, occupied by wisecracking, somewhat bored U.S. troops. "Give me something to shoot," sighs an exasperated sniper, Doyle (Jeremy Renner). The Americans are unequivocally in charge of their British subjects. "The U.S. Army is responsible for your safety," intones one of the green zone's military tour guides.

Living in the green zone and reunited with his children, Don claims a spurious authority. As he gives his son, Andy (Mackintosh Muggleton), and daughter, Tammy (Imogen Poots), a tour of the large, clean, well-appointed building where they will be living, he reveals that he has been given a custodial job by London's American overseers. Boasting, "I basically run the place," he is rebuked by Tammy who offers the sobering judgement, "you're the caretaker." Don's jokey fibbing about the importance of his job is followed by outright lying when he tells his children a version of the events surrounding their mother's death. "There was nothing I could do.... I tried to go back, but she was already gone." The scene ends with a flashback to Alice's face, filled with shock and recrimination, at the moment Don abandons her.

This scene, presenting a husband and father who is a liar and a coward, is immediately followed by one that provides us with an alternative patriarch. American chopper pilot Flynn (Harold Perraneau) has a child's drawing adorning his cockpit with the words "For Dad" emblazoned upon it. Next to it is a photograph of this father accompanied by his wife and children. In the course of the movie, Flynn will save Andy and Tammy on three occasions, obviously a more dashingly heroic figure than their own father. Flynn's friend Doyle bestows upon him the telling nickname "family man."

Having introduced us to two very different fathers, the movie presents a sequence in which British and American characters compete for space. At its climax we will discover which nationality is truly in control of London. Escaping their quarantined living quarters, Tammy and Andy slip into the forbidden zones of the capital. While their father in unaware of their disappearance, Doyle spies them through the scope of his sniper rifle, quickly dispatching Flynn to chase down these unruly "puppies." "Yeah! London's mine!" shouts Andy as the children speed through the deserted and decaying streets on a moped. For a few minutes, they wrest back from the American occupiers a sense of agency and dominion. They head for their former home, a modest suburban house a world away from the slick, shiny minimalism of their green zone domicile. In doing so, they make a stand for their version of domesticity, not the one that has been imposed upon them. Their trip to the suburbs is also a rejection of the new home overseen by their father and bespeaks a desire to reconnect with the memory of their mother, Alice. They are shocked to find, not just reminders of their mother, but the woman herself, lurking in the shadows of an upstairs bedroom, a mentally disturbed but nonviolent carrier of the rage virus.

Tammy and Andy's spree is brought to a halt by the appearance of Flynn's helicopter. "I've got your puppies," he reports to Doyle. This line, suggesting that Doyle has some sort of patriarchal claim over the pair, heralds a section of the movie in which the children's stewardship is effectively passed to him.

Their real father, Don, is no longer able to care for them after he contracts the rage virus from Alice. His first act in his transformed, rabid state is to kill his wife, using his thumbs to push her eyes into her skull. In doing so, he attempts, it seems, to erase the withering look she gave him at the moment he fled. He will spend the rest of the movie as a threat to his children. Doyle, on the other hand, will spend the rest of his remaining screen time trying to protect them. During the murderous chaos that erupts after the infected Don spreads the virus within the green zone, Doyle, and his fellow snipers, must attempt to shoot carriers of the disease and spare so-called "friendlies." The American narrowly avoids killing Andy by accident. It is this moment, he later admits, that causes him to desert his post, horrified by the possibility of killing a child. Doyle shepherds the children, and a number of other refugees from the green zone, through the treacherous streets.

If Doyle is an American patriarch, it is Chief Medical Officer Scarlet Levy (Rose Byrne) who takes on the role of American mother. Levy has realized that Alice, as an asymptomatic carrier of the virus, represents a valuable scientific resource. Following Alice's death, Levy feels it is vitally important to protect Alice's children, should they hold the secret to an antidote. As they race to find safety on the outskirts of London, the beleaguered party rests at an abandoned fairground, complete with derelict ice-cream truck. As Levy and Doyle talk quietly to each other, and the children roam between the rusty rides, the scene resembles a family outing. It is at this moment, when the children find themselves bound to reliable, efficient, American caretakers, that Andy sees fit to criticize his biological parents. "They've left us again," he complains. In comparison to Don and Alice, Levy and Doyle will prove endlessly loyal. Both will die trying to save the children.

Despite the repeated insistence that Americans are superior caretakers, the U.S. military will definitively lose control of London. The movie places blame for the ensuing chaos on an overconfident American leadership, not the rank and file soldiery. America's mission leader, General Stone (Idris Elba) is prone to hubristic pronouncements. Discussing the virus, he flatly states, "it won't come back." Challenged on his contingency plan, he adds, "If it comes back, we kill it." Levy, Doyle, and Flynn are far less sanguine, rejecting the orders of their military superiors to forge their own strategy for survival.

The movie's final movement is concerned with Tammy and Andy's attempt to escape their murderous father and reach safety by rendezvousing with the American father figure, Flynn. The chopper pilot has promised to meet the band of survivors at Wembley stadium. There is perhaps no more potent symbol of British masculine prowess than Wembley, most famous and storied of England's soccer venues. As the children arrive there, it is deserted and unkempt, a riot of long grass replacing its ritually manicured turf. This image of a crumbling national institution succinctly illustrates the movie's repeated suggestion that British masculinity has become wayward and unfit for purpose. The throngs of English soccer fans who would usually be in attendance are absent, replaced by a lone American. It is to him that the children must turn, and he does not fail them.

The movies discussed in this chapter emerged from a Britain that was hugely dissatisfied with Tony Blair's interactions with the United States. A July 2006 poll revealed that a significant section of the populace wanted

Britain to "take a much more robust and independent approach to the United States" and evidenced a "strong public opposition to Tony Blair's close working relationship with President Bush."[24] The popular conception of Blair as Bush's lackey led to his depiction, in cartoons and other satirical media, as emasculated and feminized. British cinema responded to this deluge of images by offering tales of masculine competition between British and American men. In most of these films Britons successfully stand up to U.S. presidential, diplomatic, and military might. British masculinity is redeemed in *Love Actually*, *The Special Relationship*, and *In the Loop*, fighting its way back, with varying degrees of success, from an apparently hopeless position. In *28 Weeks Later*—an exercise in masochism in which America has entirely usurped the power of the British patriarch—the males of the United Kingdom are a spent force.

There is some evidence that these movies were therapeutic texts for British viewers. *Love Actually* is remembered and celebrated for the scene in which Hugh Grant's Prime Minister proclaims that he will no longer be pushed around by President Billy Bob Thornton. His jingoistic speech became such an exemplar of anti–American bluster, that when Blair's successor, Gordon Brown, hinted that he would be less diplomatically cozy with the U.S., there was talk in the British press of "a *Love Actually* moment" in the offing.[25] If *Love Actually* had become so culturally significant, it is likely that each of this chapter's movies provided British audiences with an opportunity to reflect upon the new, highly gendered, state of the post–9/11 special relationship.

Chapter Notes

Introduction

1. Britain's global supremacy in 1930 is referred to in B.J.C. McKercher, *Transition of Power: Britain's Loss of Global Pre-eminence to the United States, 1930–1945* (Cambridge: Cambridge University Press, 1999), 1.
2. Such fraternal sentiment is discussed in Correlli Barnett, *The Collapse of British Power* (New York: William Morrow and Company, 1972), 258–59.
3. James Bryce notes that considering the fraught history of Anglo-American relations, "it is one of the remarkable events of our time that a cordial feeling should now exist between the two chief branches of the English race." He contends that Americans were just as keen to strengthen transatlantic ties as the British, noting in the U.S. "a growing sympathy for 'the old country,' as it is still called" (Bryce, *The American Commonwealth*, vol. 2 [New York: Macmillan and Co., 1895], 527, 785).
4. Rudyard Kipling, "The White Man's Burden" quoted in Chris Brooks and Peter Faulkner, *The White Man's Burdens: An Anthology of British Poetry of the Empire* (Exeter: University of Exeter Press, 1996), 307.
5. Matthew Arnold, *Civilization in the United States; First and Last Impressions of America* (Boston: Cupples and Hurd, 1888), 191.
6. F. A. McKenzie, *The American Invaders* (London: Grant Richards, 1902), 244.
7. *Ibid.*, 243.
8. Harold Nicholson, "The American Attitude of Mind," *The Listener*, 28 January 1954, 163–64.
9. Ritchie Ovendale, *Anglo-American Relations in the Twentieth Century* (New York: St. Martin's Press, 1998), 118.
10. J.B. Priestley, *English Journey, Being a Rambling But Truthful Account of What One Man Saw and Heard and Felt and Thought During a Journey Through England During the Autumn of the Year 1933* (London: William Heinemann, 1934), 300.
11. *Ibid.*, 301.
12. *Ibid.*, 301–302.
13. Hugh Walpole, "The Pretty Characterless Face—of Hollywood," interview by Danvers Williams, *World Film News*, no. 2 (May 1937): 4.
14. Alan Pryce-Jones, "A Road with No Turning," *The Listener*, 3 July 1958, 15.
15. Quoted in Peter Stead, "Hollywood's Message to the World: The British Response in the Nineteen Thirties," *Historical Journal of Film, Radio & Television* 1, no. 1 (1981): 23.
16. Irving Sarnoff, "Crime Comics and the American Way of Life," *The Listener*, 10 March 1955, 417–18.
17. Daniel Snowman in his *Britain and America: An Interpretation of Their Culture, 1945–1975* (New York: New York University Press, 1977) argues "British culture has long emphasized the virtue of self-restraint and has tended to applaud the understatement, the double negative, the qualifying phrase, the ability to try to keep calm under fire." (83–84).
18. "The Sleep Walkers," *Picture Post*, 3 December 1938, 30–31.
19. Russell Ferguson, "Hooray You're Dead," *World Film News* 2, no. 1 (1937): 4.
20. Simon Harcourt-Smith, "The Case Against Hollywood," *Picture Post*, 6 December 1947, 28.

21. Christopher Hitchens, *Blood, Class, and Nostalgia: Anglo American Ironies* (New York: Farrar, Straus and Giroux, 1990), 371.
22. Ovendale, *Anglo-American Relations in the Twentieth Century*, 127.
23. E.W. and M.M. Robson, *The Film Answers Back, An Historical Appreciation of the Cinema* (New York: Arno Press & The New York Times, 1972), 143.
24. Tony Aldgate cites a 1943 survey that noted the British cinema audience was made up mainly of "the lower economic and education groups" (Aldgate, "Comedy, Class and Containment: The British Domestic Cinema of the 1930s" in *British Cinema History* eds. James Curran and Vincent Porter. [London: Weidenfeld and Nicolson, 1983], 257).
25. "Seven Sinners," press book, British Film Institute Library, London.
26. *Ibid.*
27. "Orders is Orders," press book, British Film Institute Library, London.
28. *Ibid.*
29. "Innocents of Chicago," press book, British Film Institute Library, London.
30. Quoted by Lawrence Napper in his "A Despicable Tradition? Quota Quickies in the 1930s," in *British Cinema History*, 39.
31. "Innocents of Chicago," press book, British Film Institute Library, London.
32. "Dance Madness in the U.S.A," *Picture Post*, 5 November 1938, 25.
33. *Ibid.*
34. "Fitness Camp in the U.S.A," *Picture Post*, 15 December 1941, 16.
35. Duncan Webster, *Looka Yonder! The Imaginary America of Populist Culture* (London: Routledge, 1988), 215.
36. Kenneth Lindsay, "Understanding America," *The Listener*, 1 December, 1955, 923.
37. K.W. Grandsen, letter to *The Listener*, 20 November, 1958, 841.
38. "'No Orchids for Miss Blandish' Is Brutal, Sadistic, Tawdry," in *Picture Post*, 15 August 1942, 16.
39. *Ibid.*, 17.
40. The character trait is based on the trademark behavior of Johnnie Ray, the American "crying crooner" who toured the U.K. in 1953.
41. Jeffrey Richards, "The British Board of Film Censors and Content Control in the 1930s: images of Britain," *Historical Journal of Film, Radio & Television* 1, no.2 (1981): 95.
42. Quoted in Ralph Bond, "Cinema in the Thirties: Documentary Film and the Labour Movement," in *Culture and Crisis in Britain in the Thirties*, ed. Jon Clark, Margot Heinemann, David Margolies, and Carol Snee (London: Lawrence and Wishart, 1979), 246.
43. "Orders is Orders," press book.
44. Robert Muller, "A Seat Beside the Censor," *Picture Post*, 25 June 1955, 11.
45. *Ibid.*
46. Arthur Marwick, *Britain in the Century of Total War: War, Peace, and Social Change* (Boston: Little, Brown and Company, 1968), 223.
47. *Ibid.*, 228.
48. Sir Henry Bunbury, "A Revolution in the Past 10 Years," *Picture Post*, 2 October 1948, 20.
49. *Ibid.*, 21.
50. Such sentiment was perhaps the motivation for a comment made by Simon Harcourt-Smith in his aforementioned article, "The Case Against Hollywood." He notes "…let us never forget that the fate of the world is for the moment at least in the hands of 140,000,000 well-meaning adolescents who constitute the film audience of America." (29).
51. John F. Lyons, *America in the British Imagination*, 1945 to the present (London: Palgrave Macmillan, 2013), 153.
52. "The Yanks Are Coming," britishpicturesswww, accessed May 10, 2014, http://www.britishpictures.com/articles/yanks.htm.

Chapter 1

1. Jessie Matthews, *Over My Shoulder* (London: W.H. Allen, 1976), 147.
2. Charles Davy, ed., *Footnotes to the Film* (New York: Oxford University Press, 1937), 14.
3. Jeffrey Richards and Dorothy Sheridan, *Mass Observation at the Movies* (London: Routledge and Kegan Paul, 1987), 39.
4. *Ibid.*, 46.
5. Forsyth Hardy, ed., *Grierson on the Movies* (London: Faber and Faber, 1981), 102–3.
6. Paul Rotha, *Celluloid: The Film Today* (London: Longmans, Green and Co., 1933), 45.
7. Davy, 87.
8. *Ibid.*, 91.
9. Herman G. Weinberg, "America," *Cinema Quarterly* 3, no.3 (1935): 157.
10. Davy, 183.

11. *Ibid.*, 213.
12. Sarah Street, *British National Cinema* (London: Routledge, 1997), 119.
13. Peter Miles and Malcolm Smith, *Cinema, Literature and Society: Elite and Mass Culture in Interwar Britain* (London: Croom Helm, 1987), 170.
14. Davy, 225.
15. Miles and Smith, 175.
16. Davy, 186.
17. *Ibid.*
18. "Home Rule for Britain," *World Film News* 2, no.8 (1937): 5.
19. Marian Rhea, "The Star Whom Money Doesn't Tempt," *Photoplay* 51, no. 10 (1937): 89.
20. Davy, 182.
21. Rachael Low, *The History of British Film, 1918–1929* (London: George Allen and Unwin Ltd., 1971), 306.
22. Michael Thornton, *Jessie Matthews* (London: Hart-Davis, MacGibbon, 1974), 125.
23. John Sedgwick, "Michael Balcon's Close Encounter with the American Market, 1934–36," *Historical Journal of Film, Radio & Television* 16, no. 3 (1996): 335.
24. John Gammie, review of *It's Love Again*, *Film Weekly* 16, no. 411 (1936): 29.
25. G.A. Atkinson, review of *Gangway*, *World Film News* 2, no. 8 (1937): 23.
26. C. A. Lejeune, review of *Gangway*, *World Film News* 2, no. 8 (1937): 25.
27. Andrew Higson, *Waving the Flag: Constructing a National Cinema in Britain* (Oxford: Clarendon Press, 1995), 122–23.
28. *Ibid.*, 123.
29. Eric M. Knight, "The Passing of Hollywood," *Cinema Quarterly* 1, no. 4 (1933): 216–17.
30. This was a common pattern in British films of the 1930s. Such a comparison occurs once again in *Hey, Hey, USA* (Marcel Varnel, 1938). Will Hay, playing a British fish-out-of- water, sits next to an American gangster played by Edgar Kennedy. Hay sits straight and prim, his pince-nez balanced on his nose and his hands folded demurely in his lap. Kennedy slouches so much that he's almost prostrate, his posture a marker of masculine bravado in comparison to Hay's stereotypically feminine posture of restraint. The protagonist of *Oh Boy!* (Albert de Courville, 1938), whose name, fittingly, is Percy Flower, is a bundle of nerves and insecurity compared to self-assured American gangsters who demonstrate their masculine credentials with lines like "shoot first and ask questions later."
31. The portrayal of America as a nation skilled in violence is a recurring theme in 1930s British film. Usually the violent American is compared with a Briton who is largely inept in such matters. For instance, in *The Frozen Limits* (Marcel Varnel, 1939), soon after the protagonists—the music hall act, The Crazy Gang—arrive in Alaska they are confronted by a band of Indians. Several of the gang cower in fear. A temporarily brave member of the gang, Flanagan, asks, "You mean to say you're afraid of a handful of Indians?" "Yes!" they reply. "So am I.," Flanagan admits. Luckily a passing cowboy saves them from harm.

Hey, Hey, USA also suggests a British aversion to violence and an American affinity for it. A gangster complains, "You can't get a good fight over here. I wish I could get a crack at something so I could get my eye in shape." His criminal associate replies, "You dope, they throw guys in the can for punching people in this country."

British ineptitude in matters of violence is also mentioned in *Oh Boy!* As American gangsters burst into a British house, a servant faints. One of their number laughs, "Crime's a cinch in this country. They knock themselves out." Later, a British guard turns off the burglar alarm to the tower of London, thereby allowing the gangsters easy access to the crown jewels. "Boy these Englishmen sure are gentlemen," laughs one of the gangsters. "Yeah, they put you wise to everything" responds another.
32. James Walvin, "Symbols of moral superiority: slavery, sport and the changing world order, 1800–1940," in *Manliness and morality, Middle-class Masculinity in Britain and America 1800–1940*, ed. J.A. Mangan and James Walvin (Manchester: Manchester University Press, 1987), 250–251.
33. Eric M. Knight, "Synthetic America," *Cinema Quarterly* 2, no. 2 (1933): 87.
34. The decision to reject Hollywood in favor of the British stage is central to another 1930s comedy, Return to Yesterday (1939). In this film a British Hollywood star, Robert Maine (Clive Brook) returns to his home country to publicize his new movie. Escaping his handlers, he decides to act in a small seaside stage production, taking place in the theater where he first trod the boards. After the first night he tells his appreciative audience.

"Tonight I've rediscovered the thrill of living contact with living audiences." Having fallen in love with a girl thirty years his junior, he asks her to marry him and come to Hollywood. The film's narrative paints Hollywood as a place which will make the girl, as one character puts it, "hard and bitter." Maine decides that he cannot subject the girl to a Hollywood fate and leaves her behind, content to look like a cad rather than ruin her life.

35. Thomas Baird, "An Innocent in Harlem," *World Film News* 2, no. 9 (1937): 16.

36. *Ibid.*

37. Baird, "A Greenhorn in the Wild West," *World Film News* 2, no. 8 (1937): 6.

38. Baird, "An Innocent in Hollywood," *World Film News* 2, no. 7 (1937): 6.

39. Knight, "Synthetic America," 87.

40. "Home Rule for Britain," 5.

Chapter 2

1. Clive Bell, *Civilization* (London: Chatto and Windus, 1928), 24.

2. John Carey, *The Intellectuals and the Masses: Pride and Prejudice Among the Literary Intelligensia, 1880–1939* (New York: St. Martins' Press, 1993), chap. 3 passim.

3. David Cannadine, *The Rise and Fall of Class in Britain* (New York: Columbia University Press, 1999), 139.

4. *Ibid.*,134.

5. See Dick Hebdige, "Towards a Cartography of Taste 1935–1962," in *Hiding in the Light; on Images and Things* (London: Routledge, 1988), 46–48.

6. John Cowper Powys, *The Meaning of Culture* (London: Cape, 1930), 298; quoted in John R. Harrison, *The Reactionaries* (London: Gollancz, 1967), 26.

7. John Carey, introduction to *Brighton Rock*, by Graham Greene (New York: Alfred A. Knopf, 1993), vi.

8. Graham Greene, *Brighton Rock* (London: Penguin, 1938; New York, Alfred A. Knopf, 1993), 18–19.

9. Louise London in her *White Hall and the Jews, 1933–1948: British Immigration Policy, Jewish Refugees and the Holocaust* (Cambridge: Cambridge University Press, 2000) observes that in the years immediately following World War I, "the basis of policy had changed beyond recognition since pre-war days. Britain was no longer a country of immigration. Strict controls on aliens were now the rule." (18) J.P. May argues in "The Chinese in Britain, 1860–1914," in ed. Colin Holmes, *Immigrants and Minorities in British Society* (London: George Allen and Unwin, 1978), "Only after the Great War, when the numbers of Chinese in, or in close proximity to, Britain had increased noticeably was exception taken to the Chinese 'vices.' Before then their racial character and perceived racial characteristics were apparently of little concern to the majority of Britons." (122).

10. "…whereas before 1914 the existing frontiers of Europe had been only a formality, and could, for the most part, be crossed without travel documents, the post-war frontiers were formidable barriers" (Bernard Bergonzi, *Reading the Thirties, Texts and Contexts* [London: Macmillan, 1978], 70). Paul Fussell argues in his *Abroad: British Literary Traveling Between the Wars* (Oxford: Oxford University Press, 1980), "This multiplication and alteration of frontiers served to advertise the irrational nationalism that contributed so largely to the European tone between the wars, a nationalism borrowing vigor from the bullying vainglory of the Allied victors hot for reparations and the self-pitying whine of the German underdog." (33).

11. Karen Halttunen in her *Confidence Men and Painted Women: A Study of Middle-Class Culture in America, 1830–1870* (New Haven: Yale University Press, 1982) makes a similar argument with reference to nineteenth century America. The rapid growth of cities and an increasingly mobile populace meant that strangers were a more common presence in American life. The very fact that the stranger was an unknown quantity made him the bugbear of the bourgeoisie.

12. Jeffrey Richards, *The Age of the Dream Palace: Cinema and Society in Britain 1930–1939* (London: Routledge and Kegan Paul, 1984), 42.

13. Evidence to support such a conclusion is provided by Ralph Bond, a British documentary filmmaker active in the 1930s. He recalls, "When a copy of Eisenstein's *Battleship Potemkin* was smuggled in and shown to Eton College Students who cheered their heads off when the mutinous sailors threw their officers into the sea, the British Establishment was convinced that the end of their world had come." In the same essay, he recalls the condescending attitude of those who had the power to control images, "Filmgoers in the mass were regarded as children who must be protected against evil thoughts and tempta-

tions and it was the duty of their betters (i.e. the Establishment) to make this their responsibility" (Bond, "Cinema in the Thirties: Documentary Film and the Labour Movement," in *Culture and Crisis in Britain in the Thirties*, eds. Jon Clark, Margot Heinemann, David Margolies, and Carol Snee, [London: Lawrence and Wishart, 1979], 245–46).

14. Quoted in Jeffrey Richards, *The Age of the Dream Palace*, 116.

15. Jeffrey Richards, "The British Board of Film Censors and content control in the 1930s: images of Britain," *Historical Journal of Film Radio & Television* 1, no. 2 (1981): 99.

16. Alfred Hitchcock, "The Real Spirit of England," *World Film News* 1, no. 11 (1937): 15.

17. "[The British film star] Gracie Fields ... functioned in the narrative of the films in which she appeared to point up the inherent soundness of the community, one in which social divisions were best left as they were, with everyone happy in her/his own place" (Peter Miles and Malcolm Smith, *Cinema, Literature, and Society: Elite and Mass Culture in Interwar Britain* [London: Croom Helm, 1987], 172).

18. Matthew Arnold, *Civilization in the United States; First and Last Impressions of America* (Boston: Cupples and Hurd, 1888), 64.

19. *Ibid*.

20. Quoted in Paddy Scannell and David Cardiff, *A Social History of British Broadcasting, 1922–1939*, vol. 1, *Serving the Nation* (Oxford: Basil Blackwell, 1991), 292.

21. The characterization of Americans as upstart children was common in the British press and cinema during the 1930s. Journalist Katherine Walker claims, "It is easy to understand how these fundamentally childish people—a very young nation after all—found comfort at this time of disappointment in films like Charlie Chaplin's *City Lights* and Marie Dressler's *Min and Bill*" (Walker, "America at the Cross-Roads: Film's Mirror Nation's Moods," *World Film News* 1, no.7 [1936]: 18).

Such an attitude perhaps gave rise to scenes such as the following from the Will Hay comedy *Hey, Hey, USA*. American achievement and energy are encapsulated in the form of an unruly child.

KID: History began in 1492 when Columbus discovered America.
HAY: Why history began before America was even thought of.
KID: Not American History.
HAY: Well, we're not talking about American history. We're talking about English History. REAL history.
KID: What about our history? The Battle of Gettysburg and the Battle of Bunker Hill.
HAY: Well they weren't real battles at all. They were just newspaper talk.
[The kid refers to British battles as "lousy"].
HAY: Don't you call our battles lousy. Let me tell you that Britain fought some of the most important battles in history and won the lot.
KID: What about when she fought America?
HAY: Well that was just our second eleven playing away.
KID: And we won the Great War too.
HAY: Who did?
KID: We did.
HAY: You did? I like that! Why England won the Great War.
KID: Well why don't you pay your war debts?
HAY: Well how can we pay when we're saving up for the next war?

22. "U.S. Gunmen Loose in London," *Daily Sketch*, 3 January 1935, 5.

23. "Murder in Soho," press book.

Chapter 3

1. Angus Calder, *The People's War: Britain 1939–1945* (New York: Pantheon Books, 1969), 18.

2. Edward Hulton, "Two Nations Become One," *Picture Post*, 3 October 1942, 22.

3. Charles Madge, "How the worker's life has changed," *Picture Post*, 2 January 1943, 10.

4. Calder, 546.

5. Ruth Bowley, "Is the Middle Class Doomed?" *Picture Post*, 4 June 1949, 13.

6. *Ibid*.

7. Rachael Low points out that "the cultural and academic elite" had an "attitude of condescension to the predominantly lower and middle-class British film industry" (Low, *The History of British Film, 1918–1929* [London: George Allen & Unwin, 1971], 305).

8. Quoted in John Ellis, "Made in Ealing," *Screen* 16 (Spring 1975): 119.

9. "The Way to the Stars," press book, British Film Institute Library, London.

10. Quoted in Charles Barr, *Ealing Studios* (London: Cameron and Tayleur, 1977), 30.

11. "I Live in Grosvenor Sqaure," press book, British Film Institute Library, London.
12. "The Way to the Stars," press book.
13. Ernest Betts, "You'll Like This U.S. Sergeant in a Truly British Film," review of *A Canterbury Tale* (Eagle-Lion movie), *Sunday Express*, 14 May 1944.
14. Edward Hulton, "The Britain of Tomorrow," *Picture Post*, 2 January 1942, 26.
15. "Grantham's Surprise M.P. 'I won't sit down and I won't shut up,'" in *Picture Post*, 18 April 1942, 6.
16. *Ibid.*, 8.
17. "I Live in Grosvenor Square," press book.
18. "The Way to the Stars," press book.
19. *Ibid.*
20. "A Canterbury Tale," press book, British Film Institute Library, London.
21. *Ibid.*
22. Moore Raymond, "Soldier with a Big Film Job," review of *A Canterbury Tale* (Eagle-Lion movie), *Sunday Dispatch*, 4 May 1944.
23. Review of *A Canterbury Tale* (Eagle-Lion movie), *Evening Standard*, BFI microfiche.
24. Betts.
25. Review of *A Canterbury Tale* (Eagle-Lion movie), *Lady*, 18 May 1944.
26. Lilian Duff, "Lovely to Look At—But Not Much of a Tale," review of *A Canterbury Tale* (Eagle-Lion movie), *Sunday Graphic*, 14 May 1944.
27. Anthony Gibbs, Review of *A Canterbury Tale* (Eagle-Lion movie), BFI microfiche.
28. Ernest Betts, "You'll Like This U.S. Sergeant.
29. Moore Raymond, "Soldier with a Big Film Job."
30. "What On Earth's Going on Around Here?" *Picture Post*, 22 May 1943, 10.
31. Robert Waithman, "We Are in It Together," *News Chronicle* (London), 6 July 1942.
32. Guy Ramsey, "'Boy, Was I Scared! Said U.S. Flier When His Plane Bounced," *News Chronicle* (London), 13 July 1942.
33. Robert Waithman, "An Army in Earnest," *News Chronicle*, 20 July, 1942.
34. S.L. Solon, "What Do Americans Think of Us?" *News Chronicle*, 7 August, 1942.
35. "Hallowe'en Party for U.S. Soldiers" *Picture Post*, 14 November 1942, 21.
36. Waithman, "An Army in Earnest."

Chapter 4

1. Angus Calder, *The People's War, Britain 1939–1945* (New York: Pantheon Books, 1969), 169–70.
2. Philip Ziegler notes in his *London at War, 1939–1945* (New York: Alfred A. Knopf, 1995) that "the wardens, in the eyes of the public, became, if not villains, at least self-important nuisances." (65).
3. C.S. Lewis, *Surprised by Joy: The Shape of My Early Life* (New York: Harcourt, Brace and World, 1955), 9.
4. "Is This Why Soldiers Break Down?" *Picture Post*, 2 February, 1949, 28–32.
5. Lionel Birch, "Why Did the Salesman Really Die?" *Picture Post*, 20 August 1949, 29–30.
6. "The Snake Pit: Can It Do More Harm Than Good?" *Picture Post*, 21 May 1949, 23.
7. Jeffrey Mark, "This Is Psychodrama," *Picture Post*, 10 July 1954, 22.
8. Geoffrey Williamson, *Morality Fair, Vagaries of Social Conduct as Reflected in the Press* (London: Watts & Co., 1955), xi.
9. *Ibid.*, 147.
10. Fyfe Robertson, "Messina Trial Exposes West-End Vice and the World Mocks London," *Picture Post*, 7 July 1956, 5–7.
11. Robert Muller, "A Seat Beside the Censor," *Picture Post*, 25 June, 1955, 11.
12. Charles Hamblett, "Are We Really Free?" *Picture Post*, 28 May 1955, 15.
13. *Ibid.*
14. Edward Hulton, "The Young Decent Britons—Millions Like Them ... But Too Many Spivs." *Picture Post*, 2 January 1954, 34.
15. *Ibid.*, 35.
16. As I note in my introduction, the U.S. was consistently presented in mid-twentieth century Britain as the world authority on immoderation.
17. Such resentment can be traced in the post-war British films of American actor Bonar Colleano. During the war, censorship strictures made it difficult to present the G.I. as anything but an angel or a rough diamond. Colleano specialized in playing the latter. After the war, whether he was playing a serviceman or a civilian, Colleano was always some version of the wisecracking "yank" character he had perfected during the war. However, now he was consistently a villain. It seems that Colleano had become the whip-

ping boy for a Britain that harbored resentment for the GI.

In *Good Time Girl* (David MacDonald, 1948) he is one half of a GI criminal duo. The film, posing as social commentary but not quite able to conceal is salacious delight in its subject matter, traces the descent of a teenage girl into a life of booze, sex, and criminality. Her last port of call on the way to prison is the back seat of a car stolen by Colleano and friend.

In *Dance Hall* (Charles Chricton, 1950), Colleano rivals Phil (Donald Houston) a young British man for the affections of Eve (Natasha Perry). The film culminates in a fight scene in which Colleano is trounced by Phil who, though a lousy dancer, is a better influence on Eve.

A Tale of Five Women (Irma Von Cube et al, 1951) follows the amnesiac Colleano around Europe where he must confront the girls he left behind in order to find out who he is. *Pool of London* (Basil Dearden, 1951) finds Colleano suffering for his black market activity.

18. Although actor Kieron Moore was Irish and the character he plays is identified as Irish, Adam Lucian nonetheless embodies the "British" restrait that was consistently peddled on U.K. screens.

Chapter 5

1. The Marshall Plan, officially known as the European Recovery Programme, was an American system of financial aid to Europe that amounted to $12,000 million between 1948 and 1952.

2. William Clark, *Less Than Kin, A Study of Anglo-American Relations* (London: Hamish Hamilton, 1957), 146.

3. Quoted in Ritchie Ovendale, *Anglo-American Relations in the Twentieth Century* (New York: St. Martin's Press, 1998), 131.

4. *Ibid.*, 61.

5. Quoted in Clark, 154.

6. Edward Hulton, "The British Have Been the Best Travelers Ever But Their Freedom to Travel Has Been Stolen," *Picture Post*, 20 March 1954, 18.

7. Fyfe Robertson, "An American Invasion," *Picture Post*, 31 July 1948, 12.

8. Robert Muller, "That Date in Korea," *Picture Post*, 24 April 1954, 42.

9. Richard Goold-Adams, "Two Questions of Sovereignty," *The Listener*, 1 April 1954, 555–556.

10. *Ibid.*, 555.

11. O.R. Frisch, "Scientists and the Hydrogen Bomb," *The Listener*, 1 April 1954, 556.

12. Clark, 154.

13. Harold Nicholson, "The American Attitude of Mind," *The Listener*, 28 January 1954, 164.

14. Ruth McKenney, "What the U.S. Thinks of Britain's Crisis," *Picture Post*, 20 August 1949, 9.

15. Robert McDonald, letter to *Picture Post*, 17 April, 1954.

16. Robertson, "An American Invasion," 8.

17. Robert Muller, "New Idols Lure Britain's Youngsters Back to the Music Halls, *Picture Post*, 7 August 1954, 20.

18. Several other films of the 1950s portray newly powerful U.S. citizens. Three notable examples revolve around ingenuous Americans inheriting money and/or power. *The Million Pound Note* (Ronald Neame, 1954) finds a penniless American drifter, Henry Adams (Gregory Peck), becoming the object of a wager between two British millionaires. They wish to discover if a man with a million-pound note can live well for a period of one month without spending any of it. Their theory is that simply displaying the note will encourage shopkeepers, hoteliers, and other tradesmen to offer their services free of charge or on credit. All goes well until Peck is asked to produce the note. Finding that he has mislaid it, he causes his creditors to panic and instigate a crisis on the stock market. *A Yank in Ermine* (Gordon Parry, 1955) is the story of an American, Joe Turner (Peter Thompson) who inherits an English earldom. After initial reservations, he throws himself into his new role, mastering the very British pursuits of croquet and rugby, and falling in love with an English girl. "If only he'd fail at something for a change," she remarks. *Penny Princess* (Val Guest, 1953) concerns a Manhattan shop girl who inherits a mythical European kingdom. After learning that the country is destitute, she effects a reversal of fortune by exploiting its unique product: alcoholic cheese. Though these Americans are likable, the movies betray British anxieties regarding their fitness for power.

19. Raymond Durgnat argues in his *A Mirror for England: British Movies from Austerity to Affluence* (New York: Praeger, 1971) that the title of *The Battle of the Sexes* "is cannily misleading, for the real theme is not sexual resentment at all, but British resentment

of progress.... What's being kept out is not the woman's touch, but the American way of life" (40).

20. As the aforementioned article on Marilyn Monroe suggests, the American blonde bombshell appears to have symbolized for the British a United States that did not deserve its power and influence.

21. Robert Muller, "Marlon Brando v America," *Picture Post*, 6 March 1954, 18.

22. Ernest Hemingway, "Hemingway on Safari," *Picture Post*, 6 March 1954, 24.

23. Charles A. Oakley, "Scots Who Work for Uncle Sam," *Picture Post*, 23 April 1955, 29.

24. "Pal Joey: A Musical with a Difference," *Picture Post*, 8 May 1954, 21.

25. Trevor Philpott, "Billy Graham, the Press, Politics and God, *Picture Post*, 20 March 1954, 39–40.

26. Stressing the comforts to be found in the past and tradition, the films are akin to a number of other British movies of the fifties that cast the nation as a proudly unadventurous curmudgeon. As Christine Geraghty argues, 1950s British cinema "demonstrated a blithe resistance to change, a comic affection for tradition and a sceptical attitude to modernist claims about social and technological transformation." The era's films, she continues, gave "audiences a rest from the stress of being citizens in the grip of modernisation." (Geraghty, *British Cinema in the Fifties: Gender, Genre and the "New Look"* [London: Routledge, 2000], 36–37). The four films discussed here provide these same pleasures, but are distinguished by their insistence that the modernization sweeping the nation is a particularly American phenomenon. They made a virtue of stagnation because they resented, not just modernity, but America's insistence on dragging Britain into the future.

27. Fyfe Robertson, "Automation (1): What It Is, What It Can Do," *Picture Post*, 9 June 1956, 30.

28. Fyfe Roberton, "Would It Be a Curse or a Blessing to Have Leisure Unlimited?" *Picture Post*, 2 April 1955, 13.

29. Philip Kemp, *Lethal Innocence: The Cinema of Alexander Mackendrick* (London: Metheun, 1991), 99.

30. Kenneth Allsop, "A Modern Pilgrim's Progress," *Picture Post*, 17 April 1954, 39.

31. Honor Tracy, "The Englishman as Lover," *Picture Post*, 13 February 1954, 29.

32. *Ibid.*, 27.

33. *Ibid.*

34. Hulton, "The British Have Been the Best Travelers Ever," 15.

35. *Ibid.*, 16.

36. *Ibid.*

37. *Ibid.*

38. Quoted in Kemp, 104.

39. Edward Hulton, "Britain—Is a Wonderful Country to Visit but Bad Service and Manners Send Out Visitors On—to Paris!" *Picture Post*, 10 April 1954, 19.

40. Philpott, "Billy Graham," 39.

41. Marshall's precarious identity is noted in Kemp, *Lethal Innocence*, 96.

42. Clark, 150.

43. Muller, "Brando v America," 18.

44. *Ibid.*, 19.

45. *Ibid.*

46. "Elizabeth Taylor Meets the Elephants," *Picture Post*, 27 March 1954, 41.

47. Oakley, 32.

Chapter 6

1. A chief proponent of the idea that the national citizen is also a transnational subject is the anthropologist James Clifford. His essay "Traveling Cultures" begins to theorize how it might be possible to conceive of cultures and nations as fundamentally joined in an ongoing network of influence. Clifford argues that, although thinking of the ethnographic informant as 'native' yields much valuable information about the local/internal environment, the anthropologist would do well to regard the informant as a kind of traveler who also exists in a global/external context. The balancing act he proposes is "to rethink cultures as sites of dwelling *and* travel." (Clifford, "Traveling Cultures," in *The Cultural Geography Reader*, eds. Timothy Oakes and Patricia L. Price [New York: Routledge, 2008], 322). Travel for Clifford can be literal or metaphorical, the term providing a tool to imagine the many ways that individuals come into contact with other cultures and nations, either through face-to-face interaction or via certain media.

2. "Speech to Conservative Rally at Cheltenham," *Margaret Thatcher Foundation*, accessed February 14, 2015, http://www.margaretthatcher.org/document/104989.

3. Howard L. Malchow, "Nostalgia, 'Heritage,' and the London Antiques Trade: Selling the Past in Thatcher's Britain," in *Singular Continuities: Tradition, Nostalgia, and Identity*

in Modern British Culture, ed. George K. Behlmer and Fred M. Leventhal (Stanford, C.A.: Stanford University Press, 2000), 201.

4. "TV Interview for London Weekend Television *Weekend World*," *Margaret Thatcher Foundation*, accessed February 14, 2015, http://www.margaretthatcher.org/speeches/displaydocument.asp?docid=105087.

5. "Mr. Major's Speech to Conservative Group for Europe," *johnmajor.co.uk*, accessed February 17, 2015, http://www.johnmajor.co.uk/page1086.html.

6. Michael Smith and Steve Smith, "The Analytical Background: Approaches to the Study of British Foreign Policy," in *British Foreign Policy: Tradition, Change, and Transformation*, eds. Michael Smith, Steve Smith, and Brian White (New York: Routledge, 1988), 9.

7. *Ibid.*, 10.

8. "Interview for *Woman's Own*," *Margaret Thatcher Foundation*, accessed February 14, 2015, http://www.margaretthatcher.org/document/106689.

9. Stuart Hall, *The Hard Road to Renewal: Thatcherism and the Crisis of the Left*. (New York: Verso, 1988), 68.

10. W. M. Hagen, "Shadowlands and the Redemption of Light," *Literature/Film Quarterly* 26, no. 1 (1998): 14.

11. See chapter five for a discussion of the British Foreign Office's tendency to characterize the United States as a youthful and impetuousness nation sorely in need of Britain's sage-like guidance.

12. H.C. Allen, "Anti-Americanism in Britain," *The Contemporary Review* 200 (July 1961), 626.

13. *Ibid.*

14. *Ibid.*, 627.

Chapter 7

1. "Cartoon by Zapiro," brandonhamberwww, accessed January 12, 2015, http://www.brandonhamber.com/photos/cartoon-minime.htm.

2. JekyllnHyde, "The Week in Editorial Cartoons—Misremembering George W. Bush," dailykoswww, last modified November 13, 2010, http://www.dailykos.com/story/2010/11/14/919739/-The-Week-in-Editorial-Cartoons-Misremembering-George-W-Bush-w-Movie-Poll.

3. Illustration accompanying Hakima Abbas, "People Creating Change in Africa," *Pambazuka News*, last modified October 13, 2010, http://www.pambazuka.net/en/category.php/features/67708.

4. JekyllnHyde.

5. "Blair Will Discover How Much Influence He Has in White House," *The Guardian*, accessed December 16, 2014, http://www.theguardian.com/cartoons/stevebell/0,7371,1501724,00.html.

6. The provenance of this term has not been unequivocally established, but Blair's status as poodle was certainly so well established by 2003 that scholarly essays routinely made reference to it, e.g., James K. Wither, "British Bulldog or Bush's Poodle? Anglo-American Relations and the Iraq War," *Parameters* 33, no. 4 (2003): 67–82.

7. Hugo Young, "Blair Has Not Been a Poodle, But Poodleism Still Beckons," *The Guardian*, last modified November 13, 2002, http://www.theguardian.com/world/2002/nov/14/iraq.foreignpolicy.

8. Edward Luce, "Was Blair Bush's Poodle?" *Financial Times*, last modified May 10, 2007, http://www.ft.com/cms/s/0/1b706386fe2211dbbdc7000b5df10621.html#axzz3b7O5P8nI.

9. "Doo Naht Fer-Sake Me, Oh Mah Dah-lin'…" *cartoonstock.co.uk*, accessed November 12, 2014, http://lowres.cartoonstock.com/-president_bush-bush-george_bush-prime_minister_blair-blair-anon2_low.jpg.

10. Rebecca Carpenter, "'We're not a friggin' girl band': September 11, Masculinity, and the British-American Relationship in David Hare's *Stuff Happens* and Ian McEwan's *Saturday*," in *Literature After 9/11*, eds. Ann Keniston and Jeanne Follansbee Quinn, (New York: Routledge, 2009), 145.

11. Vicki Woods, "If Bush Is Masculine and Clinton Feminine, What Is Tony Blair?" *The Daily Telegraph*, last modified April 30, 2002, http://www.telegraph.co.uk/comment/personal-view/3576019/Notebook.html.

12. Richard Johnson, "Defending Ways of Life: The Anti-Terrorist Rhetorics of Bush and Blair," *Theory, Culture & Society* 19, no. 4 (2002): 213.

13. *Ibid.*

14. *Ibid.*, 225.

15. *Ibid.*, 226.

16. "We Are Working to Make the World More Peaceful," *The Guardian*, accessed March 24, 2015, http://www.theguardian.com/cartoons/stevebell/0,,924586,00.html.

17. Quoted in John F. Lyons, *America in*

the British Imagination, 1945 to the Present (London: Palgrave Macmillan, 2013), 164.

18. Carpenter, 145.

19. Quoted in Lyons, 164.

20. *The Special Relationship* was made for TV rather than theatrical release, and so it might not be considered a product of British Cinema. However, since it shares so many themes and concerns with *In the Loop*, *28 Weeks Later*, and *Love Actually*, I would ask temporary indulgence for this slight broadening of the term "cinema."

21. Cherie Blair's fondness for new age rituals is discussed in Nick Cohen, "Ev'rybody Must Get Stones," *The Guardian*, last modified December 8, 2002, http://www.theguardian.com/politics/2002/dec/08/cherieblair.labour1.

22. As journalist Ewen MacAskill notes, "Only weeks after the 9/11 attacks in 2001, [Bush] … said on a visit to the Pentagon: 'I want justice. And there's an old poster out west that says, "Wanted: Dead or Alive."'" (MacAskill, "Bin Laden's Death Sparks Brief Outburst of Respect from Bush-Era Republicans," *The Guardian*, last modified May 2, 2011, http://www.theguardian.com/world/2011/may/02/osama-bin-laden-death-republican).

23. An address delivered to the Chicago Economic Club on April 22, 1999.

24. Julian Glover and Ewen MacAskill, "Stand Up to U.S., Voters Tell Blair," *The Guardian*, last modified 25 July, 2006, http://www.theguardian.com/politics/2006/jul/25/uk.topstories3.

25. An eventuality discussed in Rachel Sylvester, "Not *Love Actually*, But Still Shoulder to Shoulder," *telegraph.co.uk*, last modified July 31, 2007, http://www.telegraph.co.uk/comment/personal-view/3641631/Not-Love-Actually-but-still-shoulder-to-shoulder.html.

Bibliography

Abbas, Hakima. "People Creating Change in Africa." *Pambazuka News*, last modified October 13, 2010. http://www.pambazuka.net/en/category.php/features/67708.
Aldgate, Anthony. "Comedy, Class and Containment: The British Domestic Cinema of the 1930s." In *British Cinema History*, eds. James Curran and Vincent Porter, 257–71. London: Weidenfeld and Nicolson, 1983.
Allen, H.C. "Anti-Americanism in Britain." *The Contemporary Review* 200 (1961): 625–29.
Allen, H.C., and Roger Thompson, eds. *Contrast and Connetion: Bi-Centennial Essays in Anglo-American History*. London: G. Bell & Sons Ltd., 1976.
Allsop, Kenneth. "A Modern Pilgrim's Progress." *Picture Post*, 17 April 1954, 36–40.
Anderson, Benedict. *Imagined Communities: Reflections on the Origins and Spread of Nationalism*. London: Verso, 1983.
Arnold, Matthew. *Civilization in the United States; First and Last Impressions of America*. Boston: Cupples and Hurd, 1888.
Atkinson, G.A. Review of *Gangway* (Gaumont-British movie). *World Film News* 2, no. 8 (1937): 23.
Baird, Thomas. "A Greenhorn in the Wild West." *World Film News* 2, no.8 (1937): 6–7.
_____. "An Innocent in Harlem." *World Film News* 2, no. 9 (1937): 16–17.
_____. "An Innocent in Hollywood." *World Film News* 2, no.7 (1937): 6–7.
Bamford, Kenton. *Distorted Images: British National Identity and Film in the 1920s*. London: I.B. Tauris Publishers, 1999.
Banks, Marcus, and Howard Murphy, eds. *Rethinking Visual Anthropology*. New Haven: Yale University Press, 1997.
Barnett, Correlli. *The Collapse of British Power*. New York: William Morrow and Company, 1972.
Barr, Charles. *All Our Yesterdays: 90 Years of British Cinema*. London: BFI Publishing, 1986.
_____. *Ealing Studios*. London: Cameron and Tayleur, 1977.
Baudrillard, Jean. *America*. Translated by Chris Turner. London: Verso, 1988.
Baxter, John. *The Hollywood Exiles*. London: MacDonald and Jane's, 1976.
Bell, Clive. *Civilization*. London: Chatto and Windus, 1928.
Bergonzi, Bernard. *Reading the Thirties, Texts and Contexts*. London: Macmillan, 1978.
Betts, Ernest. "You'll Like This U.S. Sergeant in a Truly British Film." Review of *A Canterbury Tale* (Eagle-Lion movie). *Sunday Express*, 14 May 1944.
Bhabha, Homi K., ed. *Nation and Narration*. London: Routledge, 1990.

Bigsby, C.W.E. *Superculture: American Popular Culture and Europe.* Bowling Green, Ohio: Bowling Green University Press, 1975.

Birch, Lionel. "Why Did the Salesman Really Die?" *Picture Post*, 20 August 1949, 29–30.

"Blair Will Discover How Much Influence He Has in White House," *The Guardian*, accessed December 16, 2014, http://www.theguardian.com/cartoons/stevebell/0,7371,1501724,00.html.

Bochner, Stephen, ed. *Cultures in Contact: Studies in Cross-Cultural Interaction.* Oxford: Pergamon Books, 1982.

Bond, Ralph. "Cinema in the Thirties: Documentary Film and the Labour Movement." In *Culture and Crisis in Britain in the Thirties*, ed. Jon Clark, Margot Heinemann, David Margolies, and Carol Snee, 241–56. London: Lawrence and Wishart, 1979).

Boorstin, Daniel J. *America and the Image of Europe.* New York: Meridian, 1964.

Bowley, Ruth. "Is the Middle Class Doomed?" *Picture Post*, 4 June 1949, 13.

Bradbury, Malcolm. *Dangerous Pilgrimages: Transatlantic Mythologies and the Novel.* New York: Viking, 1995.

Brehony, Kevin J., and Naz Rassool. *Nationalisms Old and New.* New York: St. Martin's Press, 1999.

Bryce, James. *The American Commonwealth.* Vol. 2. New York: Macmillan and Co., 1895.

Bunbury, Sir Henry. "A Revolution in the Past 10 Years." *Picture Post*, 2 October 1948, 19–22.

Burnett, Ron. *Cultures of Vision: Images, Media, and the Imaginary.* Bloomington: Indiana University Press, 1995.

Calder, Angus. *The People's War: Britain 1939–1945.* New York: Pantheon Books, 1969.

Cannadine, David. *The Rise and Fall of Class in Britain.* New York: Columbia University Press, 1999.

"A Canterbury Tale." Press book, British Film Institute Library, London.

Carey, John. *The Intellectuals and the Masses: Pride and Prejudice Among the Literary Intelligensia, 1880–1939.* New York: St. Martins' Press, 1993.

_____. Introduction to *Brighton Rock*, by Graham Greene. New York: Alfred A. Knopf, 1993.

Carpenter, Rebecca. "'We're not a friggin' girl band': September 11, Masculinity, and the British-American Relationship in David Hare's *Stuff Happens* and Ian Mcewan's *Saturday*." In *Literature After 9/11*, eds. Ann Keniston and Jeanne Follansbee Quinn, 143–60. New York: Routledge, 2009.

"Cartoon by Zapiro." Brandonhamberwww. Accessed January 12, 2015. http://www.brandonhamber.com/photos/cartoon-minime.htm.

Chibnall, Steve, and Robert Murphy, eds. *British Crime Cinema.* London: Routledge, 1999.

Clark, William. *Less than Kin, a Study of Anglo-American Relations.* London: Hamish Hamilton, 1957.

Clifford, James. "Traveling Cultures." In *The Cultural Geography Reader*, eds. Timothy Oakes and Patricia L. Price, 316–24. New York: Routledge, 2008.

Cohen, Nick. "Ev'rybody Must Get Stones." *The Guardian.* Last modified December 8, 2002. http://www.theguardian.com/politics/2002/dec/08/cherieblair.labour1.

Conrad, Peter. *Imagining America.* London: Routledge and Kegan Paul, 1980.

"Dance Madness in the U.S.A." *Picture Post*, 5 November 1938, 25.

Davy, Charles, ed. *Footnotes to the Film.* New York: Oxford University Press, 1937.

"Doo Naht Fer-Sake Me, Oh Mah Dah-Lin.'" *Cartoonstock.Co.Uk.* Accessed November 12, 2014. http://lowres.cartoonstock.com/-president_bush-bush-george_bush-prime_minister_blair-blair-anon2_low.jpg.

Duff, Lilian. "Lovely to Look At—But Not Much of a Tale." Review of *A Canterbury Tale* (Eagle-Lion movie). *Sunday Graphic*, 14 May 1944.
Durgnat, Raymond. *A Mirror for England: British Movies from Austerity to Affluence.* New York: Praeger, 1971.
Dyer, Richard, and Ginette Vincendeau. *Popular European Cinema.* London: Routledge, 1992.
"Elizabeth Taylor Meets the Elephants." *Picture Post*, 27 March 1954.
Ellis, John. "Made in Ealing," *Screen* 16, no. 1 (1975): 78–127.
Ellwood, David, and Rob Kroes, eds. *Hollywood in Europe: Experiences of a Cultural Hegemony.* Amsterdam: VU University Press, 1994.
Epitropoulos, Mike-Frank, and Victor Roudometof. *American Culture in Europe: Interdisciplinary Perspectives.* London: Praeger, 1998.
Ferguson, Russell. "Hooray You're Dead." *World Film News* 2 (May 1937): 4.
Fiske, John. *Understanding Popular Culture.* London: Unwin Hyman, 1989.
"Fitness Camp in the U.S.A." *Picture Post*, 15 December 1941, 16–17.
Freedman, Jonathan, and Richard Millington, eds. *Hitchcock's America.* Oxford: Oxford University Press, 1999.
Friedman, Lester. *Fires Were Started: British Cinema and Thatcherism.* London: Wallflower, 2007.
Frisch, O.R. "Scientists and the Hydrogen Bomb." *The Listener*, 1 April 1954, 556.
Fussell, Paul. *Abroad: British Literary Traveling Between the Wars.* Oxford: Oxford University Press, 1980.
Gammie, John. Review of *It's Love Again* (Gaumont-British movie). *Film Weekly* 16, no. 411 (1936): 29.
Geraghty, Christine. *British Cinema in the Fifties: Gender, Genre and the 'New Look.'* London: Routledge, 2000.
Gellner, Ernest. *Nations and Nationalism.* Oxford: Basil Blackwell, 1983.
Gillis, John R. *Commemorations: The Politics of National Identity.* Princeton, N.J.: Princeton University Press, 1994.
Gilmore, Michael T. *Differences in the Dark: American Movies and English Theatre.* New York: Columbia University Press, 1998.
Glancy, Mark. *Hollywood and the Americanization of Britain*: From the 1920s to the present. London: I.B. Tauris, 2013.
——. *When Hollywood Loved Britain: The Hollywood 'British' Film, 1939–45.* Manchester: Manchester University Press, 1999.
Glover, Julian, and Ewen MacAskill. "Stand Up to Us, Voters Tell Blair." *The Guardian.* Last modified 25 July, 2006. http://www.theguardian.com/politics/2006/jul/25/uk.topstories3.
Goold-Adams, Richard. "Two Questions of Sovereignty." *The Listener*, 1 April 1954, 555–556.
Grandsen, K.W. Letter to *The Listener*, 20 November 1958, 841.
"Grantham's Surprise M.P. 'I Won't Sit Down and I Won't Shut Up.'" *Picture Post*, 18 April 1942, 6–8.
Green, Martin. *Transatlantic Patterns. Cultural Comparisons of England with America.* New York: Basic Books, 1977.
Greene, Graham. *Brighton Rock.* London: Penguin, 1938. Reprint, New York: Alfred A. Knopf, 1993.
Hagen, W. M. "Shadowlands and the Redemption of Light." *Literature/Film Quarterly* 26, no. 1 (1998): 10–15.
Hall, Edward T. *Beyond Culture.* Garden City, N.Y.: Anchor Books, 1981.
Hall, Stuart. *The Hard Road to Renewal: Thatcherism and the Crisis of the Left.* New York: Verso, 1988.

"Hallowe'en Party for U.S. Soldiers." *Picture Post*, 14 November 1942, 20–21.
Halttunen, Karen. *Confidence Men and Painted Women: A Study of Middle-Class Culture in America, 1830–1870*. New Haven: Yale University Press, 1982.
Hamblett, Charles. "Are We Really Free?" *Picture Post*, 28 May 1955, 13–15.
Harcourt-Smith, Simon. "The Case Against Hollywood." *Picture Post*, 6 December 1947, 27–29.
Hardy, Forsyth, ed. *Grierson on the Movies*. London: Faber and Faber, 1981.
———. *Scotland in Film*. Edinburgh: Edinburgh University Press, 1990.
Harrison, John R. *The Reactionaries*. London: Gollancz, 1967.
Hebdige, Dick. "Towards a Cartography of Taste, 1935–1962." In *Hiding in the Light: On Images and Things*. London: Routledge, 1988.
Hemingway, Ernest. "Hemingway on Safari." *Picture Post*, 6 March 1954.
Higson, Andrew. *Waving the Flag: Constructing a National Cinema in Britain*. Oxford: Clarendon Press, 1995.
Hill, John. *British Cinema in the 1980s: Issues and Themes*. London: Clarendon, 1999.
Hill, John, Martin McLoone, and Paul Haimsworth. *Border Crossing: Film in Ireland, Britain and Europe*. Ulster: Institute of Irish Studies in association with the University of Ulster and the British Film Institute, 1994.
Hitchcock, Alfred. "The Real Spirit of England." *World Film News* 1, no. 11 (1937): 15.
Hitchens, Christopher. *Blood, Class, and Nostalgia: Anglo-American Ironies*. New York: Farrar, Straus & Giroux, 1990.
Hobsbawm, Eric J. *Nations and Nationalism Since 1780: Programme, Myth, Reality*. Cambridge: Cambridge University Press, 1992.
Hockings, Paul. *Principles of Visual Anthropology*. New York: Mouton de Gruyter, 1995.
"Home Rule for Britain." *World Film News* 2, no. 8 (1937): 5.
Hulton, Edward. "Britain—Is a Wonderful Country to Visit but Bad Service and Manners Send Out Visitors On—To Paris!" *Picture Post*, 10 April 1954, 18–21.
———. "The Britain of Tomorrow." *Picture Post*, 2 January 1942, 26.
———. "The British Have Been the Best Travelers Ever but Their Freedom to Travel Has Been Stolen." *Picture Post*, 20 March 1954, 15–18.
———. "Two Nations Become One." *Picture Post*, 3 October 1942, 22.
———. "The Young Decent Britons—Millions Like Them … But Too Many Spivs." *Picture Post*, 2 January 1954, 33–36.
Huxley, Julian. "Changing Britain: What Is Her Future?" *Picture Post*, 2 January 1943, 9.
"I Live in Grosvenor Square." Press book, British Film Institute Library, London.
"Innocents of Chicago." Press book, British Film Institute Library, London.
"Interview for *Woman's Own*." *Margaret Thatcher Foundation*. Accessed February 14, 2015. http://www.margaretthatcher.org/document/106689.
"Is This Why Soldiers Break Down?" *Picture Post*, 2 February, 1949.
JekyllnHyde. "The Week in Editorial Cartoons—Misremembering George W. Bush." Dailykoswww. Last modified November 13, 2010. http://www.dailykos.com/story/2010/11/14/919739/-The-Week-in-Editorial-Cartoons-Misremembering-George-W-Bush-w-Movie-Poll.
Johnson, Richardson. "Defending Ways of Life: The Anti-Terrorist Rhetorics of Bush and Blair." *Theory, Culture & Society* 19, no. 4 (2002): 211–32.
Kagan, Norman. *Greenhorns: Foreign Filmmakers Interpret America*. Ann Arbor, M.I.: Pierian Press, 1982.
Kemp, Philip. *Lethal Innocence: The Cinema of Alexander Mackendrick*. London: Methuen, 1991.
Kipling, Rudyard. "The White Man's Burden." In *The White Man's Burdens: An Anthology of British Poetry of the Empire*, eds. Chris Brooks and Peter Faulkner, 307–8. Exeter: University of Exeter Press, 1996.

Knight, Eric M. "The Passing of Hollywood." *Cinema Quarterly* 1, no. 4 (1933): 216–17.
_____. "Synthetic America." *Cinema Quarterly* 2, no. 2 (1933): 87.
Kristeva, Julia. *Nations Without Nationalism*. Leon S. Roudiez trans. New York: Columbia University Press, 1993.
Kroes, Rob, Robert W. Rydell and Doeko F.J. Bosscher, eds. *Cultural Transmissions and Receptions: American Mass Culture in Europe*. Amsterdam: VU University Press, 1993.
Landy, Marcia. *British Genres: Cinema and Society, 1930–1960*. Princeton, N.J.: Princeton University Press, 1991.
Lant, Antonia. *Blackout: Reinventing Women for Wartime British Cinema*. New Jersey: Princeton University Press, 1991.
Lease, Benjamin. *Anglo-American Encounters: England and the Rise of American Literature*. Cambridge: Cambridge University Press, 1981.
Lejeune, C.A. Review of *Gangway* (Gaumont-British movie). *World Film News* 2, no. 8 (1937): 25.
Lewis, C.S. *Surprised by Joy: The Shape of My Early Life*. New York: Harcourt, Brace and World, 1955.
Lev, Peter. *The Euro-American Cinema*. Austin: University of Texas Press, 1993.
Lindsay, Kenneth. "Understanding America." *The Listener*, 1 December 1955, 923–4.
London, Louise. *White Hall and the Jews, 1933–1948: British Immigration Policy, Jewish Refugees and the Holocaust*. Cambridge: Cambridge University Press, 2000.
Louis, Roger, and Hedley Bull, eds. *The Special Relationship: Anglo-American Relations Since 1945*. Oxford: Clarendon Press, 1986.
Lourdeaux, Lee. *Italian and Irish Filmmakers in America*. Philadelphia: Temple University Press, 1990.
Low, Rachael. *The History of British Film, 1918–1929*. London: George Allen and Unwin Ltd., 1971.
Luce, Edward. "Was Blair Bush's Poodle?" *Financial Times*. Last modified May 10, 2007. http://www.ft.com/cms/s/0/1b706386fe2211dbbdc7000b5df10621.html#axzz3b7O5P8nI.
Lyons, John F. *America in the British Imagination, 1945 to the Present*. London: Palgrave Macmillan, 2013.
MacAskill, Ewen. "Bin Laden's Death Sparks Brief Outburst of Respect from Bush-Era Republicans." *The Guardian*. Last modified May 2, 2011. http://www.theguardian.com/world/2011/may/02/osama-bin-laden-death-republican.
MacDougall, David. *Transcultural Cinema*. Princeton, N.J.: Princeton University Press, 1998.
Madge, Charles. "How the Worker's Life Has Changed." *Picture Post*, 2 January 1943.
Malchow, Howard L. "Nostalgia, 'Heritage,' and the London Antiques Trade: Selling the Past in Thatcher's Britain." In *Singular Continuities: Tradition, Nostalgia, and Identity in Modern British Culture*, eds. George K. Behlmer and Fred M. Leventhal, 196–216. Stanford, C.A.: Stanford University Press, 2000.
Marchant, Hilde. "The Truth About the 'Teddy Boys' and the Teddy Girls." *Picture Post*, 29 May 1954, 25–28
Mark, Jeffrey. "This Is Psychodrama." *Picture Post*, 10 July 1954.
Marwick, Arthur. *Britain in the Century of Total War: War, Peace, and Social Change*. Boston: Little, Brown and Company, 1968.
_____. *British Society Since 1945*. London: Penguin, 1982.
Matthews, Jessie. *Over My Shoulder*. London: W.H. Allen, 1976.
May, J.P. "The Chinese in Britain, 1860–1914." In *Immigrants and Minorities in British Society*, ed. Colin Holmes, 111–24. London: George Allen and Unwin, 1978.
McGee, Patrick. *Cinema, Theory, and Political Responsibility in Contemporary Culture*. Cambridge: Cambridge University Press, 1997.

McKenney, Ruth. "What the U.S. Thinks of Britain's Crisis" *Picture Post*, 20 August 1949, 9–11.
McKenzie, F. A. *the American Invaders*. London: Grant Richards, 1902.
McKercher, B.J.C. *Transition of Power: Britain's Loss of Global Pre-Eminence to the United States, 1930–1945*. Cambridge: Cambridge University Press, 1999.
Miles, Peter, and Malcolm Smith. *Cinema, Literature and Society: Elite and Mass Culture in Interwar Britain*. London: Croom Helm, 1987.
"Mr. Major's Speech to Conservative Group for Europe." *Johnmajor.Co.Uk*. Accessed February 17, 2015. http://www.johnmajor.co.uk/page1086.html.
Morrison, James. *Passport to Hollywood: Hollywood Films, European Directors*. New York: State University of New York Press, 1998.
Moser, John E. *Twisting the Lion's Tail: American Anglophobia Between the World Wars*. New York: New York University Press, 1999.
Muller, Robert. "Brando or Beefcake?" *Picture Post*, 4 June 1955.
_____. "Marlon Brando V America." *Picture Post*, 6 March 1954.
_____. "New Idols Lure Britain's Youngsters Back to the Music Halls." *Picture Post*, 7 August, 1954, 20–22.
_____. "A Seat Beside the Censor." *Picture Post*, 25 June 1955, 10–11.
_____. "That Date in Korea." *Picture Post*, 24 April 1954, 42.
"Murder in Soho." Press book, British Film Institute Library, London.
Murphy, Robert, ed. *The British Cinema Book*. London: BFI Publishing, 1997.
_____. *Realism and Tinsel: Cinema and Society in Britain 1939–48*. London: Routledge, 1989.
Naficy, Hamid, ed. *Home, Exile, Homeland: Film, Media, and the Politics of Place*. New York: Routledge, 1999.
Naficy, Hamid, and Teshome H. Gabriel, eds. *Otherness and the Media: The Ethnography of the Imagined and the Imaged*. Langhorne, Pa.: Harwood Academic Publishers, 1993.
Napper, Lawrence. "A Despicable Tradition? Quota Quickies in the 1930s." In *The British Cinema Book*, ed. Robert Murphy, 37–47. London: BFI publishing, 1997.
Nicholson, Harold. "The American Attitude of Mind." *The Listener*, 28 Jan 1954, 163–64.
"'No Orchids for Miss Blandish' Is Brutal, Sadistic, Tawdry." *Picture Post*, 15 August 1942, 16–17.
Nowell-Smith, Geoffrey and Steven Ricci. *Hollywood and Europe. Economics, Culture, National Identity: 1945–95*. London: BFI Publishing, 1998.
Oakley, Charles A. "Scots Who Work for Uncle Sam." *Picture Post*, 23 April 1955, 29–32.
"Orders Is Orders." Press book, British Film Institute Library, London.
Ovendale, Ritchie. *Anglo-American Relations in the Twentieth Century*. New York: St. Martin's Press, 1998.
"Pal Joey: A Musical with a Difference." *Picture Post*, 8 May 1954.
Petrie, Duncan. *Screening Europe: Image and Identity in Contemporary European Cinema*. London: BFI Publishing, 1992.
Petrie, Graham. *Hollywood Destinies: European Directors in America, 1922–31*. London: Routledge and Kegan Paul, 1985.
Philips, Gene D. *Exiles in Hollywood. Major European Film Directors in America*. London: Associated University Presses, 1998.
Philpott, Trevor. "Billy Graham, the Press, Politics and God." *Picture Post*, 20 March 1954, 39–41.
Priestley, J.B. *English Journey, Being a Rambling but Truthful Account of What One Man Saw and Heard and Felt and Thought During a Journey Through England During the Autumn of the Year 1933*. London: William Heinemann, 1934.
Pryce-Jones, Alan. "A Road with No Turning." *The Listener*, 3 July 1958, 15–16.

Ramsey, Guy. "'Boy, Was I Scared! Said U.S. Flier When His Plane Bounced," *News Chronicle* (London), 13 July 1942.
Raymond, Moore. "Soldier with a Big Film Job." Review of *A Canterbury Tale* (Eagle-Lion movie). *Sunday Dispatch*, 4 May 1944.
Review of *A Canterbury Tale* (Eagle-Lion movie). *Lady*, 18 May 1944.
Rhea, Marian. "The Star Whom Money Doesn't Tempt." *Photoplay* 51, no. 10 (1937).
Richards, Jeffrey. *The Age of the Dream Palace: Cinema and Society in Britain, 1930–1939*. London: Routledge and Kegan Paul, 1984.
_____. "The British Board of Film Censors and Content Control in the 1930s: Images of Britain." *Historical Journal of Film, Radio & Television* 1, no.2 (1981): 95–116.
Richards, Jeffrey, and Dorothy Sheridan, eds. *Mass Observation at the Movies*. London: Routledge and Kegan Paul, 1987.
Roberton, Fyfe. "An American Invasion." *Picture Post*, 31 July 1948, 8–13.
_____. "Automation (1): What It Is, What It Can Do." *Picture Post*, 9 June 1956.
_____. "Messina Trial Exposes West-End Vice and the World Mocks London." *Picture Post*, 7 July 1956, 5–7.
_____. "Would It Be a Curse or a Blessing to Have Leisure Unlimited?" *Picture Post*, 2 April 1955, 13–16.
Robson, E.W., and M.M. *The Film Answers Back, an Historical Appreciation of the Cinema*. New York: Arno Press & The New York Times, 1972.
Rotha, Paul. *Celluloid: The Film Today*. London: Longmans, Green and Co., 1933.
Sarnoff, Irving. "Crime Comics and the American Way of Life." *The Listener*, 10 March 1955, 417–18.
Scannell, Paddy, and David Cardiff. *A Social History of British Broadcasting, 1922–1939*. Vol. 1, *Serving the Nation*. Oxford: Basil Blackwell, 1991.
Scott, Ian. *From Pinewood to Hollywood: British Filmmakers in American Cinema, 1910–1969*. London: Palgrave Macmillan, 2010.
Sedgwick, John, "Michael Balcon's Close Encounter with the American Market, 1934–36." *Historical Journal of Film, Radio & Television* 16, no. 3 (1996): 333–49.
"Seven Sinners." Press book, British Film Institute Library, London.
"The Sleep Walkers." *Picture Post*, 3 December 1938, 30–1.
Smith, Michael, and Steve Smith. "The Analytical Background: Approaches to the Study of British Foreign Policy." In *British Foreign Policy: Tradition, Change, and Transformation* eds. Michael Smith, Steve Smith, and Brian White, 3–23. New York: Routledge, 1988.
Snowman, Daniel. *Britain and America: An Interpretation of Their Culture, 1945–1975*. New York: New York University Press, 1977.
Solon, S.L. "What Do Americans Think of Us?" *News Chronicle* (London), August 7, 1942.
Sorlin, Pierre. *European Cinemas, European Societies 1939–1990*. London: Routledge, 1991.
"Speech to Conservative Rally at Cheltenham." *Margaret Thatcher Foundation*. Accessed February 14, 2015, http://www.margaretthatcher.org/document/104989.
Stead, Peter. "Hollywood's Message to the World: The British Response in the Nineteen Thirties." *Historical Journal of Film, Radio & Television* 1, no. 1 (1981): 19–32.
Street, Sarah. *British National Cinema*. London: Routledge, 1997.
_____. *Transatlantic Crossings: British Feature Films in the United States*. London: Continuum, 2002.
Sylvester, Rachel. "Not *Love Actually*, but Still Shoulder to Shoulder." *Telegraph.co.uk*. Last modified July 31, 2007. http://www.telegraph.co.uk/comment/personal-view/3641631/Not-Love-Actually-but-still-shoulder-to-shoulder.html.
Thornton, Michael. *Jessie Matthews*. London: Hart-Davis, MacGibbon, 1974.

Tracy, Honor. "The Englishman as Lover." *Picture Post*, 13 February 1954, 27–29.
"TV Interview for London Weekend Television *Weekend World*." *Margaret Thatcher Foundation*. Accessed February 14, 2015. http://www.margaretthatcher.org/speeches/displaydocument.asp?docid=105087.
"U.S. Gunmen Loose in London." *Daily Sketch*, 3 January 1935, 5.
Waithman, Robert. "An Army in Earnest," *News Chronicle* (London), 20 July 1942.
_____. "We Are in It Together," *News Chronicle* (London), Monday, 6 July 1942.
Walker, Katherine. "America at the Crossroads" *World Film News* 1, no.7 (1936): 18.
Walpole, Hugh. "The Pretty Characterless Face—Of Hollywood." Interview by Danvers Williams. *World Film News* 2 (May 1937): 3–4.
Walvin, James. "Symbols of Moral Superiority: Slavery, Sport and the Changing World Order, 1800–1940." In *Manliness and Morality, Middle-Class Masculinity in Britain and America 1800–1940*, eds. J.A. Mangan and James Walvin, 242–260. Manchester: Manchester University Press, 1987.
"The Way to the Stars." Press book, British Film Institute Library, London.
"We Are Working to Make the World More Peaceful." *The Guardian*. Accessed March 24, 2015. http://www.theguardian.com/cartoons/stevebell/0,,924586,00.html.
Webster, D. *Looka Yonder!: The Imaginary America of Populist Culture*. London: Routledge, 1988.
Weinberg, Herman G. "America." *Cinema Quarterly* 3, no.3 (1935): 157.
Westin, Alan F., Julian H. Franklin, Howard R. Swearer, and Paul E. Sigmund, eds. *Views of America*. New York: Harcourt, Brace & World, Inc., 1966.
"What on Earth's Going on Around Here?" *Picture Post*, 22 May 1943, 10–13.
Williams, Tony. *Structures of Desire: British Cinema, 1939–1955*. New York: SUNY Press, 2000.
Williamson, Geoffrey. *Morality Fair, Vagaries of Social Conduct as Reflected in the Press*. London: Watts & Co., 1955.
Wilson, Rob, and Wimal Dissanayake, eds. *Global/Local: Cultural Production and the Transnational Imaginary*. Durham: Duke University Press, 1996.
Winston Dixon, Wheeler. *Re-Viewing British Cinema, 1900–1992: Essays and Interviews*. New York: SUNY Press, 1994.
Wither, James K. "British Bulldog or Bush's Poodle? Anglo-American Relations and the Iraq War." *Parameters* 33, no. 4 (2003): 67–82.
Woods, Vicki. "If Bush Is Masculine and Clinton Feminine, What Is Tony Blair?" *The Daily Telegraph*. Last modified April 30, 2002. http://www.telegraph.co.uk/comment/personal-view/3576019/Notebook.html.
Xu, Shi. *Cultural Representations: Analyzing the Discourse About the Other*. New York: P. Lang, 1997.
"The Yanks Are Coming." Britishpictureswww. Accessed May 10, 2014. http://www.britishpictures.com/articles/yanks.htm.
Young, Hugo. "Blair Has Not Been a Poodle, but Poodleism Still Beckons." *The Guardian*. Last modified November 13, 2002. http://www.theguardian.com/world/2002/nov/14/iraq.foreignpolicy.

Index

Numbers in **_bold italics_** indicate pages with photographs

American characters: as acquisitive 144–146; as assertive/brash 133–136; as classless 58–64; as conmen 68–70; as go-getters 64–66; as an ideal 88–91, 96–97, 103–105; as masculine 39–44; as mobile 66–68; as modern 137–139; as rash/shortsighted 143–144; rendered unthreatening 73–77; as unstable/out-of-control 115–127, 146–148; as "Yank" 89–90, 96–97; *see also* United States of America
As Long As They're Happy 4, 7, 10, 16–20, ***17***
The Avenging Hand 67–68

The Battle of the Sexes 133–153, ***152***
Betjeman, Sir John 29–30
Blair, Tony 25, 170–175, 187–188; as character in *The Special Relationship* 175–179
Brighton Rock (Grahame Greene novel) 55, 74
British characters: as antiquated 137–39; as diplomatic 148–151; as effeminate/emasculated 39–44, 139–143; as effete/ineffective 70–74; as reserved 136–137; as uninterested in wealth 144–146; *see also* Great Britain
Bush, George W. 25, 170–172, 188

A Canterbury Tale 97–103, ***99***
cartoons (political) 170–171
censorship, British 20–21, 56–58, 109
Cummings, Constance ***12***, 13, ***152***

Dead of Night 125–127
Dean, Basil 30, 44
Deste, Luli ***61***
Donlevy, Brian ***122***

84, Charing Cross Road 162–169
Eisenhower, Dwight D. 7

The Frozen Limits 51

Gangway 2, 35–48, ***37***
Great Britain: Americanization 151–154, 161–162; anti–American sentiment 7–10; class system 53–56, 78–79, 83–97, 101–103; culture of restraint 106–111, 166–169; decline on world stage 5–7; as mentor to the United States 128–131; pro–American sentiment 10–11; transnational identity 158–161; *see also* British characters
Gregson, John ***134***
Grierson, John 29

Head Over Heels 35–48
Hey, Hey, USA 51
The Hidden Room 111–115
Hollywood: British ambivalence regarding 10, 21, 28–35; British characters' rejection of 44–48, 73–77; star system 30–31; *see also* American characters; United States
Hull, Henry ***142***

I Live in Grosvenor Square 83–91, ***87***
In the Loop 179–184

Index

Innocents of Chicago 13, 14
It's Love Again 35–48, *45*

Jagger, Dean *87*
Johnson, Bob *99*

King-Wood, David *122*
Knight, Esmond *99*

La Rue, Jack *69*
Lewis, C.S. 107
Local Hero 2, 158–62
Love Actually 2, 172–175
Lynn, Vera 106

The Maggie 133–153
Major, John 155–158
Matthews, Jessie 2, 22, 27–52, *45*
Meredith, Burgess *116*
Mine Own Executioner 115–119
Moffatt, Graham *99*
Moore, Kieron *116*
More, Kenneth *142*
Morley, Robert *87*, *152*
Murder in Soho 2, 53, 59–76, *69*, 70

Non-Stop New York 67

Orders Is Orders 13, 20

Pendleton, Nat *37*
Picture Post (magazine) 131–133, 136, 139, 142–143, 146–148, 153–154
press books (movie marketing pamphlets) 11–16
Price, Dennis *99*

Priestley, J.B. 7–8
propaganda, World War II 80–81

The *Quatermass Xperiment* 119–124, *122*

The Return of the Frog 53, 59–76
Robinson, Edward G. *61*

The Secret Agent 53, 59–76
Seven Sinners *12*, 13
Shadowlands 162–169
The Sheriff of Fractured Jaw 133–153, *142*
Sim, Sheila *99*
The Snake Pit 108
The Special Relationship 175–179
Stormy Monday 2, 158–162
Suez Crisis 7

Thatcher, Margaret 24–25, 155–158
Thunder in the City 53, 59–76, *61*
To Dorothy a Son 133–153, *134*
The Tunnel 50–51
28 Weeks Later 2, 184–188

United States of America: ascendancy on the world stage 5–7; as beacon of social change 12–15; as false utopia 49–52; as inexperienced in diplomacy 128–131; use of English Language 14; *see also* American characters

Warner, Jack *122*
The Way to the Stars 91–97
Wayne, Pat *37*
Winters, Shelley *134*

Young, Robert 38, *45*, 46

www.ingramcontent.com/pod-product-compliance
Lightning Source LLC
Chambersburg PA
CBHW032056300426
44116CB00007B/765